ARAMAIC LIGHT
ON THE
GOSPELS OF MARK AND LUKE

Aramaic New Testament Series — Volume 2

Books in print by Rocco A. Errico

Setting A Trap for God: The Aramaic Prayer of Jesus
Let There Be Light: The Seven Keys
And There Was Light
The Mysteries of Creation: The Genesis Story
The Message of Matthew: An Annotated Parallel Aramaic-English Gospel of Matthew
Classical Aramaic—Book 1

Spanish publication
La Antigua Oración Aramea de Jesús: El Padrenuestro

German publication
Acht Einstimmungen auf Gott: Vaterunser

Books in print by Rocco A. Errico and George M. Lamsa
Aramaic New Testament Series—Volumes 1 and 2:
Aramaic Light on the Gospel of Matthew
Aramaic Light on the Gospels of Mark and Luke

Books in print by George M. Lamsa
The Holy Bible from the Ancient Eastern Text
New Testament Origin
The Shepherd of All—The 23rd Psalm
The Kingdom on Earth
Idioms in the Bible Explained & A Key to the Original Gospels

ARAMAIC LIGHT
ON THE
GOSPELS OF MARK AND LUKE

A COMMENTARY ON THE TEACHINGS
OF JESUS FROM THE ARAMAIC AND
UNCHANGED NEAR EASTERN CUSTOMS

Aramaic New Testament Series — Volume 2

ROCCO A. ERRICO / GEORGE M. LAMSA

Noohra Foundation, *Publisher*
Mailing Address:
4480H S. Cobb Drive SE #343
Smyrna, Georgia 30080

First Printing 2001

ISBN: 0-9631292-7-9

November 2001

As a token of appreciation for your generous
support for this volume and devotion
to Aramaic studies, I dedicate
this commentary to you
Mr. Hanny Freiwat

CONTENTS

THE COMMENTARY

FOREWORD
by Rocco A. Errico

Aramaic Light on the Gospels of Mark and Luke, like its predecessor, *Aramaic Light on the Gospel of Matthew*, acts as a Near Eastern guide, revealing to the Western mind a more intimate view of the socio-religious and psychological environment of Semitic peoples.[1] It reveals to us the human Jesus, his teaching, apostles, disciples, followers and opponents in the light of his own language, people and times.

FORMATION OF THIS COMMENTARY

Aramaic New Testament Series Volume 2 is not founded on contemporary academic analysis of Scripture. It does not use critical source/historical and literary methods of interpretation. However, on certain passages, I do make reference to some of the these findings in the footnotes.

This work is not a verse by verse commentary. Nor does it repeat the verses and comments that have already been explained in Matthew's gospel, Aramaic Series Volume 1. The reader must keep in mind that this commentary works with the received text—that is, with the gospels as we now have them in their present forms—and does not attempt to provide the reader with source/critical study. I use layman's language and not theological, specialized terminology. As much as possible, each comment is written in story form. This style is maintained throughout the volume.

All scriptural excerpts are from the King James Version of the New Testament. I have also quoted scriptural passages from *The Holy Bible from Ancient Eastern Manuscripts* by Dr. George M. Lamsa.

---

[1]See Errico and Lamsa, *Aramaic Light on the Gospel of Matthew*, "Foreword by Rocco A. Errico," pp. xi-xvi.

Each quotation is identified as the "Aramaic Peshitta text, Lamsa translation." There are other citations of Scripture in the body of the comments that I have translated directly from the Aramaic Peshitta text. These passages are identified as "Aramaic Peshitta text, Errico."

I have attempted as much as possible to avoid a collision with denominational belief systems and interpretations as well as various schools of theological implications. Nevertheless, in certain scriptural passages cited in this volume, it became unavoidable. Apparently some biblical interpreters have unwittingly created and established monumental dogmas and confusing notions on verses that were only Semitic idiomatic phrases, metaphoric expressions or biblical customs. The expressions in the gospels are Semitic; it is, therefore, helpful if we understand them from their Near Eastern, cultural perspective. (Throughout the commentary, references to Semites are to Near Eastern Semites and not Westernized Semitic peoples.)

ACKNOWLEDGMENTS AND FINAL WORD

My deep appreciation and sincere gratitude to Mrs. Nina Shabaz, niece of Dr. George M. Lamsa and proprietor of the Lamsa estate, for her kind and most gracious permission to edit, expand, annotate and prepare Dr. Lamsa's previous commentaries, *Gospel Light* and *More Light on the Gospel*, in a new format. I have also added material that he and I had only drafted before he passed from this earthly life on September 22, 1975. There is also additional information derived from my continual research into Aramaic word meanings and Near Eastern studies.

My very genuine and heartfelt thanks and gratefulness to Ms. Sue Edwards, Ms. Ann Milbourn, and Ms. Linetta Izenman for their constructive suggestions and assistance in preparing this manuscript for publication.

These comments on the Gospels of Mark and Luke are the only works based solely on Aramaic and Near Eastern Semitic culture. They were written not to leave the impression that we have not understood Jesus' gospel of the kingdom but to present a clearer picture and setting in which that gospel comes to us. May this commentary be a light and guide to those who seek to understand more fully the blessed truths which were once spoken by the Semitic, Galilean prophet and wisdom teacher—Jesus of Nazareth.

To all the readers of this commentary, I say to you: *taybootha washlama dalaha nehwoon amhon hasha walmeen.* "The grace (loving kindness) and peace of God is with you now and always!"

Rocco A. Errico
November 22, 2001

INTRODUCTION

JESUS, A SON OF THE NEAR EAST

Jesus of Nazareth was born and reared in the Near East under the influence of Semitic, Near Eastern culture and practices. He spoke in terms that the people of his time could understand. However, his spiritual genius and personality are far above everything that has been written and said about him. He is a portrait of God. Through him we can see God. The most significant truth, therefore, is this living personality who, through his miraculous powers, has transformed the life of humankind and given humanity a new hope for a greater practice and manifestation of love and harmony while on earth.

THE TORAH, THE PROPHETS AND JESUS' GOSPEL

"Thy word is a lamp unto my feet and a light to my path."[1] Holy Scripture, which we call the Bible, contains the light of God. Light is the most precious and abundant thing in the world, but God's light is even brighter, more precious and powerful. Through this spiritual illumination (understanding) we see light, whether there is sunlight or darkness. God's light has come to us through the Torah and the words of the prophets. And yet, according to the gospel of John, Jesus said: "I am the light of the world." The reason for this saying is because Jesus' gospel of God's kingdom is distilled from the teachings of the Torah (Mosaic law) and prophets.

Jesus, through his divine power and knowledge of God and humanity, simplified the visions and revelations of Israel's prophets. His teaching is clear, like water issuing from a spring. It is so simple that children could understand his message. Jesus said: "I thank thee, O my Father, Lord of heaven and earth, because thou hast hidden

---

[1] Ps. 119:105 K. J. V.

xv

these things from the wise and the men of understanding, and hast revealed them to children."[2] Jesus' gospel of the kingdom is the light of the world. He came to enlighten the hearts of people everywhere and to bring clarity to what seems to be harsh and difficult in religion. He came to recover the teachings of the Hebrew Bible that had become dormant.

Unfortunately, mistranslations and misunderstanding of biblical idioms, Near Eastern customs and mannerisms of speech have obscured the meanings of much that fell from the lips of Jesus, the great master and orator. Today, also, when a political speech or religious sermon is translated from one language to another, misunderstanding and mistranslations often occur. Sometimes the idioms of one language are literally translated into another and the meaning is either obscured or is lost completely.

JESUS' SIMPLE GOSPEL

We must understand that the four canonical gospels are as vast as an ocean. We can only partially explore them. For many years oceanographers have been probing the depths of the sea and have only begun to uncover its mysteries. And, like the exploration of the sea, it will take many more centuries before the depths of the gospels are fully understood.

However, within the four gospels of Matthew, Mark, Luke and John is Jesus' teaching. His message is plain and direct, but it is deep in its meaning and challenging in its application and implementation. For example, it is difficult for human beings, who for centuries have been hating their adversaries, to stop acting on their hatred and begin praying and loving their enemies and antagonists.

For nearly two thousand years, New Testament scholars throughout the world have been trying to understand and explain what Jesus preached, taught and demonstrated to his simple and illiterate

---

[2]Mt. 11:25, Aramaic Peshitta text, Lamsa translation.

disciples. Yet even today, the quest continues. It is the simplicity and sincerity of the gospels that make it arduous for scholars and learned men to understand it. They are accustomed to indirect and obscure terms of speech.

In the old days, the more obscure and difficult the work of a writer, the more it was admired and the more that author was esteemed as a learned man. Today, in certain areas of the Near East, when a Semite compliments a speaker, he will say: "Your talk was marvelous; but I didn't understand a word you said!" This really means: "Your talk was so deep and philosophical that it was beyond my comprehension." The speaker is pleased with this uplifting remark. (One would have to keep coming back to the very learned teacher until the lesson was understood.) To say that one liked and understood the speech would imply that the listener and speaker were equal in their learning. This is one reason why many writers choose to write and speak in abstruse and complex terminology. It shows their high education and superiority to those with less knowledge.

JESUS' STYLE OF SPEAKING

Jesus abandoned this ancient practice of speaking. He used simple words, short sentences, aphorisms, and parables. He spoke and taught in a way that would be easy to remember. He avoided qualifying clauses that often obscured meaning. Thus, Jesus' style of speaking before the masses by the lake of Galilee, in marketplaces and on hillsides created a new norm of public teaching and writing. His methods of public speaking were contrary and alien to the manner that the Pharisees, scribes and all the writers of his day were employing.

People were amazed and stunned by Jesus' clarity and authority. Even his enemies admired the way he spoke and the direct words he used. Because of the simplicity of his message of the kingdom, many people flocked to him. They came to hear him expound on the Torah and the prophets. They didn't understand what the Pharisees, scribes and other religious authorities were telling them. In addition, many of these religious authorities themselves didn't care whether the people understood them or not. The more they kept the people in the dark, the more some of these teachers could exploit them.

For example, if the priestly, religious leaders had told the people that God is a loving Father who forgives freely, then the people might have stopped bringing sacrifices and offerings to the temple. Therefore, the priests, Pharisees and scribes were angry when Jesus told the sick: "Go your way. Your sins are forgiven." He made no demand for any remuneration nor for sacrificial or any other offerings to God.

A CLEAR COMMUNICATION

The books of the law and the prophets are clearer than the writings of the elders and scribes who came centuries after them. God told Moses, "Write, and make it plain." God also told Habakkuk in a vision: "Write the vision and make it plain upon the tablets that he who reads it may understand it clearly."[3]

Communicating spiritual, practical truths in a direct style makes them easier to understand and follow. This is why Jesus spoke in parables—so that the people could understand his message of God's kingdom. God's presence was among them, but they needed clear vision to see the divine in their midst. "Delighted are those who are pure in their hearts for they shall see God."[4]

THE ARAMAIC LANGUAGE

The gospels were written in the simplest language the world has ever known—Aramaic. It was in this Semitic language that the

---

[3]Hab. 2:2, Aramaic Peshitta text, Lamsa translation.
[4]Mt. 5:8, Aramaic Peshitta text, Errico.

Hebrew patriarchs, prophets and, later, the apostles, conversed with and received inspiration from God. This Near Eastern tongue is the oldest mentioned in the Bible and is the language spoken by Abraham, Isaac and Jacob.

One must also realize that ancient languages have a limited vocabulary. In those early days, people had fewer things and, therefore, fewer words to describe them. The challenge with Aramaic is that there are hundreds of words with more than a dozen meanings behind each one. Dictionaries and lexicons are advantageous, but they cannot teach the subtle use of words—that is, their nuances. Knowing the roots of words is helpful but not the total answer. Therefore, only a native-born Aramaic speaking person could understand its real significance and its shades of meaning.

At times, even a native can be deceived by the position of the points that are placed over or under a letter to determine its meaning. This is particularly so when the manuscript has been exposed to flies and more dots may be placed on a word or words. Also, manuscripts often suffer through humidity and careless handling, thus becoming more difficult to read and interpret.

TRANSLATION CHALLENGES

On the other hand, translations of the Bible were usually made by men who only knew their own language. They translated from a text written in a language that they could read but did not speak. This is the reason translators were unable to render an Aramaic idiom with its proper meaning into Greek, or a Greek idiom into Latin or English. They took these idiomatic phrases literally.

For example, when one says in English "The banks are on the rocks," the person means "the banks are insolvent." The opposite meaning would be true when said in Aramaic. Literally translated into Aramaic, the phrase would carry the idea that "the banks were solvent."

Furthermore, when translators came to a word that had several meanings, they used only the meaning they knew. For instance, the Aramaic word *gamla,* "camel," also means a "rope." Matthew 19:24 should read, "It is easier for a rope to go through the eye of a needle" and not, "It is easier for a camel to pass through the eye of a needle." To this very day Near Easterners say, "It is like a rope and a needle's eye," meaning "it is a difficult problem."

When the man said to Jesus that he had to bury his father, Western translators took it for granted that the man was dead. They did not know that "I must bury my father" means "I must take care of my father until he dies." Had this man's father been dead, he would not have been able to come and listen to Jesus teach; he would have been busy making preparations for the burial. And Jesus would not have told the man, "Let the dead bury the dead." No one in the Near East would have spoken in such a harsh manner to a man who had just lost his father.[5]

Many Aramaic words with various meanings were translated literally. A good scriptural example is the word *ruha,* "spirit," which also means "wind, pride, rheumatism." In Luke 13:11, Jesus spoke about a woman who was suffering from rheumatism, but the translators, not knowing the meaning of the word, translated it literally that she was "suffering from the spirit." In Matthew 5:3, we read: "Blessed are the poor in spirit." It should read: "Blessed are the poor in pride," that is, the humble.

A MISLEADING TRANSLATION

One of the most misleading translations of a gospel passage is in Luke 14:26. It reads: "If any man come to me, and *hate* not his father, and mother, and wife, and children, and brethren, and sisters, yea and his own life also, he cannot be my disciple." The verse should read: "He who comes to me and does not *put aside* his father, his mother,

---

[5]For a detailed commentary on Jesus' saying, see Errico and Lamsa, *Aramaic Light on the Gospel of Matthew,* "Burying One's Father," pp. 129-130.

his brothers, his sisters, his wife and his children and even his own life cannot be a disciple to me."

The word "hate," *sna* in Aramaic, is misunderstood. Jesus would never have used such a phrase. He was a teacher of love, not hatred. This verse has been a puzzle for many sincere readers of Jesus' gospel. Communistic and atheistic writers have called Jesus a preacher of hatred because of this mistranslated verse. Interestingly, in Near Eastern countries, many people burned translations of the Bible that contained this verse. No Near Eastern Jew, Christian or Moslem would ever permit his children to read a gospel with this verse in it. People in those lands loved their fathers, mothers and children..

The Aramaic word *sna* has several meanings. It means "hate" and "put aside." It is like our English word "fair." Someone can be fair in complexion and fair in judgment. The word is spelled exactly the same but the context changes the meaning. Again, we can use the word "light" to mean light in weight or "light" meaning illuminate.

Young people of the Near East would know that Jesus was not preaching hatred. They knew he would not admonish people to hate their parents. The meaning is clear in the Aramaic language: To be a true follower of Jesus' teaching, one would have to set aside one's parents and relatives. The gospel of God's kingdom was to be uppermost for his disciples and followers; it must come first. Those who would relinquish their personal possessions for his sake would receive a hundred times more. On another occasion, Jesus said: "But first you search for the kingdom of God and his justice and all these things will abundantly be given to you."[6] Jesus was consistent in his teaching. When one puts God first, all other things will function harmoniously.

As we have said, Jesus chose to use a simple and direct style of speaking because his disciples and a large majority of the people were simple folk and slow in understanding. These country peasants and fishermen were accustomed to hearing and using idioms,

---

[6]Mt. 6:33, Aramaic Peshitta text, Errico

parables, metaphors and maxims. Therefore, through this method of speaking, provincial people could grasp abstract ideas and spiritual truths that were otherwise hidden from their eyes.

JESUS' USE OF IDIOMS

Following are a few examples of Jesus' mode of speaking: "If your hand offend thee, cut it off" means "If you have the habit of stealing, quit it. For it is better to cut out that habit than lose other members of your body." In the Near East, even today, the hands of thieves are amputated, and in some rare cases, the lips and noses of shoplifters are cut off. "If your foot offends you" signifies "If you have the habit of trespassing another man's vineyard or orchard, stop trespassing." These idiomatic terms of speech are well understood by Aramaic speaking people. In Aramaic and Arabic speaking countries, no one has ever cut off his hand, plucked out his eyes, or amputated one of his bodily members. But in other countries, countless hundreds have deliberately cut off their hands and injured themselves because they understood Jesus' words literally.

It is also true that many American idioms are understood literally by some foreigners, such as: "The baseball player died on third base." "He was in a pickle (or hot water) for over a year." "He was born with a silver spoon in his mouth." "The ladies auxiliary gave a shower for her." "The man blew his top, hit the bottle and went on the skids." "He received the information right from the horse's mouth." These expressions of speech, of course, are understood by those living in America and are not taken at face value.

AN ENIGMATIC SAYING

One of the most challenging and puzzling Semitic idioms for people of the Occidental world is the Aramaic saying in the gospel of John 6:53-54: "Jesus said to them, Truly, truly, I say to you, Unless you eat the body of the Son of man and drink his blood, you have no life in yourselves. He who eats of my body and drinks of my blood has eternal life: and I will raise him at the last day." Even some of the Jewish followers in Judea did not understand that Galilean idiomatic phrase. It was puzzling to them, so they decided to abandon him. They said: "This is a hard saying; who can listen to it? How could this man give us his body to eat and his blood to drink?" What Jesus meant was "to eat of his teaching, make it a part of their lives and to be willing to suffer the consequences of adopting his gospel of the kingdom." Jesus had suffered for their sake; now they must be willing to suffer.

Aramaic speaking people still say, "He has eaten the book," meaning, "He memorized what is in the book." Both the prophet Ezekiel and John the revelator were told to "eat the scroll." They had to remember what they read and make it a part of their predictions. When Semitic people work excessively hard or suffer, they say, "I have eaten my body and drunk my blood" or "I have eaten my father and mother." In very extreme cases they will say, "I have eaten my dead people." These sayings are so common in Aramaic speech that one can still hear them during ordinary conversations.

Jesus compared himself to the lamb that the Jews were going to eat on Passover day and the blood of the lamb that spared the lives of their forefathers in Egypt. They were symbolic of his body and blood which were to be spiritually eaten and drunk by his followers to the end of time. It was not a literal statement. Besides, Jewish law prohibited anyone from even touching the blood of a dead person. How could Jesus have literally meant for people to eat his body and drink his blood?

BIBLICAL CUSTOMS

Cultural customs and manners also present difficulties in transmitting thought from one language into another. This, of course, holds true when translating Near Eastern, Semitic, biblical thought into other languages. A familiarity with the customs and manners of the Near Eastern world is essential.

For example, in America everyone knows the hour when a bride and bridegroom will arrive for their wedding ceremony and celebration. Readers of the gospels wonder why Jesus said that just as no one knows when the bridegroom comes forth, so no one knows the hour of the son of man's coming. He used a familiar custom which everyone in the Near East could understand to illustrate his point. To explain further, we must first understand that usually Near Eastern Semites are not punctual. Time means nothing to them. Being late four or five hours is common. Second, the bridegroom and bride are bathed before the wedding ceremony and feast. No one knows when they will be ready because water is scarce and hard to procure. Therefore, no one but God knows when the bride and bridegroom will be ready to go to the wedding house.

Another custom that Jesus used was when he told the people that no one stores new wine in old skins. Even today, in many areas of the Near East, wine and oil are carried in goatskins. And when the wine is new the fermentation will cause the skins to expand and burst. What he meant by this saying is that his teaching was like new wine and the people's traditional religious education was like old skins. They could not blend or work together.

On another occasion, Jesus told his disciples to go to a town where they would find a donkey with a foal tied to the door. Some Western readers of the Bible wonder how he knew about the donkey and the foal. Was he acting as a prophet? But one does not have to be a prophet to have the answer. Up until the 1920s one could see many donkeys tied up at the doors of their owners. In the United States, this would be like knowing that there would be many taxis in front of an airport or bus station waiting to be hired.

A SEMITIC AUTHOR

Dr. George M. Lamsa was born and raised in a unique civilization that continued static from the time of Abraham to the dawn of the twentieth century—in a region where customs and manners remained unchanged and unaltered. His people conversed in his native tongue, Aramaic, in the same way that the patriarchs, Jesus and his disciples did. Amazingly, his people used the same idioms and mannerisms of speech that the writers of Holy Scripture used. They wore the same style garments, ate the same kinds of food and used the same implements for plowing and threshing as did King David.

The area where these people lived was like a little island in a great ocean. They were surrounded by millions of non-Christians and by people who spoke alien languages. Nothing new was introduced into this region until World War 1. It was only in 1965 that the Turkish government permitted tourists to enter this land. In the old days, this region of the Near East, because of its abundant water, fruit trees and vegetables, was called the Garden of Eden.

Dr. Lamsa was educated under the care of learned priests of the Church of the East who knew no other language but Aramaic. Highly educated Englishmen—graduates of Oxford, Cambridge and other famous English schools—were also his educators. He was the first native speaker of Aramaic with the knowledge of biblical customs and manners, as well as English, who has ever translated the entire Bible from ancient Aramaic texts into English. His translation is now in wide use.

THE PURPOSE OF THE COMMENTARY

The purpose of this second volume in the Aramaic New Testament series, *Aramaic Light on the Gospels of Mark and Luke,* as in the first volume, is not to present a critical source/ literary/ academic analysis of these two gospel writings. The comments are based only on the Near Eastern Aramaic culture, customs, and language that lie behind the text. The material that pertains to textual criticism is extremely extensive and cannot be dealt with even briefly in this volume or in the volumes that follow.

The endeavor of this commentary is to shed light on many obscure scriptural gospel passages. Our intent is to elucidate what appears to be harsh and difficult for Western readers to understand and to clarify and strengthen the meaning of Jesus' teaching—his glorious gospel of God's kingdom.[7]

Rocco A. Errico and George M. Lamsa

---

[7]Please see Errico and Lamsa: *Aramaic Light on the Gospel of Matthew—Volume 1* "Introduction Aramaic New Testament Series." pp. xxiii-xliv.

ABBREVIATIONS

Old Testament		**New Testament**	
Gen.	Genesis	NT	New Testament
Ex.	Exodus	Mt.	Matthew
Lev.	Leviticus	Mk.	Mark
1 Sam.	1 Samuel	Lk.	Luke
2 Sam.	2 Samuel	Jn.	John
1 Ki.	1 Kings	Col.	Colossians
2 Ki.	2 Kings	Heb.	Hebrews
1 Chron.	1 Chronicles	**Other Abbreviations**	
Ps.	Psalm	**BCE**	Before the common era, B.C.
Isa.	Isaiah	**CE**	Common Era, A.D.
Jer.	Jeremiah	K. J. V.	King James Version
Ezk.	Ezekiel		
Hab.	Habakkuk		
Zeph.	Zephaniah		
Mal.	Malachi		
1 Macc.	1 Maccabees		

ܐܬܘܢ ܬܚܠܦܘܢ ܩܕܡ ܐܬܘܪ̈ܝܐ

ܒܝܕ܂

ܝܘܣܦ ܒܝܬ ܝܘܣܦ

ܩܘܪ̈ܒܢܐ

ܘܦܪܥܣܘܦ

INTRODUCTION
The Gospel According To Mark

AUTHORSHIP

According to Near Eastern tradition, the gospel of Mark was the Aramaic preaching and writings of John Mark. He was a devout, Jewish follower of Jesus.[1] The apostles and early converts met at his mother's home after Jesus had been crucified. "And when he understood, he [Simon Peter] went to the house of Mary the mother of John, whose nickname was Mark, because many brethren were gathered there praying."[2] There is another tradition that says that Mark was the young man who fled naked when Jesus was arrested at Gethsemane.[3]

Jesus had many followers in Jerusalem, most of whom were Galilean merchants. It is probable that Mark, as a young man, had seen and heard Jesus on a few occasions when the Galilean prophet had visited Jerusalem. His mother Mary might have been one of the first converts in the historic city. Some scholars suggest that Mark was the disciple who was with Peter when he followed Jesus to the high priest's courtyard and that he was acquainted with the high priest.[4]

According to the Book of Acts, John Mark accompanied Paul and Barnabas from Jerusalem on their first missionary journey.[5] Later

---

[1]C. S. Mann in his commentary on Mark says: "In the first place, the author sees no good reason to suppose that any single writer of our four canonical gospels was any other than a Jewish Christian." *MARK: A New Translation with Introduction and Commentary*, "The Composition of the Gospels," A. The Background of the Tradition, p. 15.

[2]Acts 12:12, Aramaic Peshitta text, Errico.

[3]See Mk. 14:51-52. However, many NT scholars consider this late tradition as pure supposition.

[4]See Jn. 18:15-16.

[5]Acts 12:25.

he left them at Pamphylia. On the second trip, Paul refused to take Mark because he had left them on the first missionary journey, but Barnabas was determined to take him along. This resulted in a dispute and separation between Barnabas and Paul. Thus, Barnabas and Mark went to Cyprus, while Paul chose Silas and went through Syria and Cilicia.

Mark spent some time in Cyprus and later was with Simon Peter in Babylon in the Persian Empire. The apostle Simon had been there for some time preaching and teaching Jews and other Semitic clans. Many apostles had traveled to the East seeking "the lost sheep of the house of Israel."

Simon Peter calls Mark "my son" in his first epistle: "The chosen church at Babylon and Mark, my son, salute you."[6] (Interestingly, the patriarch of the Church of the East, whose See was at Seleucia, Persia, assumed the title *Shimon Kepa*—Simon Peter—and this title has been carried to the present day.)

TRADITIONAL BACKGROUND

Mark's gospel greatly resembles Matthew's gospel. By this time in the growing movement, Mark was in possession of most of the scrolls that contained the early preaching of Matthew. The church at Jerusalem and Antioch could hardly have sent out missionaries who were new converts without written material concerning Jesus' teaching. This certainly would be the case with new converts Paul, Mark, Luke and Barnabas. They scarcely knew anything about Jesus' message of the kingdom. This would also be true of the missionaries who followed these men. They would have had to carry Jesus' teachings wherever they went and whenever they preached about their lord's gospel of the Kingdom. American and European missionaries do the same thing on their missionary journeys today.

Mark omits Matthew's genealogy of Jesus, which was probably

---

[6]1 Peter 5:13, K. J. V.

not yet written. Usually, such material was written later when an individual became prominent. Mark stressed the messiahship, miracles and works of Jesus more than the other gospels did. It seems quite probable that when Mark was present at Jerusalem, he copied from the scrolls that Matthew had written. He added what he already knew and what he had learned from the apostle Simon Peter. If this traditional background is correct, then Mark was the man whom the high priest had known.[7] Mark was educated and had been in the Jewish schools that were under the care of the high priest. Presumably, this is one reason why Barnabas and Peter took him with them. Mark could help them in writing letters to the established churches.

Later traditions placed Mark at Alexandria. There is also a seventh century writing that puts him in Italy, where all the apostles, according to European tradition, were buried. But these European traditions are hardly credible because, with the exception of Paul, there is no mention in the gospels that any of the other apostles ever went to Italy. Mark might have died in Persia or he might have returned to Antioch, the home base of the mission. Near Eastern Christians claim and believe that all the apostles except Paul died and were buried in the Near East.

THE DATE OF MARK'S GOSPEL

When and where Mark wrote his gospel is difficult to say. Internal and external evidence on the subject is inadequate and obscure. But if Mark was not the actual writer or compiler of his gospel, he certainly was the author of the documentary sources of the material and its preaching. Some New Testament scholars suggest that it may have been written around 55 CE.[8] However, the dates range from 55 to 75 CE. Traditionally, scholars accept Rome as the

---

[7]See Jn. 18:16. (See also page 1 of this Introduction, "Authorship")

[8]See C. S. Mann, *Mark: A New Translation with Introduction and Commentary*, "The Date of Mark's Gospel," pp.72-77.

birthplace of this gospel. But others suggest Galilee, Syria, the Decapolis and the northern Transjordan. Regardless, Eastern apostolic tradition ascribes the second gospel to Mark.

Interestingly, Irenaeus states that Mark wrote his gospel after Matthew had written his and after the apostle Simon Peter had died. Origen says that it was written before the gospels of Luke and John.[9] However, modern New Testament scholars believe Mark was the first gospel and that Matthew and Luke copied Mark's gospel. Today, there is a growing movement among New Testament scholars who claim that Mark is not the first gospel and that Matthew did not copy Mark.[10] The compositional differences in style and story between the gospels of Mark and Matthew were chiefly due to the understanding and progress of the gospel message in various places. The apostles and disciples had few written, but many oral, sources.

The new Galilean movement was passing through seemingly insurmountable challenges and difficulties, so it was not possible for the early leadership and disciples to meet and decide what was to be accepted or rejected among the writings that were making their appearances. The leadership's time was taken with more pressing issues such as the defense of their movement before Jewish and other religious governing bodies as well as Roman officials. They also had to solve controversial questions about circumcision and other such matters that were rising among the followers of the new movement.

---

[9]Eusebius, His, Eccl. 6, 25, 5.

[10]See C. S. Mann, *MARK: A New Translation with Introduction and Commentary,* "Synoptic Relationships and the Supposed Priority of Mark," pp. 47-71. For a brief history of the "Two-Source Hypothesis" and the German scholar Griesbach who suggested that Matthew was the original gospel and not Mark, see Allan J. McNicol, editor with David L. Dungan and David B. Peabody, *LUKE'S USE OF MATTHEW: BEYOND THE Q IMPASSE—A Demonstration by the Research Team of the International Institute for Gospel Studies,* "Preface, Introduction," pp. xi-xiii, pp. 1-12. This was a team of 30 NT scholars who met in Jerusalem. Also see David Laird Dungan, *A HISTORY OF THE SYNOPTIC PROBLEM,* "Current Trends in Understanding How the Gospels Were Created," pp.368-391.

CHAPTER 1

THE BEGINNING OF THE GOSPEL

The beginning of the gospel of Jesus Christ, the Son of God; As it is written in the prophets, Behold, I send my messenger before thy face, which shall prepare thy way before thee. The voice of one crying in the wilderness, Prepare ye the way of the Lord, make his paths straight. Mk. 1:1-3.

According to Mark, the baptism of Jesus at the river Jordan truly begins the good news. Bishop Ishodad of Merv, in his Aramaic commentaries, says: *"We ought to know that the beginning of the Gospel is the baptism of our Lord, for these things from his conception up until his baptism are not considered to be of the Gospel, although they are additions with it to the Gospel, in order that we may learn in what way his conception and birth happened."*[1]

The Aramaic term *resha*, "beginning," refers to the new era that God brought through Jesus' ministry and his gospel of the kingdom. God had ordained and appointed Jesus for this very purpose; therefore, he was the *msheeha*—Messiah/Christ—meaning "the anointed." He was truly "God's son" in that he did the will of his heavenly Father.

Part 1—THE PROPHECIES. Mark's gospel is the only one that cites prophecy from two Hebrew prophets. (See verses two and three.) Mark quotes from Malachi first: "Behold, I send my messenger before thy face, which shall prepare thy way before thee."[2] Then he finishes with Isaiah: "The voice of one crying in the wilderness. Prepare ye the way of the Lord, make his paths straight."[3]

The beginning of verse two in the Aramaic text does not read: "As it is written in *the prophets*" as does the King James Version. It

---

[1] *THE COMMENTARIES OF ISHO'DAD OF MERV*, BISHOP OF HADATHA, (c. 850 A.D.), in Aramaic, Vol. 2, "Matthew and Mark," p. 207.

[2] See Mal. 3:1.

[3] See Isa. 40:3.

reads: "As it is written in *Isaiah the prophet.*" This agrees with both Matthew's and Luke's accounts. It is most probable that a scribe added the Malachi prophecy on the margin of Mark's scroll for preaching purposes and it was later incorporated into the text itself. Much later, however, the scribes saw that Mark's text now cites two prophets; to solve the problem, they changed the second verse to read "prophets" and dropped the line "Isaiah the prophet" in some New Testament Greek manuscripts.

Part 2—THE VOICE IN THE WILDERNESS. *Madhbrah*, "wilderness" in Aramaic, usually means a barren and silent region without habitation. (It can also mean a place where there is an oasis and some vegetation.) The human voice carries further in the wilderness than among the hills and mountain regions because the land is generally level with nothing to impede its sound. Hills and mountains often create echoes.

John's voice was like a shepherd in the wilderness calling and warning his sheep. His voice was clear and direct. He brought a powerful and persuasive message to the Jewish people. The message John proclaimed had no theological dogmas. He did not want to confuse his people. His criticisms of the behavior of the scribes, Pharisees, and soldiers were concise and emphatic. Everyone could understand him. His clear and simple demand was for genuine piety, integrity, and justice by returning to God (repentance) and good works. It is not surprising that although his ministry as a prophet was short lived, his voice (message) carried far and is still heard today.

Part 3—PREPARATION. Sanitary departments and public works were unknown in Near Eastern lands, especially where ancient customs and practices still dominated. The governments seldom built new bridges and roads and those constructed in former days were not repaired. King's highways and other thoroughfares were obstructed at the entrance to cities with piles of refuse that were usually sold to the farmers.

Commonly, people cleaned the cities and repaired the roads only when they expected an official visit of a king or prince. In addition, the citizens of the town would frequently decorate the entrance to the city and the streets through which the royal visitor was to pass with tapestry, rugs, and artistic ornaments. Often, rivalry arose among the people, who tried to outdo one another with their decorations so that they might be the special ones to receive the greater honor from the royal visitor. Local officials also took great care to make sure the royal entourage entered the city without any accidents or delays. The rise or fall of many officials depended on the attention they would give to this very important matter.

John was calling to the people of his nation to clean house. He was heralding a new era. The advent of a new age required the removal of sin through repentance and the return to good works. The Jews were to prepare themselves for the royal visitor. They were to rid themselves of false teachings and the burdensome traditions of the elders, which were obstructions to the coming king and kingdom. The Jewish nation was to prepare the way for the new laws of God's kingdom not only for themselves as a people but for all the nations of the world. In Luke 3:7-14, John very clearly and precisely tells his people what they must do to show that they were truly turning to God in preparation for the dawning kingdom and arriving king.

JOHN IN THE WILDERNESS

John did baptize in the wilderness, and preach the baptism of repentance for the remission of sins. Mk. 1:4.

Part 1—THE OPEN COUNTRY. The word "wilderness" does not always mean an arid desert where one cannot find water or vegetation. (See above commentary: The Voice in the Wilderness.)[4] At times, regions with abundant water and vegetation are called *horba*, meaning "an uninhabited region." Also, a town that is no longer inhabited or that has been destroyed is called *haraba*, meaning "desolate." In this verse, "wilderness" refers to an uninhabited area

---

[4]Also see Errico/Lamsa, *ARAMAIC LIGHT ON THE GOSPEL OF MATTHEW*, NT Series Vol. 1, "Chapter 4," part B—Wilderness, pp. 44-45.

that people used for pastoral purposes only. John did not baptize in an arid desert region but at the river Jordan, where water was abundant. We also read about Jesus leaving the cities and retreating to the wilderness for prayer and fasting. The area he went to was not an arid place. Sheep-raising people commonly live in such regions the year around.

Of course, there are areas that are nothing but arid deserts. Near Easterners call these regions *madhbra*. These places are between Palestine and the Red Sea peninsula. The desert is sandy and without water. Interestingly, nomad tribes who live in black tents inhabit most areas of the Arabian desert. They raise sheep and other animals in these regions.

Bara is another Aramaic word for "wilderness," but it literally signifies "open country." Our English word "barbarian" comes from the Aramaic word *barbara*. It is a compound word—*bar*, meaning "son" and *bara*, "of the open country." This word literally translates as "son of the open country or desert"—in other words, a "Bedouin."

Part B—BAPTISM OF REPENTANCE. The King James version reads: ". . .and preach the baptism of repentance for the remission of sins." The word "repentance" derives from the Semitic root *tuwu* (*shuwu* in Hebrew.) It means "turn, return." The Aramaic noun for "repentance," *tyawootha* (Hebrew: *tishuwa*) refers to the action of turning or returning—that is, "turn to, return to God." One must turn to God, the covenant and the practice of good works, all of which bring forgiveness of sin and salvation. "Remission (forgiveness) of sins" denotes "to be released from sins." (See also Luke 3:3.)

John's preaching was contrary to the usual manner of receiving "forgiveness of sins." According to the law, the common way people could atone for—be released from—their sins was through animal sacrifices. Remission or forgiveness of sins was through the shedding of blood. The writer of the epistle to the Hebrews confirms this belief when he says: "And almost all things are by the law purged with blood; and without the shedding of blood there is no remission."[5]

---

[5]Heb. 9:22, K. J. V.

Those who submitted to John's water baptism, which was an outward sign, and had truly repented inwardly—that is, had turned to God and were doing good works—found "forgiveness of sins."

THE KINGDOM OF GOD

Now after that John was put in prison, Jesus came into Galilee, preaching the gospel of the kingdom of God, and saying, The time is fulfilled, and the kingdom of God is at hand: repent ye, and believe the gospel. Mk. 1:14-15.

The Aramaic text reads: "Now after John had been arrested, Jesus came to Galilee and was announcing the joyful message of God's sovereign presence, proclaiming: This age has ended! God's sovereign presence is here! Everyone return to God and have confidence in the joyful message!"[6]

Whenever persecution, injustice and suffering prevail, Semites dream of better governments and laws that benefit everyone. And, when men fail to bring justice and good government, people look to God as the only true sovereign. They begin to look to God's heavenly reign as the only means for genuine justice, happiness, and prosperity. To a Near Easterner, God is a house of refuge during times of trouble and a shelter in the midst of persecution and war. With all their hearts, they place their complete trust in God. They pray continually and wait patiently for the coming of God's sovereign presence.

During the reign of the Israelite kings, Palestine was the major connecting link between Assyria and Egypt. Therefore, it was exposed to attacks from its enemies and from warring Eastern nations. Assyrians, Chaldeans, and Egyptians made it a battleground in their wars against each other. Palestinian natives were the victims of the belligerent. During these conflicts, large military battalions were transported into Palestine and the land was often left devastated.

---

[6]Mk. 1:14-15, Aramaic Peshitta text, Errico.

9

Retreating forces would confiscate cattle and sheep, and the victorious armies would levy heavy tribute on the people.

After the fall of Assyria and Egypt, mistreatment and misrule still continued to plague the Jewish people. They suffered persecutions and onslaughts during the Greek assaults in their land. They also had to endure oppressive Greek rule throughout Palestine. Then, after the Roman invasion and the annexation of Judea to the Roman empire, the people were burdened with three major forms of taxation: one to Caesar, a second to the Jewish state, and a third to the temple. They also had to pay a head tax. (During the reign of King David, the people paid only one tax.)

When the Davidic dynasty ended, the state of Judah became subjected to foreign yoke. This is when the people began to hope for a better kingdom—the heavenly kingdom of God wherein they could find peace and happiness. This would be the Messiah's kingdom on earth. Pagan rule would be overthrown and Israel would be restored to power and prosperity. Eventually, this messianic kingdom would become the great kingdom of God, where spiritual and moral character would prevail regardless of racial differences. Therefore, the Galileans were overjoyed to hear Jesus announcing God's kingdom.

According to Matthew, Jesus went throughout Galilee, teaching in the synagogues and proclaiming the joyful message of the kingdom.[7] He demonstrated the presence of the kingdom through his own life, his healing power and his social behavior. He befriended the outcasts of society and celebrated God's presence with the poor, the harlots, tax collectors and sinners. He went to their homes, eating and drinking with them. Jesus revealed that God was among the people.

Part 1—THE TERM "GOSPEL." The gospel authors use three distinct words in their writings that we usually translate as "gospel"—*swartha, evangalion, karozutha.* (1) *Swartha* comes from the Aramaic root *swr*, meaning to "hope, trust, declare, announce,

---

[7]See Mt. 4:23-25.

tell, bring news and publish abroad." One may translate *swartha* as the joyful "message, hope, or expectation." An appropriate rendering into English would depend on the scriptural context. Jesus had a joyful message (gospel) because he announced that God's reign was dawning.

(2) *Evangalion* derives directly from Greek, although some Aramaic experts dispute this notion. They claim that *evangalion* originated from Aramaic. However, Aramaic nouns that terminate in "ion" are loan words from Greek. This Aramaic word has the same meaning as the Greek *euangelion*, "good news." It also had a secondary meaning in Greek—one of absolution when a king ascends the throne. Some Aramaic linguists suggest that the word should be translated as "revelation," claiming that the ending of the word *galion* derives from the Aramaic *gilyana*, "revelation."

(3) *Karozutha* comes from the Aramaic root *krz*, meaning to "preach, declare, make known, announce, and publicly celebrate." All three words are correct when translated as "gospel," but we lose the specific meaning that lies behind each word. The gospel (*swartha*) according to Jesus is the *joyful announcement* of God's reigning presence.

Part 2—KINGDOM. The term "kingdom," *malkutha* (Hebrew: *malkuth*), comes from the Semitic root *mlkh*. It means to "advise, counsel, reign and rule." A king, *malka* in Aramaic, also means a "counselor." According to Aramaic *targumin* or targums (interpretations) of those times, God's Kingdom referred strictly to God. Therefore, the term "kingdom of God" represented God's sovereign presence. God was the ruler, king or counselor. Jesus' message was a call to recognize God's active presence in the world. He had a vision of God that went beyond the religious limits of his day. He perceived God as working among people, moving in and through their daily routine living, despite the poverty, fears, and suffering.[8] He awakened his compatriots and followers to the reign of God by

---

[8]See Rocco A. Errico, *AND THERE WAS LIGHT*, "Uncovering Jesus' Gospel," pp. 32-41.

11

telling parables that would help them to focus on the unobservable but dawning kingdom. "God's kingdom cannot be recognized by sight. No one will be able to say: Look, here it is! Or, look it is there! It is just the opposite. God's reign [sovereign presence] is present among you!"[9]

FISHERS OF MEN

And Jesus said unto them, Come ye after me, and I will make you to become fishers of men. Mk. 1:17.

The Aramaic word *sayadeh* primarily means "hunters." However, Aramaic speaking people use the same word for "fishermen" and for "those who hunt birds." It comes from the root word meaning to "hunt, chase, fish, capture, catch and take." Usually, Semites do not indulge in games, but those who do are also nicknamed *sayadeh*.

The metaphorical expression "I will make you fishers of men" means "you will catch and persuade men by your speech." For example, Jesus' enemies tried to "catch" him with their words. His adversaries hunted for words so that they could ensnare him. They would ask certain questions that they thought he could not answer. In the Near East, winning people to your ideas is generally done through debates. There are various expressions of speech that carry this idea. For instance: "He catches men with his mouth." (See Mark 12:13.)

What Jesus meant by "fishers of men" is that his disciples were to be so well tutored and versed in scripture that they could silence even the high priests and could catch men by their words and win them over to the new teaching about God's kingdom. Most of his disciples were fishermen by trade, but instead of catching fish and hunting animals, they would travel everywhere bringing in recruits for the kingdom. This was a notable position for these obscure fishermen. They were soon to stand before the high priests, state

[9]Lk. 17:20-21, Aramaic Peshitta text, Errico.

12

officials, governors and kings, testifying for their lord and proving he was the Messiah/Christ.

UNCLEAN SPIRIT

And there was in their synagogue a man with an unclean spirit; and he cried out, Saying, Let us alone; what have we to do with thee, thou Jesus of Nazareth? art thou come to destroy us? I know thee who thou art, the Holy One of God. And Jesus rebuked him, saying, Hold thy peace, and come out of him. Mk. 1:23-25.

"Unclean spirit" in Aramaic is *ruha tamtha*. It refers to a person who is unruly, mentally ill, hot tempered, an individual with bad intentions or who is inclined to do evil. Near Easterners consider any impulse to do wrong as "unclean" whether it be toward a person, with food, in a speech or teaching.

In biblical days people did not know anything about medical terms. They thought that people who suffered mentally were possessed by an evil spirit. The impulse to behave weirdly or wrongly was an "unclean spirit." *Ruha*, "spirit," in Aramaic has many meanings—"wind, temper, pride, rheumatism, inclination, impulse, a person" to name a few.

When this man who was somewhat mentally deranged saw Jesus in the synagogue, he could not control his anger toward him. He had heard some of the men who were attending the synagogue discussing and making attacks against the Galilean teacher. They had been accusing Jesus of being a dangerous prophet and an enemy of their faith. Jesus, on different occasions, had disapproved of some of the scribes, Pharisees, and religious authorities. He also had changed many of the ideas about the law and did not follow the teachings of the elders. Therefore, these men disagreed with Jesus' teachings. They looked upon him as a subversive teacher and not to be trusted, but they did not have the courage to personally confront him.

Nonetheless, the mentally ill man did cry out in a rage against Jesus. "Let us alone! What have we to do with you, Jesus of

13

Nazareth? Have you come to destroy us?" Then, in a sarcastic, despising and demeaning tone of voice he said to Jesus: "I know who you are, Holy One of God." Such remarks are also determined by facial expressions and hand gestures of the speaker. (Interestingly, in the Near East, an insane person can even rebuke a king or prince without offending him. The ruler will not punish that individual's wild and bad conduct.)

The impulsive man's erratic behavior, angry rebukes, and sarcastic remarks had no effect on the Galilean prophet. Instead, in a powerful and persuasive voice, Jesus rebuked the man and called for him to calm down. He said to him: "Hold thy peace and come out of him." The man immediately responded to Jesus' compelling, but calming, healing presence. At first the man began to convulse and shout; then an emotionally serene and stable state of heart and mind replaced the rage and shaking. Jesus restored him to sanity. As a result of this episode, Jesus' fame spread throughout the surrounding region of Galilee.

THE EVENING HOUR

And at even, when the sun did set, they brought unto him, all that were diseased, and them that were possessed with devils. Mk. 1:32.

During the summer months, the heat in Palestine is intense. Laborers do very little work; sheep are in the hill country, grazing; farmers are waiting for harvest. Most people spend the day at home so that they can avoid the heat. But in the evening, they gather on the housetops or sit under trees discussing town affairs or debating religious subjects. It is usually during the summer evenings that meetings, conferences, and social affairs take place.

The sick and infirm also remain in the house until the sun begins to sink behind the hills and the cooling shadows fall. Then, those who are ill with fever rise to perform some of their daily tasks or go to healers. Family members or friends usually bring the seriously ill out of the house, lying them on a quilt to rest beneath the shadows of

14

trees or near a wall. Near Easterners believe the sun is bad for sick people.

So, in the evening everyone is generally outdoors. It was at this time that Jesus preached to the people and healed the sick who were brought to him from Capernaum and neighboring towns. (It was the common belief that all kinds of diseases and illnesses were the activities of evil spirits—that the sickness was "possessing" the ill.)

CASTING OUT DEVILS

And he healed many that were sick of divers diseases, and cast out many devils; and suffered not the devils to speak, because they knew him. Mk. 1:34.

The Aramaic word for devil is *dewa*. *Dewana* is the adjective of *dewa* and means "insane." A similar word that Aramaic speaking people use is *shedana*. This Aramaic word means "a demented person" and refers to one whose talk is jumbled and whose mind is unbalanced. This word also describes an individual who has an uncontrollable temper, one who flares up with intense anger for apparently no good reason. At times people thoughtlessly call each other *shedana* or *dewana*. Although these terms sound strange and also refer to so-called invisible spirits called demons and devils, they are really the names of diseases known to the ancients. When we translate these terms into modern languages, we lose the original meanings just as English, Latin, and Greek medical and scientific terms lose their meanings when rendered into Aramaic. For instance, toward the end of the 19th century, a Near Eastern Semite might think of the term "radio waves" as sorcery, electricity would be something magical, and the names of medicines might appear as the designations of invisible powers.

Until the middle of the 20th century, many Eastern countries did not know anything about insane asylums and sanitariums. There still exist some areas that know nothing of these places. The mentally ill lived with their own people. They married, worked, went to church

15

and at times were apparently normal, but the townspeople still thought of them as crazy and often made fun of them. To be sure, there were moments when these mentally unbalanced persons would become violent and tear their clothes, walking naked through the town, swearing and cursing. They often broke down doors, frightening women and children, and sometimes causing injuries to the public. Even then, most of these troubled people remained free to do as they pleased because the townfolk had respect and sympathy for the relatives of these individuals. Nevertheless, when their violent acts went out of control, their own people bound them in chains.

Strangely enough, some of the mentally ill were regular churchgoers. They attended meetings and listened to the preachers not so much to learn to pray and hear the lesson but to imitate the speakers. After the meetings, they gathered curiosity seekers in the streets and lectured them, mimicking the priest or rabbi. Their families often took them to churches, sacred shrines or holy men in hopes of a cure. When healed, they changed suddenly and became very docile and agreeable. Once this happened they were ready to give everything they had, even to dedicate their lives, to the shrine or healer.

When these people find peace in their souls and complete restoration of mind, they become deeply pious. They go about telling others how they were healed, praising the man who had cured them. Naturally, some of them would exaggerate and at times embarrass the healer. For example, a man who had been crazy for only two years might add a few more years and say that he had been crazy for ten years. Another might exaggerate and say that not only was he healed of his mental illness but the healer cured his lameness. Such mendacities reflect on the healers.

Jesus did not like the publicity and fame. He wanted nothing for his healing work. Some of the mentally ill people whom Jesus healed were his acquaintances. Some of them had known him for years and had worked with him in the fields. Others knew his father and mother. They were surprised that Jesus had such spiritual healing powers. When they were healed, thinking to please Jesus, they began to spread his name everywhere and brought other cases to him. Jesus told them not to publicize his healing powers because that would take away the time he needed to teach and preach the gospel of the kingdom. This is what the verse means that reads: ". . .and suffered not the devils to speak, because they knew him." Jesus did not address invisible, evil spirits. Besides, evil spirits would not have declared his healing powers to people.[10]

TOUCHING AND HEALING A LEPER

And Jesus, moved with compassion, put forth his hand, and touched him, and saith unto him, I will; be thou clean. Mk. 1:41.

The Aramaic word for "leper" is *garwa;* in Hebrew it is *mezora* (see Leviticus 13:1-59). It means one who suffers from a skin disorder. In ancient biblical days the term "leprosy" applied to a wide range of skin ailments, among them the one that we know today as an incurable skin disease. This kind of leprosy is very contagious. When it breaks out in a community, every person is warned to be extremely cautious. As soon as a leper is pronounced unclean, even his family members refrain from touching him. The fear of this terrible disease makes a leper helpless and an outcast. If the leper happens to be wealthy or in a high position, he can remain in his own house. Those in charge keep his food and clothes separate from everyone else.

Part 1—TOUCHING. In those days, it was unlawful to touch a leper until the priest pronounced him clean.[11] Jesus was not afraid of this frightful disease. He knew that his healing power was stronger than this devastating skin disorder (which often resulted from extremely bad hygiene and uncleanliness.)

By touching the leper, Jesus proved that he was not afraid of it. This act removed fear from the mind of the leper. Semites regard healers and holy men as immune from disease, but ordinary people are afraid to touch someone with a contagious skin disease. Some

---

[10]See Mt. 4:2; Lk. 4:40.
[11]See Lev. 14.

17

seek a special blessing from a healer so that they can have protection against a possible attack of leprosy.

Jesus did not have to touch the leper to heal him. Frequently, he healed people by a word.[12] Jesus reached out and touched the leper to dispel the fear that had gained a firm grip on the man. Once the man's fear was alleviated, the healing forces could regenerate the body and cleanse the skin.

Part 2—JESUS ADMONISHED THE LEPER. "And, as soon as he had spoken, immediately the leprosy departed from him and he was cleansed. And he straitly charged him, and forthwith sent him away; And saith unto him, See thou say nothing to any man; but go thy way, shew thyself to the priest, and offer for thy cleansing those things which Moses commanded, for a testimony unto them."[13]

Evidently, while Jesus was in the synagogue preaching, healing and restoring the mentally ill, the leper came seeking healing from him. (See Mark 1:39.) When the leper was healed, he was so overwhelmed that he forgot to do his duty according to the Mosaic ordinance concerning leprosy. Instead of rushing to see the priest, who had the sole authority to declare him clean, he kept talking and boasting about his healing. Jesus knew that without the order of the priest the leper could not come and go among the people. So Jesus admonished him: "Why do you talk about it? Go and show yourself to the priest, who will give you a bill of clearance." (Leviticus 14:2-3)

Jesus had no intention of weakening the Mosaic laws and ordinances; he sought to strengthen them. This confirms what he had previously taught: "I have not come to weaken the law and the prophets, but to put them into practice." Indeed, Jesus did not wish to have any unnecessary conflict with the religious authorities.

---

[12]See Mt. 8:2-4; Lk. 5:12-14.
[13]Mk. 1:42-44, K. J. V.

18

CHAPTER 2

UNCOVERING THE ROOF

And they came unto him, bringing one sick of the palsy, which was borne of four. And when they could not come nigh unto him for the press, they uncovered the roof where he was; and when they had broken it up, they let down the bed wherein the sick of the palsy lay. Mk. 2:3-4.

Those who live in modern western cities and are accustomed to seeing tall buildings and skyscrapers would find it difficult to understand and visualize a Near Eastern house. They would probably wonder how these men could carry a sick man up to the housetop and then break up the roof so that they could lower him from the ceiling. But those who have lived in the Near East know that this was quite practical.

Most homes in the old towns of Syria and Palestine are still built in the same style as in the times of Abraham and Jacob. Dwellings are constructed of rough stones, unbaked bricks, and mud. They are built in the shape of a square box without windows but with an air chimney in the center of the flat roof. Some houses are not more than ten to twelve feet in height and have only one story. Two story houses were very rare. The back walls of homes built on a hilly slope are not more than two or three feet high, so it is easy to get on the roof without a ladder. Houses are built adjacent to each other and the roofs are so evenly arranged that they serve as playgrounds for children. They also serve as meeting places for men and women. In some instances, when a town is built on a hill or mountain slope, the roof of one house serves as a courtyard for the adjoining home.

Roofs are made of beams and branches of trees. The builders throw a layer of straw over the branches and cover the straw with earth. These roofs are so poorly constructed that when it rains, the roofs leak badly. On some housetops one can see wide open holes. Strangers could easily watch what was happening in the house below by looking through these holes or even through the chimney. Often,

19

business and social conversation passes between the people in the house and those on the roof. Therefore, it was an easy task for the four men to make a larger hole in the roof. It takes only a few minutes to remove the branches. This recalls a Semitic proverb: "When the master of the house and the thieves work together, they can steal an ox through the ceiling."

On this occasion, the house was crowded and it was difficult for the men to carry the paralytic into the home. Others who had brought their sick to Jesus were ahead of them. However, these men did not lose hope. Since they could not enter by the door, they could do so by the roof. So, these four men carried their sick friend in his bedroll up to the roof. They probably looked through the chimney or one of the wide holes to see where Jesus was seated. Then they opened a space in the roof between the beams and lowered the sick man on his bedroll.

The house was so congested with the sick and their relatives, and the noise was so great, that the owner of the house was not aware of what was happening on his roof. It was not until everyone saw the bedroll containing the paralytic hanging from the ceiling and slowly descending to where Jesus was seated that the people realized what was happening. It was quite a surprise. It was a very ingenious act and the men's faith and perseverance were so great that Jesus was deeply moved. He affectionately responded and healed the paralytic.

YOUR SINS ARE FORGIVEN

Whether is it easier to say to the sick of the palsy, Thy sins be forgiven thee; or to say, Arise, and take up thy bed, and walk? Mk. 2:9.

It was the common belief of the people at that time that sickness was the result of sin—that is, guilt. According to rabbinic sources, a prayer for forgiveness precedes the prayer for healing. To say to a man suffering from palsy "take your bedroll and walk" is far more miraculous than to say "your sins are forgiven," although forgiveness may be needed. Palsy is an extremely formidable disease to heal.

Many teachers of religion can easily say "Your sins are forgiven." Judges can forgive people their trespasses; kings and governors can commute death sentences. But to say to another human being suffering from palsy, a dreaded disease, "take up your bedroll and walk" is more challenging and difficult. Most healers would shun such a case.

The Pharisees were told that no one could forgive sins but God and that the high priest was the only one who could make atonement on behalf of the people for their sins. But God had sent Jesus and he had the power to forgive sins and to heal any kind of disease. Surely, any religious teacher endowed with such tremendous healing capability could forgive sin and heal people.

RECLINING AT MEALS

And it came to pass, that as Jesus sat at meat in his house, many publicans and sinners sat also together with Jesus and his disciples: for there were many, and they followed him. Mk. 2:15.

The Aramaic word *smikeh*, "reclining," also means "guests." It comes from the Aramaic root *smkh*. In Near Eastern countries some guests sit upright on the floor with their legs folded under them; others, more honored, recline against bedding, clothes, rugs or other objects used as cushions. Tables and chairs as we know them in the Occidental world were unknown. As soon as a guest enters a home, the women rush to bring a carpet or a quilt to put under him as a token of hearty welcome. According to Eastern etiquette, any man visiting another as a guest must have food placed before him. It does not matter what time of the day it may be or if the guest has just previously eaten somewhere else. This custom has been modified in recent years in Palestine, Turkey and Persia. They now just serve coffee or tea instead of food.

21

PUBLICANS, SINNERS AND THE PHARISEES

And when the scribes and Pharisees saw him eat with publicans and sinners, they said unto his disciples, How is it that he eateth and drinketh with publicans and sinners? Mk. 2:16.

Publicans are the tax collectors of the Near East. They function quite differently from the revenue and customs officers in America and Europe. They are not necessarily employees of the government, nor is their task solely confined to collecting customs duties. They collect taxes and revenues as agents of one who has purchased this privilege from the government.

Governments levy taxes and tribute on salt, animals, land, and on certain export and import articles. Usually, the government assigns the collection of taxes to the highest bidders. For the most part, these bidders are district leaders and powerful overlords. Since they have now contracted with the government, they, in turn, recruit shrewd and cruel men as their tax collectors so that they can fulfill their obligations and make a good profit.

Publicans must survey crops, count sheep, and levy taxes. The total issue of taxes is left entirely to their discretion. They can tax as high or low as they please. The central government has nothing to say. It is satisfied to have the contract fulfilled and the amount of money pledged by contractors paid into the treasury. Government officials are indifferent to the methods that their collectors may employ to exact taxes. Therefore, the public, especially the poor, are at the mercy of dishonest publicans who accept bribes and collect unjust and undue taxes which they share with government officials.

Commonly, they exact taxes by force and violence. When the poor fail to pay the sums assessed or if they protest the confiscation of their crops or sheep, the tax collectors will strip them of their clothes, unmercifully beat them and make them examples so that the collection of taxes from others will be easier. The publicans search homes for hidden money and goods. Women and children become panic-stricken during this time. This is the reason people hate publicans so intensely and consider them sinners. No man of high social standing accepts the post of publican. The injustice done by them is never forgiven. Furthermore, the people believe that God will never forgive them in the world to come. Men of reputation and piety are reluctant even to touch or speak to a publican on the street. He is an outcast and everyone shuns his association.

Publicans are always the target of priests and religious reformers who denounce and brand them as traitors. The publican's bread is called "the bread of blood" and many will not eat it because they perceive him and his bread as unclean. The Pharisees did not want to eat with the Publicans and sinners, because for them breaking bread was more than just sharing a meal; it was also a time for learned discussion and prayer. They also strictly adhered to the codes of purity and impurity and could not eat with sinners who were neither versed in these laws nor observed them.

Despite all this, the publicans were friendly to Jesus because he attacked the priests and Pharisees and had more respect for publicans and sinners than for those who wore religious garb and imposed taxes on the people in the name of God. These men saw a new light through Jesus' teachings and his socio-religious acceptance of harlots, tax collectors, and sinners. This was a marvel in their eyes.

ABIATHAR

And he said unto them, Have ye never read what David did, when he had need, and was an hungered, he, and they that were with him? How he went into the house of God in the days of Abiathar the high priest, and did eat the shewbread, which is not lawful to eat but for the priests, and gave also to them which were with him? Mk.2:25-26.

The high priest, during this particular episode with David, was Ahimelech, the son of Ahitub. Abiathar was Ahimelech's son and also ministered with his father and brothers. The narrative here differs in detail from 1 Samuel 21:1-6. The gospels of Matthew and Luke do not mention Abiathar. Some New Testament authorities suggest that it was an early gloss that a copyist supplied or that Mark added the name because Abiathar was well known for his association with King David.[1]

When David fled before Saul he stopped at Nob, the city of priests. He and the men who were with him were hungry and there was no bread, so Ahimelech supplied them with the sacred bread of the presence that was before the Lord in the tabernacle. Only priests could eat this sacred bread, but the emergency induced the priests to yield to David's need and demand. The moment David and his men ate the sacred bread, they broke the holy law.

This generous act toward David and his men made King Saul destroy the city of Nob and kill all the priests and their families.[2] But Abiathar had escaped with David. When David became the sole ruler in Israel, he made Abiathar the high priest. Later, Solomon sent Abiathar away and appointed Zadok the priest in his place.[3] Solomon took away Abiathar's position of high priest because of the part he played in the intrigue of Adonijah, King David's son, who had usurped the throne of his father.

---

[1]See also 2 Sam. 8:17.
[2]1 Sam. 22:17-20.
[3]1 Kings 2:26-27, 35.

CHAPTER 3

THE INSANE CONFESS JESUS

And unclean spirits, when they saw him, fell down before him, and cried, saying, Thou art the Son of God. Mk. 3:11.

The term *ruheh tanpatha* refers to individuals who are mentally deranged.[1] When the insane men approached Jesus, they felt his spiritual presence and knew he was a holy man. They fell at his feet and worshiped him as an act of reverence.

In the Near East, even violent, mentally unbalanced people honor and bow down to priests and holy men; they recognize them by the priestly garments. Quite a number of insane men usually attend prayer meetings. Evidently, these men had, on some occasion, seen Jesus preach, teach and heal or had heard about his healing powers. They called him "Son of God," because they wanted to honor him as a holy man. "Son of God" here simply means "you are a God-like or godly man." It was these mentally ill men who cried out and not some evil, invisible spirits.[2] Had it been the unclean spirits, they would never have confessed Jesus as "the Son of God."

SCRIBES AND RELATIVES ACCUSE JESUS

And when his friends heard of it, they went out to lay hold on him: for they said, He is beside himself. And the scribes which came down from Jerusalem said, He hath Beelzebub, and by the prince of the devils casteth he out devils. Mk. 3:21 22.

Part 1—JESUS DENOUNCED BY RELATIVES. The Aramaic word *hyanaw* means "his relatives." The word for "friends" is

---

[1]See Mk. 1:23-25, commentary "Unclean Spirit."
[2]See Lk. 4:41.

kariwan and *rahmeh*. It was Jesus' relatives who came to seize him and not his friends. His relatives thought that he had lost his mind. We are also told of other occasions when his brothers did not believe in him.[3] Others said that he had a devil—that is, he was crazy.[4]

Jesus' actions and claims to messiahship were an embarrassment to his relatives. They were afraid of the religious authorities who might expel them from the synagogue. Jesus had said: "No prophet is without honor except in his own town and among his own relatives." It is probable that this was the reason he did not go out to meet his mother and his brothers when they called on him.[5]

Part 2—TRUE AND FALSE HEALERS. There are both genuine and fake healers in the Near East. Semites believe that their power either comes from God or from Satan. This is based on the ancient belief in dualism that holds there is one god of good and another god of evil. They also believe that either angels or demons influence humankind. Today we know that many bad influences come from ignorance and superstition. In ancient days, people even offered their children as burnt offerings on the altars to idols. But neither God nor evil forces were responsible for such human sacrifices.

A human being under God's power is able to prophesy, work miracles and heal the sick. When individuals are under the power of evil, they practice sorcery, curses and black magic—common practices in the Near East. At times, it can be difficult to discern between people who possess these powers because both can work miracles and wonders. Those who are really charlatans claim that they are working for God and that the public seeks their help. For example, compare the works of Moses and those of the Egyptian magicians. Also compare the struggle for supremacy between Elijah and the prophets of Baal.[6] The charge against Jesus that he had an

---

[3] See Jn. 7:5.
[4] Jn. 10:20.
[5] See Mk. 3:31-35.
[6] See Ex. 7:11 and 1 Kings 18:21.

unclean spirit classed him in the same category as the medium of Endor.[7] It was not true, but it was advanced to discredit his mission and his miraculous powers. It was an attack by Jesus' enemies. However, Jesus emphatically denied that he derived his power from Satan. He said one devil could not cast out another without destroying his own realm. How could a kingdom remain if it was divided against itself?[8]

JESUS' RELATIVES

There came then his brethren and his mother, and standing without, sent unto him, calling him. Mk. 3:31.

Jesus' relatives did not follow him because they were afraid of being expelled from the synagogue. When he pronounced himself as the Messiah, at the synagogue in Nazareth,[9] the people took him out to throw him from the edge of the hill,[10] but he escaped and fled to Capernaum.

At the outset, Jesus' relatives did not want to have any part in his mission and messianic claims because of their fear. A Jew would choose to die rather than be excommunicated and disowned by his people. When Jesus became popular and began to gain friends in the cities around the Lake of Galilee, his relatives came to see him, but he did not go out to greet them. He knew they had branded him as an insane person and he did not want to interrupt his discourse. (See Mark 3:21.) He pointed to his disciples and told the crowd that these disciples were his relatives. They had left everything and followed him. Jesus' relatives, friends and the inhabitants of Nazareth knew him as a child, as a youth and as a mature man. They did not believe he could be the long awaited promised one—the Messiah.

---

[7]See 1 Sam. 28:7.
[8]Mt. 9:32-34, 12:25-26; Lk. 11:14-15.
[9]Lk. 4:18-23.
[10]Lk. 4:29.

CHAPTER 4

SECRETS REVEALED

And he said unto them, Is a candle brought to be put under a bushel, or under a bed? And not be set on a candlestick? For there is nothing hid, which shall not be manifested: neither was anything kept secret, but that it should come abroad. Mk. 4:21-22.

The Aramaic text reads: "And he said to them, Is a lamp brought and put under a basket or under a bed? Is it not put on a lampstand? For there is nothing hidden which will not be uncovered; and nothing done in secret which will not be revealed."[1]

The reference here is to the Jewish religion. "Lamp" means the light of God which was the Torah. Israel was to share the light of God with its neighboring nations. It was to be put on a lampstand so that it might give light to all those who were living in darkness. The Jewish religion had its cultic side with the priesthood and the temple. The worship of God was enshrined in great mystery, rituals, and ceremonies. How could Israel part with the mysteries of its religion? All religions in those days were mystical, esoteric, and clannish. All priests and learned men used magic as part of their religion. According to the book of Acts, Moses had been trained in the art of magic. The Egyptian priests had also been trained in magic. They were able to duplicate the same wonders that Moses performed before Pharaoh.

Jesus told the people that secrets could only be kept for a short while but not forever. In the Near East what is often done in secret is sooner or later discussed in the marketplaces and on the housetops and private matters are usually subjected to public scrutiny. Jesus understood human nature and knew (as is true in all cultures) that when told a secret, people can hardly wait to tell a friend.

When Jesus healed someone, he usually told the person not to tell anyone. But, the one who was healed told it all the more. If you

---

[1]Mk. 4:21-22, Aramaic Peshitta text, Lamsa translation.

should tell a Near Easterner to go and tell a secret, his reply will be: "Why don't you go and tell it yourself?"

Jesus was soon to reveal all the hidden secrets of the Jewish religion and would be sharing the "lamp of God," holy scripture, with the Gentile nations. What had previously been whispered in the dark, dim temple would be discussed openly on the housetops. The light of God—like air, water and heat—is universal and is given by God, not to be kept a secret, but to be shared with all humanity. We cannot hide the revelation of God. We cannot keep secret that which God intended to be made known and to benefit all humankind.

THE MEASURE

And he said unto them, Take heed what ye hear; with what measure ye mete, it shall be measured to you; and unto you that hear shall more be given. Mk. 4:24.

A wheat measure is a square wooden box about two feet wide and fourteen inches deep. Most wheat growers in the Near East have one or two wheat measures varying in size. This creates mistrust on the part of the buyers. Some shrewd buyers prefer to select their own measures before they purchase wheat.

Once the price of the wheat is settled between the seller and buyer, the owner kneels down and places the wooden measure between his knees and the wheat is poured into it until it is filled. However, before they settled on the fixed price for the wheat, they had to agree as to whether the measure will be shaken or not. Good and generous sellers of wheat shake it and let the wheat flow over it, but some sellers resent having the buyer touch the measure or shake it.

When borrowing wheat, the borrower selects the same measure and uses the same methods of measuring when returning it to the owner. If the measure was shaken down when he borrowed the wheat, he will do the same.

In the Near East, cheating by measure is a frequent occurrence.

29

At times, people buy with one measure and sell with another. Even in dry goods shops, merchants who still use the arm as the standard means of measuring generally cheat customers in a shop by having one partner with long arms and another with short arms. The man with long arms buys material goods made in the homes and the man with short arms sells the same material in his shop.

Weights and balances are also very unreliable. Every family has its own weights that consist of one or two pieces of stone or two or three bricks. These pieces are apt to break off at the edges because children often play with them.

Jesus had seen so much cheating and dishonesty in business that this warning against deception was quite appropriate. In his kingdom true measures were to be practiced.[2]

LAKE OF GALILEE

And there arose a great storm of wind, and the waves beat into the ship, so that it was now full. And he was in the hinder part of the ship, asleep on a pillow: and they awake him, and say unto him, Master, carest thou not that we perish? And he arose, and rebuked the wind and said unto the sea, Peace be still. And the wind ceased and there was a great calm. Mk. 4:37-39.

The Lake of Galilee, although small in size, is often and suddenly visited by terrible windstorms. As quick and unexpected as the wind- storm comes, it can also go. The lake is situated in a valley six hundred feet below sea level. Strong winds blow from the north toward the Dead Sea in the south and agitate the waters of the lake. Such storms are dangerous because Easterners are poor mariners and are easily frightened when a tempest overtakes them.

Semitic people have faith in their holy men. They believe that these men can rebuke storms and sickness as well as bless, curse, bring or stop rain. During a storm, holy men quote scripture, then

---

[2]See Mt. 7:2 and Lk. 6:38.

command the winds to be calm. When someone is ill, they read passages from scripture that tell of God's sovereignty over evil. After the reading, they rebuke and command the disease to leave the sick.

Jesus was a holy man and a great healer. When his disciples became frightened because of the sudden windstorm, they called on their master to save them. Jesus was sleeping, so they awakened him. He arose, rebuked the winds, and commanded the waters of the lake: "Peace, be still." The storm suddenly disappeared as quickly as it had appeared and the waters of the lake were peaceful.

CHAPTER 5

MY NAME IS LEGION

And he asked him, What is thy name? And he answered, saying, My name is Legion: for we are many. Mk. 5:9.

"He cast out demons" is an Aramaic colloquialism. It means that he healed the mental illness and restored the person to sanity. *Shedah* is the Aramaic word for "demon." Aramaic speaking people apply this word to anyone who has weird ideas, behaves strangely, talks incessantly or whose actions do not follow the socially acceptable and approved way of life. They also frequently use the term *shedana* to express the same ideas. Mothers, at times, call their little children *shedana.* They do not mean that their children are literally "devils" or "demon possessed" but that they are misbehaving.

Brothers and sisters call each other *shedana* without intending any offense. Religious people and elders use the term commonly in conversation without the slightest idea of some sort of supernatural being. On one occasion, Jesus called Simon Peter *satana,* "Satan." This was a formal rebuke and did not mean that the apostle Shimon had become some sort of demon.

As Jesus was traveling and preaching, people brought the mentally and emotionally troubled to him. Some of these men and women were not severely afflicted with insanity but simply could not think straight. Others had a very bad outlook on life. Some hated their neighbors and relatives for no reason; others were very difficult to live with because they were overly temperamental. Jesus quietly talked with these people; some he had to rebuke. He would uproot and correct their delusional imaginings and help them to reason clearly and differently. Through this method, he could dismantle their faulty thinking and misguided emotions. As a result of being with Jesus their actions changed and they were healed.

In this instance, Jesus had encountered a severe case of mental derangement. No one could bind this man, not even with chains.

Jesus, at first, rebuked the man and called for him to calm down. He said: "Come out of the man, unclean spirit." Then he asked the lunatic his name. The man replied: "My name is legion, for we are many" meaning, "I have many spirits in me." This does not mean, however, that he actually had a host of evil spirits living in him. One demon would have been sufficient to take care of him if that were truly the case. What the man meant was that he had numerous things wrong with him and was hopelessly lost in a maze of crazy notions and conflicting emotions. He felt totally dominated by uncontrollable thoughts and forces within his heart and mind. He felt that his mind was gone and there was no hope for restoration. Jesus helped the man and healed him of his mental and emotional disorder. The man was so grateful that he wanted to follow this great healer and teacher. Jesus told him that he should go home and tell what great things God had done for him.

TOUCHING HIS GARMENT

And Jesus, immediately knowing in himself that virtue had gone out of him, turned him about in the press, and said, Who touched my clothes? Mk. 5:30.

There was a woman who needed healing. She had tried to see Jesus but found it difficult to come near him. (See Mark 5:25-28.) The crowds that were following Jesus were large. Generally, Near Eastern women are shy and reluctant to approach a holy man, especially when so many men surround a great teacher. In some areas women are so shy that they completely veil their faces when they stand before a holy man. Also, cultural customs discourage women from approaching a prince, nobleman, or holy man.

This woman's faith in Jesus was so strong that she believed that if she could only touch his garment, it would be sufficient to heal her infirmity. Her faith was enhanced by the fact that she knew she would not have an opportunity to see Jesus and discuss her problem with him. The Aramaic phrase "touch his garment" in verse 28 does not mean that she simply touched his cloak. She held the hem of his garment in her hand and tugged, which means, "I urgently need to see you." Jesus felt the pull and knew that someone was behind him and needed him, but he didn't know who had tugged on his clothes.

The expression "that virtue had gone out of him" means that he felt some "strength, power or vibration" going out of him. When one person touches another, feelings pass between them. We also might say that a vibration passes between them. The woman's touch was like an Eastern beggar knocking at the door. The family on the inside of the house knows the difference between a beggar's knock and a guest's or relative's knock. A beggar knocks softly and the sound of the knocking indicates that he is in need. The woman's sincere touch for help indicated that she needed him badly. Jesus responded to her cry and her hemorrhage dried up. Her protracted illness of twelve years was healed.

JESUS SOUGHT NO PUBLICITY

And he charged them straitly that no man should know it; and commanded that something should be given her to eat. Mk.5:43.

How Jesus meant this command cannot be easily explained without having seen his face or having heard his tone of voice. Near Eastern speakers often warn, "don't tell this to anyone," but the listener knows the intended meaning by the motion of the hands, the facial expression and the voice inflection of the speaker.

Of course, some people who wish to publicize something make a secret of it, telling people not to repeat it, thus making sure it will be told. But in this case, Jesus was being cautious because of the reaction from religious authorities. On another occasion, however, he told his disciples and followers, "What I tell you secretly, preach in the market places and from the housetops."

There was nothing secretive about raising this little girl from death; such a miracle could hardly be hidden from the people. There were times when Jesus' popularity and his miraculous cures were

34

opposed by certain religious authorities, who thought that these miracles were exaggerated. They accused Jesus of using the power of Beelzebub. Some of these authorities felt that he was deceiving the public and therefore sought to arrest him. In other words, it was wise at certain times to keep quiet about the healing. God and the one who was healed knew what had taken place, and this was more important than the publicity.

When Jesus raised Lazarus from death, the religious leaders were alarmed, took cognizance of his work, and decided to have him arrested. In the Near East, it is not a wise thing to boast about healing and miracles, for the healer is sure to incur the anger of religious authorities. The exception would be if the religious powers had authorized the healer to practice; then it would be safe. On the other hand, true healers shun publicity and do their work quietly. They do not receive any reward for their healing. Nor do they charge for their services. Freely they have received and freely they give.

CHAPTER 6

CARPENTER

Is not this the carpenter, the son of Mary, the brother of James, and Joses, and of Juda, and Simon? And are not his sisters here with us? And they were offended at him. Mk. 6:3.

Before the introduction of Western civilization in Palestine, Syria and Asia Minor, carpentry was an insignificant occupation and still is in many countries. Although the art of the blacksmith and silversmith is very old and for unknown centuries has been handed down from father to son, carpentry, until the turn of the 20th century, was not an art. In many areas of the Near East where tables, chairs and other wooden objects are unknown, one does not find carpenters. Amateur workers meet the very small demand for this trade.

In other regions, one may find a certain man known as a "carpenter" whose advice is sought in wood construction. Generally, this kind of carpenter has a few crude tools made by hand, consisting of a saw, hammer, and plane. The whole outfit is stored in a little bag that, at times, the family uses for a pillow when short of bedding.

The carpenter's task is to fix broken doors and ploughs and make wooden spoons, but there is little demand for these things because nearly every family makes their own. Some of them seek the services of a man who is more familiar with the trade and who has assumed the title of carpenter. They seek him out because this man will have the tools that are scarce and valuable. A carpenter in some of the ancient lands of the Near East has nothing to sell; nor is he permanently engaged in this occupation. Most of them are farmers, sheep raisers, and merchants. Carpentry is done in the evening or when an article breaks and needs immediate attention.

The Aramaic for "carpenter" is *nagara*. It also means "workman, handyman." Joseph was not a carpenter in the sense that we understand the work of a carpenter in the United States. Like any other Near Easterner, Joseph had his sheep and cattle. Neighbors sought his services as a carpenter to fix doors, make wooden keys and help in the construction of houses. Such services are rendered without charge; at times, the carpenter is given a good meal or a few eggs and some cheese. Among Easterners, when a man builds a home his neighbors help him, because they expect him to help them when they build their own houses.

Some Western writers unfamiliar with these Near Eastern customs visualize Joseph and Jesus as master carpenters, working in a shop, making ploughs and yokes and other articles for sale. Such articles are never sold in the Near East. Yokes and ploughs are cut from trees and made in the field by the farmers themselves. There is no reason to believe that Jesus worked as a carpenter. Nothing in the gospel leads to this conclusion. Jesus did not make any references to saws or hammers in his teachings and parables. He did make references to all forms of pastoral pursuits and farming.

The expression "son of Mary" refers to the fact that Joseph had other wives. What the people were saying is: "Don't we know this man, his brothers and sisters and his mother Mary [as distinguished from Joseph's other wives]?" There is also another possibility here. Originally, it could have read, "Is not this the son of the carpenter [*bar nagara*] and Mary. . . . ?" as in Matthew's text.[1]

A PROPHET WITHOUT HONOR

But Jesus said unto them, A prophet is not without honour, but in his own country, and among his own kin, and in his own house. Mk. 6:4.

Not honoring a prophet of their own nationality is characteristic of Assyrian people, who were the ancestors of the Galileans. Assyrians are noted for jealousy and envy toward each other. An Assyrian dislikes seeing a fellow countryman attain prominence. He welcomes and listens with respect to the prophets and leaders of other

---

[1]See Mt. 13:55 and *ARAMAIC LIGHT ON THE GOSPEL OF MATTHEW*, "The Sons of Tamar," p. 9 and "Mary, the Mother of Jesus," p. 10.

countries but does not care for his own.

When an Assyrian gains wealth or becomes well known, some of his own people attempt to pull him down; but when a man is poor, everyone pities him. English missionaries who have worked for many years among the descendants of the Assyrians in the mountains of Kurdistan noticed this weakness and called it a disease. Undoubtedly, this jealousy has been one of the main reasons for the decline of this once powerful nation.

If Jesus had been in America or Europe, he would not have said these words. Usually Americans and Europeans are proud of their statesmen and great leaders in science and religion and do all they can to help advance them. This is also true of the Jewish people who not only help each other but are proud to know when one of them becomes a great leader. This is not to say that Americans, Europeans or Jewish people have no jealousy, but they are proud of their own.

Jesus was raised in Galilee and the Galileans had Assyrian customs.[2] Resentment and jealousy were dominant then as they are today among the remnant of Assyrians. The people of Nazareth would not object to a religious leader from another town, but they would not tolerate greatness in a Nazarene. Strangely enough, Jesus' brothers were jealous of him, doubting and denouncing him. They even called him crazy.[3]

A STAFF

And commanded them that they should take nothing for their journey, save a staff only; no script, no bread, no money in their purse. Mk. 6:8.

In this case, Mark's account is more accurate than the gospel of Matthew. (See Matthew 10:10.) A man can travel in the Near East without money, a bag, or other necessities because he relies on the hospitality of the people. But, he must have a staff to protect himself

---

[2]2 Kings 17:24.
[3]Mt. 13:57; Jn. 4:44.

from bandits and from dogs that often bark at and bite strangers as well as against wild animals and serpents. Additionally, travelers used the staff to help them climb steep hills and cross streams of water.

The Aramaic word for "staff" is *shawta*. A staff occupies a very important place in the life of Semites. One often hears them say: "We have rested the staff" meaning "we have reached the end of the journey." Every traveler carries a staff even if he has other weapons. "A staff is a friend on the road" is a Semitic proverb. Sometimes the use of a staff is merely a habit as when one carries a small staff while walking on the roofs in Near Eastern towns.

Jesus commanded his disciples not to carry anything but a staff. In this manner they were to detach themselves from material interests and give themselves completely to the preaching of God's kingdom. They represented a new way of life. In their need and weakness they were to be rich and strong through their practice and vision of eternal realities.

SODOM AND GOMORRAH

And whosoever shall not receive you, nor hear you, when ye depart thence, shake off the dust under your feet for a testimony against them. Verily I say unto you, It shall be more tolerable for Sodom and Gomorrah in the day of judgement, than for that city. Mk. 6:11.

In Hebrew *Sadam* means "a place of lime." Sodom and Gomorrah were two prosperous ancient cities, near the Dead Sea, that flourished in biblical days. A heavy rain of brimstone destroyed this region. There was a terrible earthquake, an eruption from the sulfur pits in that area, that brought total devastation to these powerful cities. In the Near East, such catastrophes are always interpreted as a punishment for the wickedness of the people. These cities were on the route between Egypt and Assyria and became very rich because of their commercial advantages. One of the theories concerning their downfall is that the great mercantile route was finally abandoned.

Jesus mentioned these two cities as a warning of impending disaster that was to befall Capernaum, Bethsaida and other towns around the Lake of Galilee. Sodom and Gomorrah had no prophets to warn them. If there had been messengers of God warning them, they would probably have repented like the people of Nineveh. The Hebrew prophets had constantly guided and warned Israel of any political disasters. But Israel's political leaders would not listen; therefore, they persecuted and murdered many of their prophets. And, in the end, other nations conquered them.

The destruction of the Galilean cities was, therefore, to be more serious than that of Sodom and Gomorrah. Capernaum and Bethsaida were destroyed in the early centuries C.E. and are still in ruins. A portion of the walls of the synagogue at Capernaum, where Jesus preached, still remains. Today tourists visit this site in the holy land.

HEROD ANTIPAS

And King Herod heard of him; (for his name was spread abroad:) and he said, That John the Baptist was risen from the dead, and therefore mighty works do shew forth themselves in him. Mk. 6:14.

Herod Antipas was one of the sons of Herod the Great. After his father's death, he was appointed with the title of tetrarch over a portion of the kingdom that comprised the territory of Galilee and Paraea. He married Herodias, wife of his brother Philip, who was tetrarch of the regions of Iturea and Trachonitis. He executed John the Baptist because John did not approve of his marriage.

Although Herod was an Idumean by race, he was a Jew by faith and was subject to the biblical laws of Moses. The Mosaic law prohibits a man from marrying his brother's wife unless his brother has died and left no male heir. Philip and Herodias had children; therefore, Herod Antipas married Herodias contrary to biblical law.

Interestingly, Jesus had called Herod Antipas a "fox," which in Aramaic means "shrewd or clever." When Jesus was on trial, Pilate sent him to Herod because Jesus was a Galilean and Pilate had no jurisdiction over Galilee.[4]

GREAT SIGNS WANTED

For they considered not the miracle of the loaves: for their heart was hardened. Mk. 6:52.

The Aramaic text reads: "Neither did they understand the miracle of the loaves of bread, because their hearts were confused."[5] The thinking of some of Jesus' disciples was confused. When Jesus had suddenly appeared to them on the water (see verses 47-51) and then climbed in the boat, they were mystified and alarmed. They did not expect to see him. (Some Eastern writers maintain that, on such occasions, it was the Christ who appeared to them rather than the man Jesus.)

Evidently some of the disciples and followers either did not think about the miracle of the bread or else discounted the miracle. Hebrew prophets also multiplied bread. In the Near East, when people go to see a religious man, they always take food with them as a gift.[6] People wanted Jesus to perform a greater miracle than just feeding the crowds who came to hear him.

Other men who had witnessed the miraculous event when Jesus fed the 5000 wanted to know, when they met him at Capernaum, where he had been. Jesus said to them: "You seek me not because you saw the miracle, but because you did eat of the loaves."[7] And later they said to him, "What miracles do you perform, that we may see and believe in you?"[8] In other words, even those who had seen the miracle of the multiplication of the bread did not take it seriously.

People in Palestine were looking for greater and more spectacu-

---

[4]Lk. 13:32.
[5]Mk. 6:52, Aramaic Peshitta text, Lamsa translation.
[6]See 1 Kings 14:1-4.
[7]See Jn. 6:25-26.
[8]Jn. 6:29.

41

lar signs. They wanted something that they had never seen before. They expected the Messiah to perform miracles, wonders, and signs to surpass anything that the prophets had done before him. But Jesus refused to do anything spectacular. He did what the Hebrew prophets had done, and even greater healing works than they. Although his own disciples were confused, he had told them that they would do greater things than he had done. Jesus' gospel of God's kingdom is not proved by miracles or signs, but by the changing of human hearts and conditions.

CHAPTER 7

JEWISH PURIFICATION CEREMONIALS

And when they come from the market, except they wash they eat not. And many other things there be, which they have received to hold, as the washing of cups, and pots brasen vessels, and of tables. Mk. 7:4.

The Aramaic text reads: "For all the Jews, even the Pharisees, unless their hands were washed carefully, would not eat, because they strictly observed the tradition of the elders. Even the things from the market, if they were not washed, they would not eat. And there are a great many other things which they have accepted to obey, such as the washing of cups and pots and copper utensils and the bedding of dead men."[1] These teachings were based on the "traditions of the elders," that is, the Oral Law and not the Written Law.

Today in the Near East not only are religious men of different faiths not permitted to sit at the same table and eat together; they are also considered defiled if they touch each other. One must wash fruits and vegetables bought at the market before eating them. The reason for this is that they may have been touched by members of other faiths who are declared unclean. Religious authorities also declare foodstuffs such as meat and cheese as taboo unless they were purchased from merchants who are of the same faith. In the name of God these religious authorities declare all these prohibitions as binding. Those who break these taboos not only become defiled but also fall under a curse. For example: a Jew may not buy meat from a Gentile butcher; Moslems or Christians would find themselves defiled if they ate Jewish bread; an Armenian may not eat Jewish cheese.

This is an ancient form of Eastern boycott, only it is done more effectively and carried to extremes. It is worse than the boycotts of today because it is done in the name of God and religion by men of

---

[1] Mk. 7:3-4, Aramaic Peshitta text, Lamsa translation.

43

one faith against another. It has existed for ages and its evil effects are so deeply rooted and strongly felt that, at times, it arouses people of one religion against another.

Part 1—THE WASHING OF HANDS. The Pharisees and the elders instituted most of the traditions. These external observances made the religious authorities appear as very pious. They often forgot the weightier matters of the law but were always careful about carrying out their traditions. They washed foods and other articles brought from the marketplace and very carefully washed their hands and feet before eating. But some of them broke the true law by oppressing the poor, accepting bribes, and embezzling the property of widows and orphans.

Pharisees, elders, and priests were all amazed because Jesus and his disciples failed to purify themselves in the traditional manner before eating. And, worst of all, they ate with publicans and sinners. These religious leaders thought that if Jesus were a man of God he would have some respect for the traditions of the elders. According to Jesus, these external religious observances were foolish and not important because they needlessly produced bitterness and hatred between Gentiles and Jews. As far as Jesus was concerned, it was not what goes into a man that defiles him but what comes out of a man's heart, such as adultery, theft, murder and so forth. (See Mark 7:18-23 and Matthew 15:2.)[2]

Part 2—THE BEDDING OF THE DEAD. So called "beds" and bed clothes were a few quilts and hand woven rugs. Beds as we know them in the United States and Europe were unknown. Even today in certain Near Eastern areas, the people are still not familiar with Western style beds. They sleep on quilts or rugs spread on the floor.

According to custom, when a person dies his body is immedi-

---

[2]According to Jewish biblical research, this strict ceremonial purification precept about the washing of hands was binding for priests only during the time of Jesus. They claim that it became binding on the laity toward the end of the first century. Regardless, this story reveals Jesus' attitude toward religious bans that detracted from the true meaning of religion such as justice, harmony, acceptance, and peace in the human family.

ately declared unclean. The bed clothes that were once worn and the bedding on which the person slept are also unclean. They will not be used until they are washed. All articles that the dead had once used must be cleaned and sanctified.

CORBAN

But ye say, If a man shall say to his father or mother, It is Corban, that is to say, a gift, by whatsoever thou mightest be profited by me; he shall be free. Mk. 7:11

The Aramaic text reads: "He said to them, You certainly do injustice to the commandment of God so as to sustain your own tradition. For Moses said, Honor your father and your mother; and he who curses father or mother, let him be put to death. But you say, A man may say to his father or his mother, what is left over is *Corban* (my offering); And yet you do not let him do anything for his father or mother. So you dishonor the word of God for the sake of the tradition which you have established; and you do a great many other things like these."[3]

Qorban is an Aramaic word and typically Semitic. Aramaic speaking people express deep affection and reverence by using this word. The term implies that the person so addressed is sincere and pious and that he is worthy as a sacrifice to God—that is, pure and clean. They also say *qorbani,* "you are my sacrifice,"or *qorbanekh,* "I am your sacrifice." These two expressions are remarks of the highest devotion.

Fathers and sons use the term *qorban* more frequently than anyone else. They do this to show their fervent loyalty, implying that they are ready to die for one another if necessary. But, because of its constant use, it often becomes merely a conventional phrase and means nothing.

Jesus disapproved of such vain and worthless compliments

---

[3]Mk. 7:9-13, Aramaic Peshitta text, Lamsa translation.

because people used them deceptively to avoid their actual duties and responsibilities. He disliked the fact that many of the Pharisees sanctioned this form of flattery and that they also practiced it. The Pharisees also approved of a son using this strong and affectionate term *"qorban"* with his parents although that son might not support them and care for their welfare.

In this passage of scripture, however, the word *qorban* has yet a different meaning. The *qorban* was also a "gift and pledge to God." It was the amount of income that was left over after all expenses were paid. This was generally put aside for the care of the parents. There are three major points to consider: (1) According to Near Eastern cultural tradition, children are to support their parents when their mother and father retire. (2) The fourth commandment reinforces this cultural custom. (3) The Pharisees changed this custom to benefit themselves. They claimed that the money put aside for the parent's retirement could be donated as an offering, "gift," to the temple thereby exempting the children from their obligation to support their parents. Thus, according to some of these Pharisees, to say to one's parents *qorban* is far more important than actually honoring and caring for the parents. As long as the sons simply say *qorban*, "a gift to God," the sons shall be free of their obligations. In other words, they "gave to God" what should have gone to the parents. This was hypocritical and Jesus denounced this absurdity. He pointed out how much more important it was to literally help and support one's parents.[4]

---

[4]See Mt. 15:5 and ARAMAIC LIGHT ON THE GOSPEL OF MATTHEW, "Jewish Ordinances," p. 208. There is also another interpretation to this verse than the one given above. Jewish scholars say that *qorban* in tannaitic literature means an "oath." The idea is that a son can take an oath against a biblical edict, such as the one to care for the parents. Once the "oath" is taken he need not be responsible for fulfilling his obligation to the parents. He is absolved. Regardless of which interpretation one may accept, Jesus was against this absolution. No one can take a vow against a biblical precept nor neglect one's parents.

A CHALLENGE

The woman was a Greek, a Syrophenician by nation; and she besought him that he would cast forth the devil out of her daughter. But Jesus said unto her, Let the children first be filled; for it is not meet to take the children's bread, and to cast it unto the dogs. And she answered and said unto him, Yes, Lord: yet the dogs under the table eat of the children's crumbs. Mk. 7:26-28.

Part 1—A SYRIAN WOMAN. The Aramaic text reads: "But the woman was a heathen from Phoenicia in Syria; and she besought him to cast out the demon [*sheda*] from her daughter."[5] Matthew, in his gospel, calls the woman a Canaanite from the borders of Tyre and Sidon.

Jesus' disciples urged their master to grant her request so that she would no longer bother them. At first he refused because she was a *hanp'tha*, "pagan." His reply was: "I am not sent except to the sheep which went astray from the house of Israel."[6] (According to Mark's gospel, the woman came into the house where Jesus was, but Matthew says she met them on the road.) One reason Jesus refused to have anything to do with the woman was because of his loyalty to the Jewish faith. He knew the prejudice of his people against Syrian foreigners and they would be scandalized if he, a Jewish prophet, treated pagans with the same consideration he showed his own people. He wanted first to minister to the people of his own faith and then to the Gentiles. This was why he selected his disciples from members of the Jewish faith and why he did most of his work among Jewish people.

There is something more to consider about this episode. Semitic teachers and healers often test the faith and sincerity of those who come to them. This woman not an Israelite. Jesus was testing her to see if her faith was powerful enough to overcome fear and doubt. But when she told Jesus about dogs receiving crumbs, he knew she

---

[5]Mk. 7:26, Aramaic Peshitta text, Lamsa translation.
[6]Mt. 15:24.

possessed a firm and persevering faith. He had never felt or seen such faith in "all Israel."

Part 2—DOGS DESPISED. As a general rule, most Europeans and Americans like their dogs and domesticate them. But Easterners regard them as unclean animals. Some Semites think that if a dog should touch them, they would become defiled and unclean. If a Moslem is accidently touched by a dog after his prayer, he becomes defiled and must say his prayers again. Dogs are often cruelly treated and seldom fed. They roam the streets searching for food. They eat meat that men are forbidden to eat by religious law and they eat the carcass of any animal.

Semites did not use tables. Food was served on a tray and placed on a cloth spread on the floor. When the tray is lifted, small pieces of bread often fall from it. Dogs patiently watch people eating; they know that the remaining crumbs will fall from the tray after it has been lifted. However, Near Easterners usually give these crumbs to beggars. They feel it is a sin to throw bread to dogs because bread is sacred and scarce. They also think of dogs as an abomination. No one would like to see their children hungry and the dogs well fed.

In the Near East, members of one faith consider members of another faith as dogs. The reason for this is that each faith has its own beliefs that permit its members to eat meat that is unlawful for others to eat. For instance, Moslems think of Christians as unclean and call them dogs because Christians usually have no dietary restrictions.

Jews thought of their heathen neighbors—that is, Syrians, Greeks, and Idumeans—as dogs because they ate swine meat, which was an abomination for them to eat. They called them dogs simply because dogs ate all kinds of meat without any discrimination. Jesus was merely using the expression of his day.[7]

---

[7]See Mt. 15:26-27. See also *ARAMAIC LIGHT ON THE GOSPEL OF MATTHEW*, "Racial Antipathy," pp. 210-211.

EPHPHATHA

And looking up to heaven, he sighed, and saith unto him, Ephphatha, that is, Be opened. Mk. 7:34.

The Aramaic text does not read "that is." It just reads: "And he looked up to heaven and sighed, then he said to him, Be opened!"[8] The actual Aramaic word for "be opened" is *ethpathakh.* The word *ephphatha* as it appears in our Western versions of the New Testament is neither Aramaic, Hebrew nor Greek. It simply has no meaning.

Undoubtedly, the Greek translator or the copyist made this error accidentally. The pronunciation and spelling of the word prove the error could easily be made, especially if the translator or copyist was unfamiliar with Aramaic. Among Aramaic speaking people today, this word is used in common everyday speech and means "to open."

---

[8]Mk. 7:34, Aramaic Peshitta text, Errico.

CHAPTER 8

OUTSIDE THE VILLAGE

And he cometh to Bethsaida; and they bring a blind man unto him, and besought him to touch him. And he took the blind man by the hand, and led him out of the town; and when he had spit on his eyes, and put his hands upon him, he asked him if he saw ought. Mk 8:22-23.

Near Eastern villages and towns are usually surrounded by a wall. Jesus took the blind man outside the village to avoid the curiosity seekers. On such occasions, Eastern people generally mob the healer. The crowd is composed of admirers and enemies. All gather around the healer—some to see the miracle, others to make fun and shout insults. This distraction confuses the healer's mind.

Jesus had to work with this blind man where it would be quiet and where a crowd could not disturb him. He had to ask the man some questions. This could not be done in the village. It might have been difficult and even embarrassing for Jesus to spit on the eyes of the blind man in the midst of a crowd. In the Near East, expectorating is a great insult. Only holy men could spit on a wound. Religious authorities would have resented Jesus' act because they did not believe he was a prophet.

When a holy man spits on a wound or disease, he rebukes the sickness and the evil that brought on the trouble. This practice is a repudiation of the power of evil. Jesus followed these practices because they were common among the people. Some sufferers would not believe unless the healer used this outward form of rebuke. Today, in Kurdistan and neighboring countries, healers whom the people recognize as genuine spit on the face or other diseased areas of the body as a healing method. These healers would not hesitate to practice this, even on a nobleman. Everyone accepts this method and does not feel it is an insult. (See Mark 7:33.)

CHAPTER 9

WIND OF SICKNESS

And one of the multitude answered and said, Master, I have brought unto thee my son, which hath a dumb spirit; And wheresoever he taketh him, he teareth him; and he foameth and gnasheth with his teeth, and pineth away; and I spake to thy disciples that they should cast him out; and they could not. Mk. 9:17-18.

In the olden days when causes of sickness and mental disorders were unknown, people believed that they came from the attacks of evil spirits. To say that "the spirit seized him" means that the person had a sudden convulsion. The Aramaic word *ruha*, "spirit," also signifies "wind" and "rheumatism." When a particular disease becomes an epidemic, people often say: "There is a wind of sickness." When a person has a series of illnesses, they say: "A wind of sickness has attacked him."

Part 1—THE BOY WITH SEIZURES. When the man brought his boy to Jesus, the young lad suddenly fell to the ground in an epileptic seizure (see verse 20). Jesus asked the boy's father several questions. Then he said to the father: "If you can believe, everything is possible to him that believes." However, the father did not reply to Jesus "I believe, help thou my unbelief" as the King James Version translates the verse. The Aramaic text reads: "I do believe, help my little faith."[1]

This is a typical Semitic expression of modesty and gratitude. It does not imply "unbelief." The father very clearly and emphatically said, "I do believe!" He responded to Jesus in a modest manner but with a heart full of faith for his boy's recovery. Jesus, in turn, responded to the genuine faith of the father and the son was healed.[2]

Part 2—THE SPIRIT OF DUMBNESS AND DEAFNESS.

---

[1]Mk 9:24, Aramaic Peshitta text, Lamsa translation.
[2]See Mt. 17:15-16; Lk. 9:38-40.

51

"When Jesus saw that people were running and gathering about him, he rebuked the unclean spirit, and said to it, O deaf and dumb spirit, I command you, come out of him, and do not enter him again. And the epileptic cried out violently and was tortured, and the spirit went out; then the boy became as if dead, so that many said, He is dead. Then Jesus took him by the hand and lifted him up."[3]

The deaf and dumb spirit refers to the cause of the disease. (See the comment above—Part 1.) *Ruha,* "spirit," also means "wind." For example, when Semites speak about wheat that is diseased, they say: "Spirit has attacked the wheat." They mean that a prolonged wind has dried the wheat. Semites often say: "There is a wind of infirmity going around." When Jesus said "do not enter him again," he was assuring the boy's father that the disease would not attack or come back on the boy again.

FASTING AND PRAYING

And he said unto them, This kind can come forth by nothing, but by prayer and fasting. Mk. 9:29.

The Aramaic text reads: "And he said to them, This kind cannot be cast out by anything except by fasting and prayer."[4] Generally, Near Easterners overeat during feasts and weddings and then suffer the consequences by becoming ill. Healers recommend fasting from food so that the body can rest and repair itself. And they also recommend that a person pray when ill. Prayer brings peace to a disturbed mind. It also stimulates the soul and quickens spiritual desires. Through prayer one is brought into closer communion with divine power. Eastern Semites always fast and pray as a means of restoring their bodies and for the forgiveness of their sins. Healers also fast so that they can receive God's power for the work of healing the sick. The disciples were novices and were afraid. They were not

---

[3]Mk. 9:25-27, Aramaic Peshitta text, Lamsa translation.
[4]Mk. 9:29, Aramaic Peshitta text, Lamsa translation.

prepared as Jesus was to heal the disease that held the boy in its grip. They had not yet learned to heal in absolute faith through prayer.

RECEIVING A CHILD

Whosoever shall receive one of such children in my name, receiveth me; and whosoever shall receive me, receiveth not me, but him that sent me. Mk. 9:37.

The Aramaic text reads: "Whoever receives a child like this in my name, he receives me; and he who receives me, does not receive me, but him who has sent me."[5] "Receive a child in my name" is a Near Eastern saying meaning, "receive a child the way I would receive him." Children are chased away when they appear in the presence of holy men, government officials or other dignitaries. Servants of the official or host usually rebuke the children and tell them to stay away and sometimes even curse them. It is an embarrassing situation for a host to see children playing in the house, talking or watching his guests as they recline at the meal. Neither women or children sit down to eat with important guests or holy men.

When children began to gather around Jesus, as they almost always did when seeing a prominent man walking or entering a town, his disciples rebuked them and chased them away. Jesus became indignant. So he took one of the children in his arms and said: "One must become like a child so that he may enter God's kingdom." Then he told them that those who do a favor for a child, even to the extent of troubling themselves to give a child a cup of water, would receive their reward.

This may be difficult for Western people to understand. But Near Eastern Semites know that Jesus placed such importance on a cup of water because water is very scarce in Palestine. An honorable guest or a high official may have plenty of water on the table, but children often go thirsty. This is the reason that biblical writers mention water

---

[5]Mk. 9:37, Aramaic Peshitta text, Lamsa translation.

and thirst so often in Scripture. In the Near East, giving a cup of water to a thirsty child is a great favor.[6]

JESUS SHARED HIS TEACHING

But Jesus said, Forbid him not; for there is no man which shall do a miracle in my name, that can lightly speak evil of me. Mk. 9:39.

The Aramaic text reads: "Jesus said to them, Do not forbid him; for there is no man who performs miracles in my name who will hastily speak evil of me."[7] Near Eastern trades and professions are generally handed down secretly from father to son. Many silversmiths, blacksmiths, and other tradesmen never disclose the secrets of their trades to strangers. On the other hand, when an artist discovers the secrets of some famous tradesman, other artists will favor and praise him, especially when these secrets come from a well-known and skilled artisan.

Jesus knew that the men who performed miracles in his name, which means by his method, would hardly speak against him. These miracle workers knew that if they did speak against Jesus, it would weaken their position. Jesus' disciples, who reported this event to him, wanted these men to stop healing because they were not a part of their group. The disciples were unaware of how Jesus thought about this, for they were fishermen and did not understand certain matters. All those who were performing miracles in the name of Jesus were helping to spread his gospel and his fame.

From this we learn that we should welcome and encourage those who do what we do and who say what we say. We should not concern ourselves with whether those who do these things give us credit or not, for as Jesus said: "Whoever is not against us is for us."

---

[6]See Mt. 10:42, Lk. 9:48.
[7]Mk. 9:39, Aramaic Peshitta text, Lamsa translation.

54

SALT

For every one shall be salted with fire, and every sacrifice shall be salted with salt. Salt is good: but if the salt have lost his saltiness, wherewith will ye season it? Have salt in yourselves and have peace one with another. Mk. 9:49-50.

Part 1—SALTED SACRIFICE. When Near Easterners killed an animal for food, they salted the meat immediately because there were no refrigerators or other devices to preserve meat. Flies and intense heat cause rapid decomposition. Eastern people salt almost any kind of food before cooking, but they use no salt when the meal is eaten. Generally, women know how much salt to use and some women are praised for salting the family meal precisely right. This custom evolved because of the scarcity of salt.

When they sacrificed animals, the meat was salted before it was offered so that it might have a good flavor. Most shrines were located on high places some distance from the town. They took the animal to the shrine while it was alive. The man who had made the vow carried the salt with him. He would then slay the animal, salt its flesh, and roast it on the stone altar of the shrine. Country folk would gather from the vicinity to partake of the sacrifice.

Part 2—SALT IS PRECIOUS. To Near Eastern Semites, salt is a sacred token of friendship. When they eat salt together, they pledge their lives for each other. When kings and princes enter a city, they are greeted with an offering of salt as a sign of welcome and sincerity.

Salt is also a precious article and in some regions very scarce. From ancient times to the present day salt has been a medium of exchange in some Near Eastern countries. It seems very probable that salt was the first medium of exchange before certain nations discovered the use of gold, silver, and copper.

Small deposits of salt had been discovered in mountains, but because of crude mining methods, a sufficient quantity could not be secured for human and animal consumption. Therefore, salt became a valuable possession. Taxes were paid in salt. Buying and selling, in some areas of the Near East, are still conducted through the medium of salt. We are told that salt preserves life and no human life can be sustained for any length of time without it.

"Have salt in yourselves, and have peace with one another." Salt symbolically represents faithfulness. Having salt in onself means to be truthful and faithful and to be at peace with others. In other words, be friendly. The custom among Semites of sharing "bread and salt" means that people will be at peace with each other.

Another interesting Semitic custom is the salting of newborn infants. According to the custom, a mother or a midwife first bathes the newborn infant, then gently rubs the baby with a very small amount of salt that has been finely pulverized in a stone mortar for this great occasion. Near Easterners believe that putting salt on the baby's body will make the flesh firm. This little ceremony represents a symbolic testimony that the parents will raise the child to be truthful and faithful.[8]

---

[8]See Mt. 5:13; Lk. 14:34.

CHAPTER 10

THE CROSSING PLACE

And he arose from thence, and cometh into the coasts of Judaea by the farther side of Jordan: and the people resort unto him again; and as he was wont, he taught them again. Mk. 10:1.

The Aramaic text reads: "And he departed from thence, and came to the border of Judea, at the crossing of the Jordan; and a great many people went to him there, and he taught them again as he was accustomed to do."[1] The Aramaic word *ewra* derives from *abar*, "to cross." *Ewra* means "crossing place" where the caravan crosses the river Jordan. At this place, people traveling in the caravan unload their beasts of burden so that they may rest. The travelers also rest and refresh themselves. Friends and enemies meet. It is a place where a man can make many acquaintances with natives as well as foreigners.

This was a vantage point where Jesus could meet many people. It was a central place where the water was shallow and well known to all travelers. Caravan routes extended from Egypt to Babylon. John the Baptist also sought such places because he could deliver his message to a large and diverse company of people. A small remnant of his followers known as "the people of St. John" are still found in Baghdad and in southern Mesopotamia. No doubt the news of John's baptisms was carried from there by converts.[2]

LOVE OF MONEY

It is easier for a camel to go through the eye of a needle than for a rich man to enter into the kingdom of God. And they were astonished out of

---

[1]Mk. 10:1, Aramaic Peshitta text, Lamsa translation.
[2]See Mt. 8:18, 19:1-2.

measure, saying among themselves, Who then can be saved? And Jesus looking upon them saith, With men it is impossible, but not with God; for with God all things are possible. Mk. 10:25-27.

Verse 25 in the Aramaic text reads: "It is easier for a *rope* to pass through the eye of a *needle* than for a rich man to enter into the kingdom God." The term "camel" is a mistake. Translators made this error simply because the Aramaic word *gamla* means both "rope" and "camel." Needles in the early days were large and made of oak. Women could thread a cord through the eye of a wooden needle.

In Aramaic literature we read that when an individual strikes an easy and instant friendship with another, he says: "When we met, it was like a needle and a thread," that is, "we understood each other right away and became friends immediately." But when it takes a long time for two people to understand one another before they become friends, they say: "Our meeting was difficult, like a rope passing through the eye of a [wooden] needle."

When a thick cord or heavy thread is passed through a needle, some of its fibers come off. A rich man must, therefore, learn to share some of his luxuries. He must surrender his overt love for money, which creates greed, so that he may enter into the kingdom of God. "To enter the kingdom" means to participate in the principles of the kingdom. This can be very difficult and challenging for some rich men. Thus, the saying, "It is easier for a rope to pass through the eye of a needle, than it is for a rich man to enter the kingdom of God." It was not impossible, just difficult.

Jesus, in this instance, was censuring certain types of rich men who had made wealth their God, were free from paying taxes and who oppressed the poor. As a prophet, Jesus was not against riches but against an all-consuming love of riches. These men abused their position of wealth; therefore, it would be difficult for them to practice the principles of the kingdom. Jesus said: "How hard it is for those who have wealth to enter into the kingdom of God!" (See Mark 10:23-24.)

Jesus' disciples thought that this was a very harsh saying. If the acquisition of money or wealth was evil, nobody could enter God's kingdom. Who can be saved? They felt it would be difficult for people to become followers of Jesus' teaching, especially if they had to give away their fortunes.

Time and time again the disciples misunderstood their master-teacher. God can help people surrender any bad habits and love of money. In other words, God can set free those whom greed has possessed. According to scripture, Matthew, who was originally a tax collector, gave up his wealth and accepted the gospel of the kingdom. (St. Francis of Assisi renounced all his father's wealth and went barefoot, preaching the gospel.) What is impossible for man is possible for God—the creator of the universe.[3]

Jesus contradicted the ways of the greedy rich of his day, who very often did not pay their laborers proper wages nor share their wealth. He never spoke against the ways of the pious rich. These men of integrity were true agents of God, who were entrusted with God's wealth so that they might distribute their gains among the needy and poor.

LEAVING RELATIVES

And Jesus answered and said, Verily I say unto you, There is no man that hath left house, or brethren, or sisters, or father, or mother, or wife, or children, or lands, for my sake, and the gospel's, But he shall receive an hundredfold now in this time, houses, and brethren, and sisters, and mothers and children, and lands, with persecutions; and in the world to come eternal life. Mk. 10:29-30.

Semites have no regular working hours. Laborers work from sunrise to sunset. Shepherds and servants, while performing their duties, have hardly any time to see their wives and children. Shepherds work day and night, eating and resting at intervals. They

---

[3]See Jer. 32:17; Mt. 19:24, *ARAMAIC LIGHT ON THE GOSPEL OF MATTHEW*, "The Needle and the Rope," p. 246-247.

leave their homes and children while they care for the flocks. Servants are required to be on duty all the time. They must also be ready for service throughout the night. They are practically slaves. They eat and live in the master's house and visit their own homes at rare intervals and only with permission from their master. Their time and attention are with their lord's obligations and household affairs. They must attend to the needs of his wife or wives and his children. Their own families are secondary.

When a young man desires to learn a trade, he leaves his home and family and eats, sleeps, and lives at his master's house. He often becomes more attached to his master's family than to his own. He does everything to please his lord and teacher so that he can win his favor and learn the secrets of the trade. Servants and apprentices who live in their own homes find little favor in the eyes of masters. The master-teacher cannot entrust everything to them. He looks on the apprentices as strangers who may some day become his competitors. He keeps from them the most important secrets of his trade. The faithful and loyal servants and apprentices live at the home of their master, often marrying his daughters, inheriting his business and other property.

Part 1—UNDERSTANDING DISCIPLESHIP. "Leaving one's family" does not mean forsaking them. Jesus' disciples and followers were not told literally to forsake wives and children. What he meant is that they were to be closely attached to him as much as possible. They were to be deeply concerned with the work of teaching and practicing the principles of the gospel of the kingdom before any other interests. They were to forget their wives, children and material goods for the time being so that they might win the confidence of their master-teacher. They were to learn the secrets of his teachings. Their own families were to take second place and later the disciples would be rewarded one hundredfold for their faithfulness.

Instead of just their own people loving them, the whole community and world would come to appreciate and care for the disciples. After they had attained a spiritual understanding, all material possessions would be at their disposal. This meant that kings and princes would bow down to them and offer them abundant gifts.

Part 2—THE REWARDS OF JESUS. Verse 30 in the Aramaic text reads: "Who shall not receive now, in this time a hundredfold, houses and brothers and sisters and *maidservants* and children and fields and *other worldly things*, and in the world to come life everlasting."[4] The words "mothers" and "maidservants" are written almost alike in Aramaic but pronounced differently—*aemhatha*, "mothers," *amhatha*, "maidservants." However, when these words are written in the singular, they are different—*emma*, "mother," and *amta*, "maid-servant."

The writer omits the reference to "father" that is in verse 29 and replaces "mothers" with "maidservants" in verse 30. The reason for this is that a man cannot be rewarded with other fathers and mothers when he loses his own parents. Nor is it probable for a man to have two fathers and two mothers. However, he can be rewarded with brothers and sisters, maidservants, children, fields and other worldly goods.

The words "with persecutions" in verse 30 are also a mistranslation of the Aramaic word *rdopyah*. It comes from the root *rdp*, meaning to "pursue, follow, and persecute." In the psalms, according to the Aramaic Peshitta text, we read: *"taybootakh wrahmaikh radpoonee,* "Your loving kindness and compassion *have pursued* me."[5] In verse 30, one may also translate the final words "lands and other pursuits."

If a man had ten sheep and his lord asked him to go to war, his lord would promise him twenty or more sheep. If he left behind twenty bushels of wheat in the field, he would receive double that amount. In this verse Jesus promises his disciples, while they were following him, more than they were then receiving.

---

[4] Mk. 10:30, Aramaic Peshitta text, Lamsa translation.
[5] Psalm 23:6, Aramaic Peshitta text, Errico.

61

CHAPTER 11

CURSING A FIG TREE

And on the morrow, when they were come from Bethany, he was hungry: And seeing a fig tree afar off having leaves, he came, if haply he might find anything thereon; and when he came to it, he found nothing but leaves; for the time of figs was not yet. And Jesus answered and said unto it, No man eat fruit of thee hereafter for ever. And his disciples heard it. Mk. 11:12-14.

In many Near Eastern lands, fruit trees growing along the roadside or in a field near the road belonged to travelers and the poor. Some of these trees grew naturally; others had been planted by unknown people. Therefore, people thought of these trees as public property. (Until the middle of the 20th century, this ancient custom still prevailed in Kurdistan.) It often happened that a field belonged to one man and the trees to another. If a man planted a tree on another's field and that tree bore fruit, both tree and fruit belonged to the one who planted it and not to the owner of the field. But, if the identity of the man who planted it is lost, then it became public property.

A traveler on the road cannot obtain any food. So, hungry travelers are constantly on the lookout for roadside fruit trees. They not only eat from these trees that are along the road but from all those that may be at a distance from the road. They will also fill their *tarmaleh*, "bags," with fruits. In many instances, they will pick the fruit even before it is ripe. Thus, such trees soon lose their fruit. A traveler might pass only once on a particular road. He feels, therefore, that he should take his share while he has the opportunity. When the season arrives, these trees may have a few leaves but no fruit. While the leaves are coming out in fullness, the tiny figs appear and when the fig season is over both leaves and figs fall at the same time.

While Jesus was on his way from Bethany to Jerusalem, he became hungry. Semites never eat an early meal. They leave the house fasting. Jesus saw the fig tree a distance from the road and thought he might pick a few figs. He went to the tree seeking food to satisfy his hunger, just like any man would, and not as God, the creator of fruit trees. He did not use divine power to find out whether the tree had fruit on it or not. He was simply living and thinking as a normal human being. On his arrival at the tree, he was disappointed to find plenty of leaves but no fruit. It was the season for figs but there were none to be had. Other travelers on the road before Jesus had, undoubtedly, picked all the fruit. Hunger and disappointment drew a typical, Semitic, emotional remark or "curse" from Jesus' lips—"From now on and forever let no man eat of your fruit."

The cursing of the fig tree has been difficult and challenging to understand. Many preachers and Bible students wonder why Jesus had pronounced a curse on the tree. Some say it was the fruit season, but the tree was late in bearing its fruit. This could hardly be the case, for all trees are under the same natural law. These people fail to see that a tree by the roadside suffers at the hands of hungry travelers. If Jesus had gone to this tree looking for food, many others had done the same and probably with better success.

Cursing something out of disappointment is again typical of Semitic temperament and is often thoughtlessly done. Nearly always when a Semite looks for something and fails to obtain it, he gives expression to his annoyance and dissatisfaction. Through this form of expression he relieves that particular pent up emotional frustration. For example, if someone was dying of thirst and searching for water and then found a brook but discovered it had dried during the summer months, the person would say: "Remain dry, no water shall spring out of you from now on."

However, it is true that Semites still believe in the efficiency of a curse spoken by a holy man, just as they believe in the good effect of blessings uttered by them. Vineyards and flocks are still cursed or blessed by certain holy men. In this case, it is not the casual cursing of the fig tree that is important but the lesson of faith we learn from the story.

The phrase "for the time of figs was not yet" is a marginal note

63

and was originally not a part of the scripture. A scribe or learned man probably wrote the note along the side of the scroll. No doubt, he thought that the season for figs had not yet arrived. Years later, this marginal note, like many others in the gospels, was copied and made an integral part of the scripture and gospel writing. There are many such marginal notes in the Hebrew Bible as well as in the New Testament.

Besides, we know that Jesus, with his knowledge of the country and its agricultural and pastoral life, would not have gone to a fig tree searching for figs out of season. Not even an ignorant desert dweller would do such a thing. (Interestingly, up until the middle of the 20th century, fig trees were still present on the road between Jerusalem and Bethany. And the fruit of these trees was still being picked by travelers as in biblical times.)

The tree served as a great lesson for his disciples. Jesus told them that if they had faith, they not only could make a tree wither, but they could also remove mountains. "Removing mountains and making trees wither" means that they would conquer insurmountable challenges and problems through their faith in God.[1]

---

[1]See Errico and Lamsa, *ARAMAIC LIGHT ON THE GOSPEL OF MATTHEW*, "Lesson from a Fig Tree," pp. 259-261.

CHAPTER 12

JEWISH SECTS

And they send unto him certain of the Pharisees and of the Herodians to catch him in his words. Mk. 12:13.

There were three important factions at that time in the Jewish faith—the Pharisees, the Sadducees and the Herodians. The scribes are not included here; however, all three major groups employed the scribes. There were also other small and peculiar sects in existence.

The term "Herodians" refers to those Jews who supported Herod's royal dynasty. Herod himself was an Edomite who became a usurper and took the kingdom from the Hashmonians (Maccabees). Most of the Jewish religious leadership resented, and some hated, Herod because they looked upon him as a foreigner. He was a very cruel man, who even put his own sons to death. But many Jews who were employed in the state government under Herod and in the service of the imperial government of Rome openly supported Herod. They did this so they could keep their government positions; but in their hearts they were his enemies, as were other Jews.

Jesus' teachings were so revolutionary that they undermined all these parties. When the party leaders saw that many of the Jews were flocking to Jesus, they became alarmed. Fearing they would lose their positions, they forgot their differences for a while and became united against Jesus. They took counsel to see how they could stop him from attacking their way of life, religious customs, and ideologies.[1]

LIKE ANGELS

For when they shall rise from the dead, they neither marry, nor are given in marriage; but are as the angels which are in heaven. Mk. 12:25.

---

[1]See Mt. 22:15; Lk. 20:20.

The term "as the angels" in this instance means "spiritual," that is, without physical bodies. "Angel" in Aramaic also signifies "God's counsel." Hebrew sages and prophets in their discourse with simple people tried to explain invisible, spiritual ideas by using physical and known ideas. Thus, they gave visual imagery and form to angels. God is pictured as a Near Eastern ruler with emissaries around the throne.

These sages and biblical writers did this so that unlearned people might understand spiritual realities. Scripture tells us that angels are spirits: "He made his angels spirits." "Spirit" in Aramaic means "omnipresent, all-embracing, everywhere." God's presence is everywhere and, therefore, God's counsel or thoughts are everywhere.

In the heavenly realm, marriage does not exist because there is no physical form of life as we now know and understand it. In the hereafter, men and women will be like angels, free from their physical forms, desires and limitations. The new life is celestial and spiritual, but as an attempt to understand this kind of life, we visualize the heavenly dimension with what we see and know in our earthly life. Jesus simply said that people will be like angels, that is, heavenly and spiritual.

THE UPPER SEATS

And he said unto them in his doctrine, Beware of the scribes, which love to go in long clothing, and love salutations in the marketplaces, And the chief seats in the synagogues, and the uppermost rooms at feasts. Mk. 12:38-39.

The Aramaic text reads: "And in his teaching he said to them, Beware of the scribes, who like to walk in long robes and love to be saluted in the streets, And take the front seats in the synagogues and the head places at banquets."[2] This practice concurs with Near Eastern customs. Banquets are held in the large room of a house. The

---

[2]Mk. 12:38-39, Aramaic Peshitta text, Lamsa translation.

reference here is to the prominent seats and not to rooms. According to Semitic etiquette, honorable guests, such as priests, politicians and rich men, must take the chief places at banquets. Here the food is more plentiful and the distance from the door is greater.

The guests are arranged according to social standing. The least important guests, such as beggars and musicians, sit near the entrance to the room. If, perhaps, a distinguished guest enters late, a servant or master of the house immediately notifies one of the other guests to take a lower place. He will say to him: "Rise and go down, an honorable guest is coming." It often happens that a distinguished guest who arrives late will take a lower seat, but the servant promptly ushers him to a higher place as a token of great honor.

Jesus instructed his disciples to notice how the scribes conducted themselves but not to follow their examples. They were to avoid this kind of behavior and take the lower seats at banquets. They were to be present at feasts but not as important dignitaries. They were simple men who represented a new kingdom and principles that did not lend themselves to their present cultural system. They were also to avoid the unseemly embarrassment and confusion if asked to take a lower seat.[3]

---

[3]Mt. 23:5-7; Lk. 14:7.

CHAPTER 13

THE TEMPLE OVERTHROWN

And Jesus answering said unto him, Seest thou these great buildings? There shall not be left one stone upon another, that shall not be thrown down. Mk. 13:2.

This prophecy was fulfilled when General Titus captured Jerusalem and destroyed the temple in the year 70 CE. All the great stones and pillars of the first temple that King Solomon had built, and which was later rebuilt by Zerubbabel and Herod the Great, were removed to a town in Lebanon called Baalbek, about 160 miles north of Jerusalem.

It seems that the Romans tried to build a temple to Zeus or Jupiter, but something happened—probably a war with Persia—and the construction of the temple was abandoned. Possibly, the temple was built and then later destroyed.

The town of Baalbek was invaded by many conquerors, who coveted the most beautiful mountain in the known world, Mount Lebanon. Jesus' prophecy was fulfilled. Not one stone was left upon another. (See Luke 19:43-44; Matthew 24:1-2.)

WHAT TO SPEAK

But when they shall lead you, and deliver you up, take no thought beforehand what ye shall speak, neither do ye premeditate; but whatsoever shall be given you in that hour, that speak ye; for it is not ye that speak, but the Holy Ghost. Mk. 13:11.

Until the 1920's, lawyers were unknown in Near Eastern lands and are still not known in parts of Turkey, Iraq and Persia (Iran). In these places authorities practice the old way of force or arbitration in settling disputes and quarrels. The rich and the noble are urged to make peace and the poor are forced by the authorities to settle their differences or pay heavy fines.

When a person is charged with a serious offense, such as murder, treason or highway robbery, he has to appear in person before the authorities and defend himself. The whole process of trial is conducted orally and in most instances the parties concerned, including the judge, are illiterate. They do not keep any records and do not quote precedents. Everything depends on the words of the defendant and the honesty of the judge.

The presence of the officials and the weight of the charge bewilder and terrify the persons involved, especially if they have never been before authorities. In such cases, they are generally coached by experienced men who are familiar with the unwritten law and understand the demeanor of the officials. They are taught how to answer certain questions and avoid others, or, in answering, to place the blame for the crime on someone else. The authorities are aware of these professional instructors and their system of bribery, and if they are discovered, the judge is more severe with the accused.

Jesus knew his disciples would be accused of false teachings and treason against the government. He knew they would be approached by instructors with the thought of receiving money from them. He did not want his followers relying on such advisors for help. They must trust in the power of the Holy Spirit. He explained that it would be easier on them to tell the truth than to rely on unscrupulous men and possibly become confused and finally convicted of false testimony. Since they were not guilty, they would not require instruction and need not be afraid of facing anyone. Their minds were to be completely free of any concern. They were innocent and the spirit of truth that was a part of them would speak for them.[1]

---

[1]Mt. 10:19-20; Lk. 12:11-12.

BROTHER BETRAYING BROTHER

Now the brother shall betray the brother to death, and the father the son; and children shall rise up against their parents, and shall cause them to be put to death. Mk. 13:12.

When a Near Easterner becomes a convert to a rival faith, he also renounces his family. The sacred family ties are broken. His parents and brothers and sisters disown him because he has brought disgrace on the family and the race by his conversion. They are ready to avenge his renunciation and some would not hesitate to take his life. His father or his brothers would like to be the first ones to lay their hands on him and willingly kill the apostate son or brother for changing his religion.

It often happens that Assyrian and Armenian girls marry Moslems against their parents' wishes. To do this, they must renounce their faith and in such cases, if they are found, their relatives will kill them. Moslems do the same to those who renounce their faith and become Christians. In the Near East, they do not consider this a crime.

Jesus knew that his teachings would create dissension and friction among family members. Some would cling to the old faith; others would accept the new teachings. Jesus told his followers that the faithful would be persecuted for accepting him as their lord. Their relatives would also seek to kill them. This has continued throughout the centuries.

THE HOUSETOPS

And let him, that is on the house top not go down into the house, neither enter therein, to take any thing out of his house; And let him that is in the field not turn back again for to take up his garment. Mk. 13:15-16.

Housetops in the Near East are flat and serve as playgrounds for children during the day and as meeting places for men and women.

During the summer months people sleep on the housetops to escape the heat and fleas. Family members work, eat, and sleep on the roof because the house is not only warm but uncomfortable. They keep their animals in the house for protection from robbers, making it utterly impossible to destroy the ravaging fleas that make sleeping miserable. These fleas inflict tortures on the sleepers, especially helpless children. People keep clothing, valuables and other possessions in the house when they sleep on their roofs. They lock their doors and place the keys under their pillows Some men take only working clothes on the roof; others go up to the roof only in their undergarments.

In the summer, farmers sleep in the fields, especially during the threshing season when the wheat has to be protected from robbers. The workers sleep in the straw. They keep their good clothes and other belongings between the sheaves. Some workers spend weeks and months at the threshing place. Their wives or daughters bring them their food twice a day. The fields and threshing floors are usually about a mile from town. As there are no laws to protect property, each farmer must be responsible for his crops. Farmers watch their crops from the time they ripen until the fruit and wheat are ready to be stored in their barns.

When unexpected enemies suddenly attack and invade a town from all directions, those sleeping on the roofs flee in confusion. They have no time to go down, open the door and retrieve their garments. This would expose them to attack by the enemies who are lying in wait to kill the people and plunder their homes. Workers in the field are cut off from their homes. They dare not return because the enemy is already in possession of the town. Near Eastern robbers attack towns to plunder the valuables. They are not concerned with the fields unless a town is to be occupied permanently; then the wheat and other supplies on the farms are seized.

The fall of Jerusalem was prophesied to be very sudden. With tranquility and peace reigning, people living in luxury, buying and selling, marrying and giving in marriage, sleeping on comfortable housetops with no thought of fear, the catastrophe would come like a sudden dark cloud covering the blue sky, bringing an unexpected storm. The Jews would not have time to settle their differences with Rome and avoid the impending disaster. The fall of the city would be so sudden that those who were asleep on the housetops would not have time to go down for clothing but would have to flee in their undergarments. Those who were in the fields would not dare return home but must flee for their lives, seeking refuge in the mountains. Every family would be separated and scattered without hope of reunion.[2]

A GREAT CALAMITY

But in those days, after that tribulation, the sun shall be darkened, and the moon shall not give her light, And the stars of heaven shall fall, and the powers that are in heaven shall be shaken. Mk. 13:24-25.

"The sun will be darkened and the moon will not give its light" is an Aramaic saying that is symbolic of a great universal disaster. In the Near East, when people lament the death of a great ruler or some other tragedy, they say: "The sun became dark and the moon refused to give its light; the stars did not appear." This means the calamity was so great that the universe shared in the tragedy. Readers of the Bible find these kinds of sayings throughout holy scripture. Such poetic statements also appear in Semitic Near Eastern literature.

According to Jesus' teachings, when the end comes there will be a universal upheaval; everything will collapse. There will be a new world and a new heaven. God's own light will surpass the light of the sun, moon, and stars. The prophet Zephaniah predicted: "That day is a day of wrath, a day of trouble and distress, a day of confusion and desolation, a day of darkness and gloominess, a day of clouds and thick darkness."[3] (See also Luke 21:25-26 and Matthew 24:29.)

---

[2]Mt. 24:17-18; Lk. 17:31.
[3]Zeph. 1:15, Aramaic Peshitta text, Lamsa translation.

THIS GENERATION

Verily I say unto you, that this generation shall not pass, till all these things be done. Mk. 13:30.

The reference here is to the continuation of the Jewish race that was to survive and witness these predictions as a testimony to the truth of what Jesus had foretold. When biblical Israel was one nation, the Assyrians invaded and took captive the ten northern tribes. These ten tribes had been scattered throughout ancient Assyria and became known as the lost tribes of Israel. But the tribe of Judah was to survive regardless of the changes in dynasties and governments that were to come and go in the Near East, especially in Palestine.

Jesus did not refer to the term "generation" as a period of time but to the continuation of a race. In those days, races were easily assimilated, exterminated and obliterated, such as the Hittites, Amorites and other Palestinian tribes that the Jewish people had abolished. The tribe of Judah would remain until the end.[4]

---

[4]See Mt. 24:34, *ARAMAIC LIGHT ON THE GOSPEL OF MATTHEW*, "The Jewish Race," pp. 303-304.

CHAPTER 14

SIMON THE LEPER

And being in Bethany in the house of Simon the leper, as he sat at meat, there came a woman having an alabaster box of ointment of spikenard very precious; and she brake the box, and poured it on his head. Mk. 14:3.

It is a common Near Eastern practice to give people nicknames to distinguish them from others who bear the same names. This is partly due to the limited number of names. Some nicknames are suggested by physical defects of the persons so named. Usually they use the word that describes the defect in the form of an adjective either before or after the proper name.

For example, they say: "This is blind Jacob," or "This is Simon the leper." If a man's eyes are weak or one of his eyes is blind, they will still call him "blind so and so." It doesn't matter if he may only be suffering from defective eyesight. This custom of distinguishing people by the diseases they had contracted or by the defects of their bodies is still followed today in the Near East.

Simon was nicknamed "the leper" because he previously had been afflicted with leprosy. At this time, however, he had been healed and no longer had leprosy. There was no way he could have entertained Jesus if he still had the disease. Jewish law did not allow lepers to remain in society. People nicknamed him "Simon the leper" to distinguish him from others who also carried his proper name, Simon, and because, in his past, he had contracted the unfortunate disease.[1]

---

[1]Mt. 26:6.

JUDAS ISCARIOT

And Judas Iscariot, one of the twelve, went unto the chief priests, to betray him unto them. Mk. 14:10.

Semites use very few names. Sometimes there will be several children in a family with identical names. In a village, probably about one-third of the names are either Simon, Abraham or Judas. These names were, and still are, popular. People distinguish between those in the same town with the same name by mentioning the father's name—for example, *Shimon Bar Yona*, "Simon son of Jonah." When speaking of people with the same name but from different towns, the name of the town is used instead of the father's name. This applies to Judas (Judah), who is called Judas Iscariot, and also to Mary of Magdala.

A MAN CARRYING WATER

And he sendeth forth two of his disciples, and saith unto them, Go ye into the city, and there shall meet you a man bearing a pitcher of water: follow him. Mk. 14:13.

Carrying water, cooking, and all household tasks are woman's work in Near Eastern countries. It would be a disgrace for the men of a family to be seen doing these domestic duties. When there is no woman present in a household, women from other families help bring in the water supply.

Generally, large towns and cities maintain a lodge for strangers, foreigners and members of other faiths who, because of their different beliefs and customs, cannot be entertained in the homes of the general populace. Often, families are reluctant to open their homes to single traveling men because men and women, guests and strangers have to sleep in the same room.

Certain *khans* (inns) and lodges cater only to male guests. These places employ a male servant to carry water and to take care of the

75

guests. It is against Near Eastern custom to hire a woman for this task. No woman would dare enter a house or lodge with only the presence of male strangers. Usually women carry jars of water on their heads or in their hands. These women bring water taken from wells and springs outside the city. Male servants carry water in large goat skins on their backs, making frequent visits to wells and springs, especially during feasts and banquets.

Jesus told his disciples to find and follow the man who was carrying water. They had to follow him because streets were crooked and wound around in the city. Streets did not carry names and numbers, so this was the easiest way to direct his disciples to the lodge for men only. His disciples were probably unfamiliar with Jerusalem. For some of them, it might have been their first visit to the Holy City. Jesus had to find a *khan* because the city was crowded and no one could possibly offer a room in his home to care for thirteen men. Years ago, strangers unfamiliar with a city questioned shepherds, vineyard workers and water carriers about a place of abode. Abraham's servant did the same when he inquired of Rebekah. (See Genesis 24:23.)

PASSOVER CELEBRATION

And as they did eat, Jesus took bread, and blessed, and brake it, and gave to them, and said, Take eat: this is my body. And he took the cup, and when he had given thanks, he gave it to them: and they all drank of it. And he said unto them, This is my blood of the new testament, which is shed for many. Verily I say to you, I will drink no more of the fruit of the vine, until that day that I drink it new in the kingdom of God. Mk. 14:22-25.

Part 1—THE LORD'S SUPPER. The synoptic gospels (Matthew, Mark, and Luke) state that the Lord's Supper was celebrated on the fifteenth of Nisan according to the Jewish calendar. This was on a Thursday during Holy Week and is in harmony with Jewish customs observed at festivals. The days of preparation for the feast and the days immediately following are regarded as holy, but

Passover day is the holiest of all. Assyrian Christians observe the Jewish feast of Passover on Thursday and the resurrection of Christ on Sunday. The *Qorbana*, "Eucharist or Thanksgiving," is observed on both days, but Easter is the greatest day of the festival for Assyrian Christians.

Jesus and his disciples left Bethany on Thursday morning, and preparations were made for the evening. Every Jew observed Passover to commemorate the exodus from Egypt led by Moses. This religious custom continues to the present day. Jesus' disciples secured a room at an inn for men only. There was no rental charge for use of the room, only the cost of the bread, lamb, wine, and other foods. They purchased these supplies for the meal from the owner of the inn.

When the meal was ready, the group sat on the floor in typical Near Eastern manner. Lamb and bread were placed on a cloth spread on the floor. There were no knives and forks. The flat bread was broken by hand and was used to pick up the meat from the common dish (tray). During the supper the meat and bread (sop) or portions of food were exchanged as a token of friendship.[2] Since there was so much camaraderie and brotherly bonding at the meal, especially with the sharing of food, Judas thought that Jesus did not know who was to betray him.

Jesus took the bread in his hands, blessed it, broke it and gave it to his disciples, saying: "Take and eat; this is my body." Before this time, Jesus and his disciples had celebrated Passover by eating bread and lamb in commemoration of the lamb slain in Egypt. They were also celebrating Israel's deliverance from Egyptian oppression. Now Jesus himself was to become the slain lamb. "This is my body" means "I will be slain like this lamb." In other words, "When you celebrate this meal again, do it in memory of me and not of the lamb slain in Egypt." Jesus was now ready to become the Deliverer from bondage and oppression for all peoples and nations.

After they had eaten the bread, he took the earthen jar that had

---

[2]See Gen. 43:34.

been filled with red wine and poured it in a cup. Semitic custom is to drink after eating and not during the meal. Jesus omitted the usual cordial exchange of greetings with his disciples when beginning the custom of sharing the cup. Instead, he gave thanks and immediately shared the cup of wine with his disciples. For Jesus, the rich, red wine resembled blood, which he was soon to pour out on the cross. This was a cup of sorrow, instead of joy, for the prophet from Galilee.

As the master-teacher began to pass the cup, he said: "This is my blood of the new testament which is shed for many." When the Israelites were slaves in Egypt, God had sent Moses to deliver them. On the final night before their departure from Egypt, Moses had instructed his people to smear the blood of the lamb on their door-posts. This action would save them from the slaughter of their firstborn throughout the land of the Egyptians by the death angel. Now the blood of Jesus, that was to be shed on the cross, would save both Israel and Gentile nations. Jesus would free them from the devastating power of sin and corruption. He was to make an everlasting offering, a sacrifice of love. Humanity was about to make Jesus their sacrifice not to appease God but to gratify themselves.

Prophets had long declared that the blood of slaughtered animals was not sufficient for the remission of sins, nor did God ever demand ritual sacrifice for atonement.[3] God wants justice and compassion and not sacrifice. Repentance[4] and doing good works are what God desires.

Jesus' death on the cross was to open the way for humanity to participate in everlasting life and to have power over sin, sickness and death. From then on, Jesus' disciples were to drink of this cup in memory of their master's triumph over death and to celebrate his glorious resurrection. The bread and wine are symbolic of the spiritual body and blood of Jesus. (See Matthew 26:26-29; Luke 22:19-20.)

Part 2—FRUIT OF THE VINE. "Verily I say unto you, I will

---

[3]See Jer. 7:21-23; Isa. 1:11-18, 66:1-3; Hosea 6:6; Mic. 6:6-8.
[4]"Repentance" means "turn to God and away from evil deeds."

drink no more of the fruit of the vine, until that day that I drink it new in the kingdom of God."[5] The Aramaic word *hamara*, "wine," has many other meanings. Metaphorically, it signifies "joy, inspiration and teaching."

This verse has been a stumbling block to many theologians and readers of the Bible. Some Bible students use it to support their belief in a physical life hereafter. They believe there will be wine in heaven because "Jesus said so," and since there will be wine, why not other physical things? Again, this is a misunderstanding of Semitic speech.

The term "fruit of the vine" means "the vine's product," that is, "wine." What Jesus meant was this: "I shall not have this joy with all of you again until we are together once more in God's kingdom." Scripture tells us that wine makes the heart merry. Jesus was to face crucifixion very soon; this was the last time he would taste "the fruit of the vine," that is, the joy he was experiencing with his beloved disciples.

On other occasions, Jesus used the expression "wine" to indicate "teaching." He said: "No one puts new wine in old skins."[6] "New wine," in this instance, refers to Jesus' teachings. "The old skins" refer to the old religious beliefs. Additionally, Semites refer to the teachings of their Church as "the wine of the Church." Near Easterners understand such figurative speech. The problem is that Western people do not use these metaphors in their languages; therefore, the Occidental world takes these Semitic expressions literally and misunderstands them.

MEETING IN GALILEE

But after that I am risen, I will go before you into Galilee. Mk. 14:28.

Jesus' faith in God—whom he called *Abba*, "Father"—was so strong and unshakeable that he knew he would triumph over death

---

[5]Mk. 14:25, K. J. V.
[6]Mt. 9:17.

and the grave. Death would not be able to silence him or his powerful message of God's kingdom. He was so sure of his rise from the grip of death and the grave that he told his disciples to meet him in Galilee after his crucifixion and before they returned to their own villages. (Note: All Jesus' disciples, with the exception of Judas, were Galileans; after Passover, they were to return home with others to Galilee.)

However, Jesus' disciples took this saying lightly and perhaps even misunderstood it. In the first place, they did not believe that their master would die on the cross. Secondly, they could not believe that anyone would be able to rise from the dead. This is the reason for their doubts when some disciples began to experience and proclaim Jesus' resurrection after his crucifixion. They thought that it was only a rumor and were reluctant to accept and believe in such a notion.

The phrase "I will go before you into Galilee" makes his resurrection a sure and definite appointment. It would be as one person would say to another when making an appointment: "Don't worry, I'll see you in your own homeland." The messenger who appeared at the sepulcher repeated this phrase when he told the women to tell Jesus' disciples that their master would meet them in Galilee: "But go away and tell his disciples and Peter that he will be before you in Galilee; there you will see him, just as he has told you."[7]

RABBI

And as soon as he was come, he goeth straightway to him, and saith, Master, master; and kissed him. Mk. 14:45.

The Aramaic text reads: "And immediately he approached him and said to him, *Rabbi, Rabbi*; then he kissed him."[8] The term *Rabbi* is Aramaic. Jewish people acquired this term during their captivity in

---

[7]Mk. 16:7, Aramaic Peshitta text, Lamsa translation.
[8]Mk. 14:45, Aramaic Peshitta text, Errico.

Chaldea (Babylon). *Rabbi* is equivalent to our English term "doctor of divinity" or "professor." It derives from the Aramaic root *rab*, "great." Thus to call one *Rabbi* means, "my great one (doctor or Master-Teacher)." This title is given only to learned men. The Aramaic word *malpana* also means "professor or teacher."

Jesus was an educated man. He had studied at the synagogue and could read and write. Luke tells us that Jesus read from the scroll of Isaiah when he attended synagogue and that he also explained the scripture to them. Had he been uneducated, he could not have taught in the synagogues.[9] Even Jesus' enemies called him *Rabbi*.

Jesus spent many years of his early life, from childhood to age 30, studying Holy Scripture. Nearly all of his teaching is based on the Mosaic law and the prophets. He quoted from them because he knew these scriptures by heart.

Evidently Jesus, while immersing himself in the Hebrew Bible, made notes just as we do today. He always spoke with authority because he quoted directly from the Written Word. Matthew might have had access to these notes when he wrote his gospel. This is why Matthew's version is the first record of Jesus' teachings. Matthew had been a chief tax collector. One must read and write to be appointed to such an important position.

Judas addressed Jesus as he had greeted him on many other occasions. Near Eastern students always address their teacher as "*Rabbi*—My teacher."

TEACHING IN THE TEMPLE

I was daily with you in the temple teaching, and ye took me not: but the scriptures must be fulfilled. Mk. 14:49.

"Teaching in the temple" does not mean preaching to a congregation within the main area of the temple. It means Jesus was teaching those who were in the outer courtyard of the temple. These

---

[9]See Lk. 4:17-22.

people would have to stop and listen to him. As public halls were unknown, Semites often gathered in church courtyards to discuss religious and political affairs. Only religious worship services were held in the church.

Jesus was not teaching in the temple proper nor did he debate anywhere near the holy of holies or other places where the high priests preached to their congregations. This would have been impossible. The high priests would not have allowed this kind of teaching to be conducted in these areas. It would have been against the established custom. Jesus constantly denounced the hierarchical system and the improper use of the temple.

The temple was composed of many units. The sole person to enter the holy of holies and other sacred worship areas was the high priest. Only Jewish people could enter certain sacred places to pray and listen to the preaching of their priests. In the outer courts or Gentile courts, people from all parts of the Eastern world could gather for worship and prayer. It was here that the priests transacted temple business. Jews and Gentiles carried on their occupations, settled their differences, held debates and social meetings within the confines of the Gentile courts. This is where Jesus preached and taught his gospel of God's kingdom. The synagogue had developed after the Chaldean (Babylonian) exile and did not follow the temple plan. Nonetheless, the synagogue also became a preaching center. (See Matthew 26:55.)

A YOUNG MAN

And there followed him a certain young man, having a linen cloth cast about his naked body, and the young men laid hold on him: And he left the linen cloth, and fled from them naked. Mk. 14:51-52.

The "certain young man" might have been one of the followers of Jesus who had accompanied him and his disciples to the Garden of Gethsemane. Or, he might have been a young man who just happened to be there at that time. There is no indication that he was

82

one of Jesus' disciples.

Gethsemane is a public park. Many wayfarers and strangers who cannot find lodging in the city on feast days spend the night there, sleeping under the olive trees. When Jesus was arrested, his disciples fled, so the young man fled too, fearing he might be implicated.

Many poor people in Palestine, especially in those early days, had only one garment, or a large piece of cloth, which covered their bodies. Such poor people are still found in many villages of India, North Africa, and Palestine. Undoubtedly, this young man was poor; that is why he was spending the night in Gethsemane.

Some commentators think that the "young man" was John Mark. This could not be true. Mark was a young boy or, as some suggest, perhaps not even born yet. He was a disciple of Paul and *Shimon Kepa* (Peter), and as a young man he traveled with them, sharing their itinerary. Most likely, the gospel writer does not tell us who the fleeing young man was, because he was not a disciple or relative of Jesus or even a relative of one of the disciples. No one really knows who this young man was. He could have even been a foreigner who had come to celebrate the feast of Passover.

COVERING THE FACE

And some began to spit on him, and to cover his face, and to buffet him, and to say unto him, Prophesy: and the servants did strike him with the palms of their hands. Mk. 14:65.

Jesus was condemned for the blasphemy of making himself equal with God. When a man was condemned for a crime or blasphemy, everyone present would have the right to spit in his face. They do this to show that they have no part in his guilt and actions. People considered him unclean and not to be touched or his face looked at. Holy men who think of themselves as pious would have felt defiled if they had accidentally looked at a condemned man. The high priest and other Jewish dignitaries would have refused to look on the face of one who had made himself "the son of God." When these men passed by Jesus, they turned their faces away from him so that they could avoid seeing him. This was after the high priest had convicted him and condemned him as a blasphemer.

Jesus' face was hooded or covered because it was smeared with blood. The Jewish leaders and people did not like to see blood. It was also a common Near Eastern custom to cover the face of a man condemned to death. (See the story of Haman in Esther 7:8, whose face was also covered.)

EXPOSED BY SPEECH

And he denied it again. And a little after, they that stood by said again to Peter, Surely thou art one of them: for thou art a Galilean, and thy speech agreeth thereto. Mk. 14:70.

Part 1—NORTHERN AND SOUTHERN ARAMAIC IN PALESTINE. The apostle *Shimon Kepa,* "Simon Peter," spoke northern, Galilean Aramaic, a dialect somewhat different in pronunciation and expression from southern, Chaldean Aramaic that the Jews spoke in Judea. Peter understood what the maid said to him, but he tried to avoid an answer so that he would not arouse suspicion. In verse 68 of this chapter, Peter said he did not understand, but the maid insisted he was one of Jesus' followers. She deduced this from his style of speech. The Aramaic text reads: ". . .for you also are a Galilean, and even your speech is like theirs." Any Galilean found in the high priest's courtyard on that occasion would have been suspected of being a follower of Jesus. It was too late; Peter's speech betrayed him. His sudden burst into cursing was characteristic of Assyrian and northern Aramaic speech. Today many disputes are settled by cursing and swearing. When a young man wants to evade an issue, he will swear and say that he does not understand what you are saying.[10]

---

[10]See Mt. 26:70; Lk. 22:55-60; Jn. 18:17.

In Palestine Aramaic the dialect of Galilee was different from that of Judea, and as a result of the religious separation of the Jews and the Samaritans, a special Samaritan dialect was evolved, but its literature cannot be considered Jewish. For eastern Aramaic whose most distinctive point of difference is "n" in place of "y" as the prefix of the third person masculine of the imperfect tense of the verb, belong the idioms of the Babylonian Talmud, which most closely agree with the language of the Mandaean writings.[11]

Part 2—THE GALILEAN DIALECT. Aramaic has three major dialects. The Assyrians spoke the northern or Galilean Aramaic. It gained much importance and became known as the *lingua franca* because of the rise and growth of the Assyrian Empire during the 11th century BCE. Princes and noblemen of neighboring lands used it as the medium for diplomacy and commerce.[12] After the fall of the Assyrian Empire, this language was so deeply established that it continued as the major language of Chaldea (Babylon). The Persian conquerors used it in their communications with officials in Palestine, Asia Minor, Egypt, and Arabia. It has remained the literary language of the Assyrians to the present day. Many Assyrians and Chaldeans still speak Aramaic in such nations as the United States, Australia, Iraq, Lebanon, Russia, Israel and many other lands.

The Jews in Judea whose forefathers had been carried captive into Chaldea (Babylon) spoke southern or Chaldean Aramaic. Western Aramaic, known as an Aramean tongue, was the language of the Syrian kingdom as far back as the days of Abraham. (Syria's true name is Aram.) However, northern Aramaic displaced western Aramaic after the Assyrians conquered Syria in 722 BCE.

This northern dialect of Aramaic was the language of Galilee from the days when the ten tribes of Israel were carried away into Assyria and large Assyrian colonies transported to Galilee and

---

[11]W. Bacher of "Aramaic Language among the Jews." By special permission from The Jewish Encyclopedia, Vol. II, Funk & Wagnalls, New York & London.
[12]See 2 Ki. 18:26, Lamsa translation.

Samaria.[13] This was the dialect that Jesus and his disciples spoke. The difference between these three dialects are in pronunciation and colloquial expressions rather than in grammatical syntax. For example, the northern Aramaic consonant *heth* is pronounced with a strong guttural sound, but in southern and western Aramaic it is a soft guttural sound. In western Aramaic the letter *alep* when ending a word is usually pronounced as an "o" as in *m'sheeho* instead of the northern and southern Aramaic *m'sheeha,* meaning "Messiah/Christ."

Then there are the colloquial and idiomatic expressions of speech that cause confusion and misunderstanding. For example, a man speaking southern Aramaic would say: "I have given birth to wealth and many sheep," meaning his sheep and money have increased. Those who speak northern Aramaic would not understand such a saying. By the same token, a southern Aramaic speaking person would find it puzzling to hear: "I have eaten my body and drunk my blood to build this house." What this means is that the man has made many sacrifices and endured many hardships to build his home.

Peter spoke the northern dialect of Aramaic which has its own peculiar accent. This roused the suspicions of the high priest's maid servant who spoke southern Aramaic. She knew Peter was not Judean but Galilean. Although Peter emphatically denied his lord, he could not disguise his nationality and speech.[14]

---

[13]See 2 Ki. 17:24.
[14]See Mt. 26:73; Lk. 22:59.

CHAPTER 15

PILATE MARVELED AT JESUS

But Jesus yet answered nothing; so that Pilate marveled. Mk. 15:5.

Jesus gave no answer simply because he knew that his time had come and that his destiny was the cross. All the accusations against him were false. Both his accusers and Pilate, the governor, knew that Jesus had committed no crime. If Jesus had answered the governor, it would have been to no avail; it might even have implicated him all the more. The Hebrew prophet Isaiah had predicted that the Messiah would not open his mouth or protest.[1] In the Near East, an accused individual is judged by his words. Semites believe that the less an accused talks, the better it will go for him. Jesus had said: "By your words, they shall judge you."

When false charges are brought against an innocent man, Near Easterners feel that the charges do not deserve a reply or answer. Pilate was already aware of the fact that Jesus had never said he was a political king. The governor could see that the haggard and poorly clad Galilean who stood before him was far from being a political revolutionary. He posed no threat to Rome. Therefore, Pilate needed no answer; the case spoke for itself. The innocence of a person is sometimes evidenced by not attempting a defense. Self-defense throws some doubt on one's innocence. Besides, Jesus also knew that the Roman governor was helpless and that his political position meant more to him than justice. (See John 19:9.)

VICTIMS SCOURGED BEFORE EXECUTION

And so Pilate, willing to content the people, released Barabbas unto them, and delivered Jesus, when he had scourged him, to be crucified. And

---

[1] Isa. 53:7.

the soldiers led him away into the hall, called Praetorium; and they called together the whole band. Mk. 15:15-16.

It was Palestinian custom to scourge victims before they were crucified. After prisoners were condemned, they were turned over to the soldiers, who would mock them and beat them with whips. Some governors would watch these unfortunate prisoners while the soldiers were afflicting them. Others never saw them again once the sentence had been pronounced.

On such occasions, some Easterners would not restrain their temper and hatred toward a condemned man. They would like nothing better than to participate in punishing the convicted prisoner. Many times the soldiers would allow them to do as they pleased. Therefore, the convicted and condemned were severely flogged before their execution; at times, they would die by the hands of the mob before their sentence was carried out. When the punishment was stoning to death, everyone would willingly throw stones at the condemned. Even women and little children took an active part in stoning.

This is the reason Jesus could not carry his cross to Golgotha. He had been physically weakened from the severe and cruel treatment he had endured by the hands of the soldiers and the crowd at the palace of the high priest. As soon as Pilate had pronounced the sentence, he handed Jesus over to the soldiers to receive the scourging. The entire crowd participated in punishing and beating him. In their eyes, Jesus was a heretic and blasphemer who had made himself one with God. They readily shared the responsibility of making him pay for his acts against their religion. (Matthew 27:26; John 19:1.)

WINE MIXED WITH MYRRH

And they gave him to drink wine mingled with myrrh: but he received it not. Mk. 15:23.

Before the convicted were crucified, soldiers would offer the victims wine mixed with myrrh to lessen their pain and suffering. This drink is similar to a shot of novocaine or morphine that a dentist or a medical doctor might give to a patient.

Jesus was thirsty. He had nothing to drink since his arrest that Thursday evening. Prisoners in the Near East, especially those charged with political crimes, are not treated kindly. Very seldom will they even be given water or food. They are not treated like condemned prisoners are in America.

Jesus had already lost much blood from his flogging and crown of thorns. This made his thirst even more intense. He asked for water, but there was no water on this hill of the crucified. Who would go down to the town well and secure a jar of water for this blasphemer? Therefore, the soldiers offered him the wine mixed with myrrh that was already at hand. But Jesus refused to drink it. He needed and wanted water. And, although it would lessen his pain and suffering, he did not want to drink anything that would deaden and stupefy his senses.[2]

HOUR OF CRUCIFIXION

And it was the third hour, and they crucified him. Mk. 15:25.

According to Mark's gospel, Jesus' crucifixion began at the third hour—that is, about nine in the morning. This method of keeping time is still used in many regions of the Near East. Matthew says "from the sixth hour"(around twelve noon) darkness covered the land until three in the afternoon. Luke's gospel agrees with Matthew's text.[3]

The gospel of John mentions the hour when Pilate told the Jews: "Behold, your king!" In other words, John's gospel mentions the time when the sentence of death was pronounced on Jesus.[4] We must

---

[2]See Ps. 69:21.
[3]See Mt. 27:45.
[4]Jn. 19:14.

remember that John was the only disciple who was at the scene when Jesus was crucified. Luke and Mark were probably children when this final episode in Jesus' life took place.

The authors of the gospels, like all Semites, were not interested in providing the reader the exact hour and minute of the events that had transpired on that suffering Friday. (Time is not relevant or important for Semitic Near Easterners. Actually any time will do as long as it is a bit reasonable. In the Near East, someone who has waited for a friend for an hour or so might say to the arriving friend: "I have been waiting for you all day.")

Jesus' disciples were not present at the governor's palace. Nearly all of his disciples, except for John, had fled. What the gospel authors wanted to say was that Jesus' crucifixion took place on Friday, the sixth day of the week, and the exact details of time did not matter to them. (See Matthew 27:45 and Luke 23:44.)

JESUS' DEATH FORETOLD

And at the ninth hour Jesus cried with a loud voice, saying, Eloi, Eloi, lama sabachthani? which is being interpreted, My God, my God why hast thou forsaken me? Mk. 15:34.

Part 1—PALESTINIAN AND CHALDEAN DIALECTS. The Aramaic Peshitta text reads: "And about the ninth hour Jesus cried out in a loud voice, and said: "*'el, 'el, lmana shwaqtani!*, that is, *Alahi, Alahi, lmana shwaqtani!*"[5] Mark translates Jesus' words that he uttered from the cross from Palestinian Aramaic into the Chaldean, or southern, Aramaic. Mark is not interpreting the phrase; he is

---

[5] I left the text in an Aramaic transliteration because I wish the reader to see the subtle difference between the two Aramaic phrases. Dr. Lamsa translates the verse as: "Eli, Eli, lemana, shabathani! which means, My God, my God, for this I was spared (kept)!" For a detailed study on the first Aramaic phrase see Errico/Lamsa, *ARAMAIC LIGHT ON THE GOSPEL OF MATTHEW*, New Testament series, Vol. 1, "Jesus' Triumphant Cry," pp. 346-352.

merely going from one dialect of Aramaic to another. The expression in the King James Version, "which is being interpreted," is not a proper rendering. The Aramaic word *deetey* simply means "that is."

Mark was with Peter; Near Eastern scholars and tradition teach that both Peter and Mark were preaching the gospel of the kingdom in Chaldea (Babylon). For some time when Jesus had been traveling and teaching his disciples, he told them to go first to the lost sheep (tribes) of Israel that were scattered throughout the Middle East. These were the tribes whom the Assyrians had taken captive to their homeland in 722 BCE and the two Jewish tribes, Benjamin and Judah, who had been in Chaldea (Babylon) since 586 BCE. Most of the well-to-do and prosperous Jews had remained in Babylon after the restoration. They did not want to return to Palestine under Ezra and Nehemiah. There was a large Jewish colony in Chaldea; the Babylonian Talmud was written there and the city was a center of learning for the Jews for many years. This is the reason for Peter's and Mark's presence in that great city.

Matthew's gospel uses Palestinian Aramaic when recording the words of Jesus from the cross. Matthew does not explain the phrase. The people in Palestine would understand the meaning of Jesus' exclamation. In Mark's gospel, the words *'el, 'el,* "O, God, O God," are translated into Eastern Aramaic *alahi, alahi,* "My God, my God! To what an end or purpose you have kept me!"

We must not forget that when Jesus made this outcry, his lips were parched with thirst, and he had lost much blood. His words were not too clear. This is the reason that those who stood by the cross thought Jesus was calling on Elijah. The Aramaic word for "God" and the word for "Elijah" are written almost alike and they almost sound alike as well. "God" is *'eli,* and "Elijah" is *'elia.* One would actually have to hear it and see it in the Aramaic letters to appreciate the subtle difference between the two words. The Chaldean or Babylonian word for "God" is *Alaha* and "my God" is *Alahi.* The final letter "i" shows the possessive case, meaning "my God." Biblical writers used the Semitic term *El,* "God," throughout Scripture. Two examples of this are: (1) *El Shaddai,* "The great God" or "God Almighty and (2) *Bethel,* "The house of God." (Jacob changed the name of the town, which was originally called *Luz,* "Almonds," to *Bethel.*)

Those of the Near Eastern tradition know that Matthew, being a Palestinian Jew, wrote for the people of Palestine in their vernacular and that his gospel was the first written gospel. Mark was probably just a young boy when Jesus died on the cross. Mark, at the outset, was a disciple of Paul and later joined Peter. Paul had never seen Jesus. He was converted to the Galilean movement some years after Jesus' death.

As we have said, Mark translated the words Jesus uttered from the cross into the dialect of the people where he and Peter were preaching. They were addressing the Jews in Babylon who had been expecting the promised Messiah. The New Testament does not tell us that either Mark or Peter visited Rome, although Western tradition teaches that Peter died in Rome. Assuredly, the gospel of Mark was written prior to the apostles' visit to Rome.

Evidently, Mark's gospel is a transcription from the earlier scrolls of Matthew. This is the reason Mark's gospel does not contain the account of Jesus' birth and genealogy. Undoubtedly, the genealogy was written later, after Jesus' kingdom movement had spread into many regions of the Near East. People wanted to know more about his early life and background. All biographies and genealogies of great men are written after they become famous or have died. Had Mark written his gospel in Rome, he would not have translated the words on the cross into the Chaldean Aramaic dialect. The Jews in Rome were Palestinians who had been dispersed by the Romans.

Part 2—JESUS NOT FORSAKEN. The ancient Aramaic speaking writers of the Church of the East tell us that God was with Jesus when he was in the womb, on the cross, and in the grave. God never forsook him. Jesus suffered, died, and was buried as a man. His divinity (spirituality)—or God within him—never suffered and died on the cross or underwent burial. Jesus the human being and Christ the God nature were inseparable but distinct.

Jesus had often told his disciples that he would be rejected, condemned to death and crucified—that Scriptures which foretold his death must be fulfilled. Isaiah, the great Hebrew prophet, had predicted Jesus' rejection and death.[6] Jesus had also assured his disciples that in spite of the cruel death he was to face, he would rise from among the dead on the third day. On their last journey to Jerusalem, Jesus predicted that his disciples would leave him and flee for their lives: "For behold, the hour is coming, and it has now come, when you will be dispersed, every man to his own country, and you will leave me alone; and yet I am never alone, because the Father is with me."[7]

Also, when Jesus was praying in Gethsemane, he had placed himself completely in God's hands and became willing to drink the cup of death. He could have asked God for help, and we are told that many legions of angels would have been sent to his aid, but Jesus was not afraid of death. He was ready to reveal that the awesome power of death and the fearful grave were not a barrier between human beings and God. He was going to show that humanity is immortal and indestructible, because a human being is the image and likeness of God—and God is indestructible. Through his death on the cross, Jesus was to triumph over death; through his resurrection, he would give life a new meaning.

A famous Near Eastern writer and commentator, Isho'dad of Merv, Bishop of Hadatha, says that these words were uttered on the cross to make known Jesus' immeasurable love and faith in God. Jesus was obedient to God to the extent that he shed his blood on the cross for the sake of humanity. How could God as a loving Father forsake his obedient son, who gave his life for the sake of God's children?

Furthermore, this Semitic writer says that God had not forsaken Jesus but that the prophet from Galilee was willing to suffer for our sakes. In his commentary on Matthew 27:46, he very clearly

---

[6]Isa. 53:1-5.
[7]Jn. 16:32, Aramaic Peshitta text, Lamsa translation.

interprets the words of Jesus as God being with him in suffering, on the cross, in death, and in the grave. He also informs us that the sun and the moon darkened as a sign of mourning. This was typical Semitic poetic style of writing, indicating that the entire universe was sharing in this great tragedy.

God allowed (Aramaic: *shawaq*) Jesus to die on the cross so that he might demonstrate that there is resurrection and life hereafter. Jesus' death on the cross was to reveal the secrets of life. Jesus could have escaped death as he had done before. Instead he chose to face the cross. Therefore, God raised him from death.

Again, Jesus in the garden said: "O my Father, deliver me from this hour, but for this cause I came to this very hour."[8] In other words, he was saying, "This is my destiny, to die for the sake of the truth." He said almost the same thing as he stood before Pilate: "For this cause came I into the world, to bear witness concerning the truth."[9] The expression "bear witness" in Aramaic means "to die for the sake of the truth." Many people understand martyrs as those who have come to bear witness with their lives. Surely, death on the cross was the fulfillment of Jesus' destiny.

Jesus cried on the cross: "My God, my God, for this I was spared!" None of the people standing near the cross thought that Jesus had said that God forsook him. To this very day, Near Eastern Semites when they suffer tragedies say, "I was spared by God to see this tragedy with my own eyes." Such phrases are very common in Semitic speech and the people understand them quite well. The ancient Greek texts also use the term "spared" or "allowed."

Had Jesus said that God had forsaken him, his enemies could then have declared that this Galilean had finally confessed that he was a sinner—God forsook him. Scripture tells us that God does not forsake the righteous; nor does God forsake those who trust in Him. The Jews near the cross said, "He trusted in God; let us see if God will deliver him." How is it that the people who stood around the

---

[8]Jn.12:27, Aramaic Peshitta text, Lamsa translation.
[9]Jn. 18:37, Aramaic Peshitta text, Lamsa translation.

cross did not say that God had forsaken him? How can it be that translators of the New Testament, who lived 1600 years later in England, knew more than the people who stood on the hill of Golgotha and witnessed Jesus' death? And they also heard his cries in their own language! Without doubt, the testimony of those who stood near the cross is greater than that of all the scholars in the world.

Part 3—THE WORDS *"LMANA SHAWAQTANI."* The challenge and difficulty in translating *"lmana shawaqtani"* was due to a misunderstanding of the Aramaic intended use of the terms and their various meanings. The word *shawaq* can mean "to spare, leave, desert, forgive, allow, permit, keep." Also, the translators mistook the word *l'mana,* which can mean "why, for what, for this." In vernacular Aramaic, people use the word *lamodi* or *lamodmindi*—"for what cause," "for this reason or cause." Usually when *l'mana* is used to mean "why," it is preceded by the word *mittol. Mittol l'mana* appears throughout a book that was written by a great soldier and physicist named Job, of the Church of the East, in the ninth century CE.

Shawaq is one of the most difficult words to translate, especially by foreigners who read but cannot converse in Aramaic. The words *l'mana shawaqtani* that appear in Matthew and Mark mean "For this cause, or thing, I was spared," that is to say, "This is my destiny." At times, Aramaic speaking people use this expression as an exclamation, with a shaking of their heads—"To what an end or purpose you have kept me!"

Throughout his life, Jesus trusted in God, who guided and directed him in everything. He never doubted or questioned his Father's wisdom. He was always in accord with God and never felt that he was alone or without God's presence.

After his resurrection, Jesus reminded some of his disciples that he had told them many times that as the Messiah he must suffer and die but would rise on the third day. Prophecy must be fulfilled. From the day on which Jesus embarked on his mission to preach his gospel, he knew and was mindful of his death on the cross. He very clearly understood that his controversial message of the kingdom, based on loving kindness and meekness, would find rejection among religious authorities and political leaders. He knew that he would meet death for speaking against the doctrines of the elders. But he was also confident of his ultimate victory over death and the triumph of his gospel. This is the reason that his very last words and cry from the cross were: "Father, into your hands I commend my spirit." He entrusted his spirit (life) to the hands of his heavenly Father.

IN A SPONGE

And one ran and filled a sponge full of vinegar, and put it on a reed, and gave him to drink, saying, Let alone; let us see whether Elias will come to take him down. Mk. 15:36.

The reference here points back to Mark 15:23. Wine mixed with myrrh was given to Jesus in a sponge fastened on the end of a reed, rather than in a cup, because the cross was so high.[10]

Generally, victims were given this mixture before they were crucified. But in this case, the drug was administered to him after he cried aloud: "My God, my God, for this I was kept!" Those standing by the cross thought that Jesus was calling upon the prophet Elijah. So they were waiting to see if Elijah would come and take him down from the cross.

---

[10]See Mt. 27:48; Jn. 19:29. See also the comment on Mk. 15:23, "Wine Mixed with Myrrh," pp. 88-89.

CHAPTER 16

WOMEN AT THE SEPULCHER

And very early in the morning the first day of the week, they came unto the sepulchre at the rising of the sun. Mk. 16:2.

It is an old established custom among Semites to visit the graves of the dead on the third day after their passing. They believe that the soul of the departed returns on the third day to say a final farewell to the body. At this reunion, the dead returns to life for a short time and realizes he is dead and buried in the grave. Relatives and friends of the deceased never fail to go to the cemetery and wait at the grave on this day.

Generally, the ceremony is attended by a group of women mourners who burn incense and sit in a circle around the grave. While the incense is burning, the women weep mournfully. They call the dead by name and converse with them as if they were alive, believing that they see them and hear their words even though the women cannot see the departed ones.

Jesus died on Friday. The women came to the tomb site early Sunday morning, the third day. They wanted to burn incense and say goodbye to their beloved lord. They did not expect that he would rise from the dead although he had told them that he would die and rise again so that the Scriptures might be fulfilled. To their amazement, they found the tomb empty and were greeted by an angel who told them Jesus had risen. (Matthew 28:1; Luke 24:1; John 20:1.)

AN ANGEL AT THE TOMB

And entering into the sepulchre, they saw a young man sitting on the right side, clothed in a long white garment; and they were affrighted. Mk. 16:5.

Angels appear as human beings to pious men and women while they are in a trance or in a vision state. For instance, Scripture tells us that angels had appeared to the Hebrew patriarchs, Gideon, Samson's mother, the prophets, Mary, Joseph and to some of the apostles. God always guides and directs those who believe in and walk in God's way. God also guides, counsels and admonishes men and women, and answers their prayers by sending messengers to them so that they may receive comfort. Jesus' followers were bereaved and sad.

White is symbolic of purity. Kings, princes and priests wore white linen garments. No matter how the angel appeared, it appeared only to Jesus' disciples and followers. Others who might have been there could not see it, just as Jesus revealed himself, after his resurrection, only to those who believed in him and were mourning his death. Those who had no relationship with him or did not believe in him never saw him. (See Luke 24:3.)

THE BELIEVER IN JESUS

And he said unto them, Go ye into all the world, and preach the gospel to every creature. He that believeth and is baptized shall be saved; but he that believeth not shall be damned. Mk. 16:15-16.

A true believer is not the one who merely says, "I believe in Jesus." Anyone who acts on the belief and practices the works of Jesus' gospel of the kingdom is a true believer. Today, literally millions of people believe in Jesus and invoke his name but do not follow his teaching. One who truly believes practices Jesus' teaching of the kingdom—loving kindness, meekness, peacemaking, compassion and inclusiveness of others.

Jesus' reference here is to those who believe in his gospel, actualize his principles of the kingdom, and are baptized in his name. When one is baptized in his name, it means that he or she has become a participant of his way of life. In biblical days, members of various sects and cults were known by certain marks on their bodies or by secret words. Jews were distinguished from other Semitic races by

98

the ordinance of circumcision. Some of the pagans made marks, cuts on their cheeks; others removed their front teeth. All these wounds identified them as belonging to a certain religious group. Certificates and membership enrollment were unknown and in many areas are still not known.

Baptism by water was the mark or identification of a believer in Jesus. It was the simplest method ever given for identification because it symbolized cleansing or purification. John the Baptist had initiated this method to show one was cleansed and ready to begin a new way of life. The Aramaic word *mamudita*, "baptism," comes from *amadha*, "to become a pillar." *Amudha* means "pillar." By means of water baptism, a believer becomes a pillar in the church of Jesus Christ. As pillars sustain temples, a religion or movement is supported and sustained by faithful men and women who are strong pillars.

There are regions in the Near East where water is very difficult to procure and is so scarce that bathing is not practiced. Because of the lack of water, Jesus' disciples who preached in Arabia could not have baptized by immersion those who had accepted Jesus' gospel. If possible, they sprinkled them with water. In arid places where water is nearly non-existent, the new disciples were not denied their place in the gospel of Jesus Christ. However, where there was ample water, they practiced baptism by immersion.

The word "damned" in the King James Version is not translated correctly. The Aramaic word implies that these persons have been judged by their own refusal to practice the principles of the kingdom. If they continue in their evil deeds, their actions judge and condemn them. According to Mark, the risen Christ spoke these words in reference to those who know the truth but have rejected it. They see the light and yet continue to practice erroneous actions harmful to themselves and others.[1]

---

[1]Many modern NT scholars today believe that Jesus as the risen Christ never uttered these words. This was a practice of the early followers in recruiting converts into the Church (Assembly). Jesus never threatened people. He only

GREAT WONDERS

And these signs shall follow them that believe; In my name shall they cast out devils; they shall speak with new tongues. Mk. 16:17.

Part 1—MIRACLES. The Aramaic word for "miracle" is *tedmorta*. It derives from the root *damar,* "to be seized with astonishment or surprise." The Arabic word *aajeeba* means "wonder." In Aramaic speech, the phrase "it is a miracle" is very common; it does not mean that something supernatural has happened. Anything that causes wonder is called a "miracle." The solution to a problem or the accomplishment of a difficult task is regarded as a miracle. When a sick person recovers, Semites say it is a miracle. They use the same expression when a woman is able to economize with the limited family budget and feed her family and guests well with just a few loaves of bread.

It is important to make a distinction between genuine miracles—such as healing the sick, raising the dead and opening the eyes of the blind—and wonders that are acts of nature. In the realms of the spirit, faith, prayer and practicing the principles of living in the kingdom are the means through which we can perform true miracles. It is as much a miracle today for a blind person to receive sight as it was when Jesus restored sight to the blind.

We also need to distinguish between the miracles that Jesus worked to help suffering humanity and his persuasive teaching through his parables that impressed and amazed his listeners. The followers of Jesus' gospel and teachings have exhibited miraculous powers through the centuries. (Matthew 21:15; Luke 23:8.)

Part 2—SPEAK WITH NEW TONGUES. "They shall speak with new tongues" means that the disciples were to speak the languages of other races and people who were to receive Jesus' gospel of the Kingdom. That is to say, when Jesus' disciples were to go as missionaries to other lands far away from Judea, the Holy Spirit

---

warned them of the dangers of bad actions and behavior.

would help them to learn to speak the new tongues which before this time were unknown to them. People who happened to be moved by the Holy Spirit would understand despite the speaker's incomplete knowledge of the language. (Today, American missionaries speak in languages which until recently were unknown to them.)[2]

The Holy Spirit was to facilitate the learning of idioms and new expressions of speech. Jesus' disciples and followers were soon to converse in Arabic, Persian, Greek, Latin, Chinese, and other languages, some of which they had never heard before. Jesus also assured his disciples that the Holy Spirit would continuously guide and teach them everything they would need to know. All the needs of these early followers and missionaries, who had dedicated their lives to God and were willing to die for Jesus' gospel of the Kingdom, were to be supplied. It is interesting to know that most of the languages spoken today—such as English, German, French, Italian, Spanish, Russian, and many others—were unknown at that early time,

The expression "a new tongue" has other meanings, as well, in the Near East. For example, when a new teaching is proclaimed, it is often referred to as a "new tongue." Jesus' gospel of God's kingdom, a gentle and peaceful message full of hope, was a "new tongue." In a different allusion, when a king reprimands his subjects, Semites say, "He is speaking in a strange tongue" or "He speaks in an unknown tongue," meaning "He speaks in a harsh tone." Near Easterners still use such expressions of speech in their many different dialects and languages.

HANDLING SERPENTS

They shall take up serpents; and if they drink any deadly thing, it shall not hurt them; they shall lay hands on the sick, and they shall recover. Mk. 16:18.

---

[2]See Acts 2:4, 10:46, 19:5.

Part 1—SNAKES, ONE'S ENEMIES. It is not unusual to see snakes and scorpions crawling on the floor of Near Eastern houses. The ceilings made of straw and branches of trees often harbor the nests of birds and snakes. Snakes enter a house in search of food and water. Little children pick them up and play with them. The snakes very seldom harm the children. Some families are so accustomed to these unwanted intruders in their homes that they do not bother the snakes, nor do the snakes hurt them. Others who try to exterminate them are frequently bitten.

"They shall take up serpents" should not be taken literally. It does not mean that people should attempt to pick up serpents to see whether the scriptures are right or wrong or to test their faith. This would be tempting God. The reference here is to those who pick up a snake by mistake or tread on one unknowingly. In such cases, if the person has faith in God, he or she will be protected. Paul was bitten by a viper, but the poison did not affect him. The Aramaic text reads, ". . .and bit his hand. . . . but [Paul] felt no harm."[3] Snakes are wise. (See Matthew 10:16.) They know that a person who picks them up in error does not intend to harm them; therefore, the serpents will usually not attack them. When an individual deliberately picks up a snake, he maintains fear and this fear makes the snake suspicious and afraid.

"Handling serpents" is an Aramaic idiom that is also very common in other Eastern languages. It means "overcoming one's enemies." Semites call an enemy a "serpent" or "snake" because he acts slyly. Near Eastern Semites still use this idiom today. They say: "When you go to a certain city, be careful. There are many snakes (enemies) there."

The apostles had many enemies who were opposed to the teaching of their lord. But Jesus assured them that the Holy Spirit would help them overcome all opposition and dangers that were ahead of them. The third chapter of the book of Exodus tells us that God commanded Moses to pick up a serpent by its tail. This meant

---

[3]See Acts 28:3-6.

that Moses would overturn and defeat Pharaoh.

Today, certain American religious groups who take Jesus' words literally do handle snakes and are sometimes bitten by them. Some Western scholars have deleted a number of verses from this chapter, stating that Jesus could not have encouraged his followers to handle snakes and drink poison.

Part 2—DRINKING POISON. "If they drink any deadly thing, it shall not hurt them" means "dealing with and conquering attacks against one's character." These harmful attacks were not to reflect on the character of the disciples, nor would they hinder the progress of the gospel.

When wanting to dispose of their enemies easily, Near Easterners generally invite them to their homes and then poison their food or drink. Sometimes, guests who have been poisoned are not affected. Others recover because they are unaware of the poison in the food or drink; therefore, they are not afraid of their sickness and feel they will become well. When a man drinks poison and knows it is poison, he will begin fearing the effects. This fear destroys the vitality and resistance of his body and results in death.

There is nothing in the gospels to show that Jesus ever attempted to pick up serpents or drink any deadly poison to prove what he said was true. He never attempted to change stones into bread when he was hungry and fasting in the desert, nor did he ever do anything purposely to show his divine power. He always had faith in God, his Father, who is aware of the dangers and needs of those who trust him.

AMEN

And they went forth, and preached every where, the Lord working with them, and confirming the word with signs following. Amen. Mk. 16:20

Amen is an Aramaic word. It means "to make firm" and refers to anything that is true, lasting, never-ceasing, eternal, perpetual, continual and faithful. As a proper name and noun *ameena* refers to a "faithful one, truthful one, and sincere person." Interestingly, the

Aramaic words for "believe" and "faith" derive from the root *amen*. So, believing and having faith denote standing firm.

Amen means so much more than just "so it is" or "so be it." Its adverbial form is *amenait*, "always." When a priest or a prince makes a statement, the people generally respond by saying "*amen*." This indicates their ready acceptance and belief. When oral laws are enacted and proclaimed, the people raise their hands and say "*amen*" as a mark of approval and loyalty.

The phrase *Amen, amen*—"Truly, truly" or "verily, verily"— often appears in the gospels. The writers use this phrase to emphasize the importance of what is about to be said. Words are repeated in Aramaic and Hebrew for emphasis. The word "*Amen*" placed at the end of documents, books, and letters, is the equivalent of a seal. When said at the end of a prayer, it indicates that the one praying will stand by his or her part in the prayer. It means the person will be responsible and back the prayer. (See Matthew 6:13.)

ܥܠܝܬܐ ܘܪܚܝܐ

ܕܡܪܝܐ

ܐܬܐ ܕܡܠܐܟܐ

ܕܩܘܝܘܬܐ

ܕܝܠܘܕܐ

INTRODUCTION
The Gospel According To Luke

AUTHORSHIP

Near Eastern tradition teaches that Luke was an early Semitic convert to the Galilean movement that was spreading throughout Palestine, Syria and other Eastern countries. There are no reliable historical records that tell us anything about his early life, background and conversion.[1] Eusebius informs us that Luke was from Ephesus.

Paul, in his letter to the Colossians, refers to him as a healer or physician: "Luke, our beloved healer and Dema greet you."[2] Some writers assert that he traveled with Paul, attending him as a doctor. This assertion can hardly be true. Paul was not a wealthy man; he had to work his trade while he was traveling on his missionary journeys. He also endured many hardships and privations. Paul could not bear an additional expense of taking a traveling physician with him, although, at times, he complained of sickness. The apostles and early missionaries never dreamed of such comforts. They knew they would have to face trying circumstances and imprisonments because of the teaching of their lord.

According to the Aramaic Peshitta text, Luke carries the title *asyah*, meaning "healer." He was not a surgeon or a physician as we understand a doctor to be in the Occidental world. He did not dispense medicine. It is most probable that he was a spiritual healer like some of the religious men in the Near East today. Or, he may have been a certain kind of spiritual healer who also manipulated the

---

[1]There exists a tradition that comes to us from the pen of Ishodad of Merv, an Aramaic speaking Bishop of Hadatha, 850 CE. He says that Luke was from Antioch and that he had been a disciple of Galenus. After his conversion to Jesus' gospel, he became a preacher of the joyful message of God's kingdom and after a long time of great struggles, he died in peace in the great city of the Thebais.

[2]Col. 4:14, Aramaic Peshitta text, Errico.

body, adjusting dislocated bones. Such professions are not acquired by medical training but are handed down from father to son. Nor do spiritual healers depend on their practice for their living. Some healers are engaged in farming, raising sheep or in other businesses. Luke was most likely this kind of Near Eastern healer. He was the only companion of Paul in Rome.[3] Paul, in his epistle to Philemon, calls him "my fellow worker."[4]

Luke's authorship of the third gospel is basically supported by external evidence. Irenaeus, Clement of Alexandria, Tertullian and the Muratorian canon all say that Luke was the author of the third gospel and also the Acts of the Apostles. However, some modern New Testament scholars believe that these assertions are not based on facts but are conjectural and debatable. Unfortunately, this does not help to solve the problem of authorship of these two valuable documents. Since this commentary is not a critical source/analysis of the gospel of Luke, the accumulation of scholarly theories for or against Luke's authorship cannot be discussed in this volume.

Regardless of the varying theories, Dr. Lamsa and I believe there is no reason to doubt that Luke was the author of both his gospel and the book of Acts. Luke, as an evangelist, had been on many missionary journeys. He must have been in possession of documentary evidence and other sources written or dictated by some of the apostles. Some of these documents could have been none other than the gospels of Matthew and Mark.[5]

It is also inconceivable that Paul would have carried any other Christian writings with him. This helps explain his references to the teaching of Jesus. Luke was with Paul when the latter wrote to Timothy from Rome asking him to bring Mark with him and the books or scrolls that he had left with Carpus at Troas.[6] Near Eastern

---

[3] 2 Tim. 4:11
[4] Philem.1:24.
[5] See *LUKE'S USE OF MATTHEW: Beyond the Q Impasse*, Allan J. NcNicol, David L. Dungan and David D. Peabody, editors.
[6] 2 Tim. 4:13.

108

Christian Semites have never questioned Luke's authorship.

STYLE AND DATE

The style of the gospel is similar to the book of Acts. It was either copied from scrolls for a prominent man named Theophilus or composed from material with which Luke was familiar. The author used other oral and written sources that are not found in the other gospels. He omitted what he found to be objectionable to the people for whom his gospel was intended.

This practice is still characteristic of missionaries. For example, an American missionary could not easily introduce a gospel to the Armenians if it contained some material favorable to the Turks. However, another missionary of the same denomination who happened to be working among the Turks would probably stress this more than any other portion of the scriptures.

Interestingly, Luke traces the genealogy of Jesus to King David through Nathan and not Solomon. He avoided the royal line through Solomon because his gospel was written for the Jews in Galilee, Syria, and Asia Minor. These Jews had lost their national aspirations, and some of them despised the kings of Judah. They blamed these kings for the downfall of the state of Israel.

Most New Testament scholars date Luke's gospel anywhere between 75 to 95 CE. Nevertheless, there are some scholars who place the dating of this gospel before the siege of Jerusalem in 70 CE. Again, all dates are conjectural.

CHAPTER 1

EYEWITNESSES

Forasmuch as many have taken in hand to set forth in order a declaration of those things which are most surely believed among us, Even as they delivered them unto us, which from the beginning were eyewitnesses, and ministers of the word; Lk. 1:1-2.

The reference here is to the scrolls containing Jesus' sayings and parables as well as some narratives that were written concerning his birth, baptism, crucifixion and other episodic life experiences. Luke also refers to many oral traditions that were handed down by those who had been with Jesus and were eyewitnesses and ministers. According to Luke, these eyewitnesses, who were not only familiar with the current testimony concerning Jesus but who also had actually heard him preach and seen him die on the cross, were the authors of his material. It was from them that Luke derived most of the material not found in the gospels of Matthew and Mark.

The early sacred writings were the basis for other documents produced about the life and teaching of Jesus. As additional material became known, it was embodied in these earlier writings, but in each case the scribes examined it very carefully before adopting it. In those rudimentary days of the Jesus' movement under the apostles, disciples and followers, what we call "New Testament" scripture was just beginning. These writings had not yet been canonized. Scribes and owners of manuscripts were at liberty to omit or add to their own scrolls or books. At that time there was no established church to pass judgment on these documents and other newly discovered materials about Jesus and his teaching.

LUKE AND THEOPHILUS

It seemed good to me also, having had perfect understanding of all things from the very first, to write unto thee in order, most excellent Theophilus, That thou mightest know the certainty of those things, wherein thou hast been instructed. Lk. 1:3-4.

The prologue, verses 1-4, in the Aramaic text reads: "Since many have desired to have in writing the story of those works with which we are familiar, According to what was handed down to us by those who from the beginning were eyewitnesses and ministers of that very word, And since these were seen by me also because I was near and considered them all very carefully; I will, therefore, write to you everything in its order, most honorable Theophilus, So that you may know the truth of the words by which you were made a convert."[1]

Part 1—LUKE'S QUALIFICATIONS. We said in the introduction that Luke was Semitic. Others claim that he was a Semite of the Jewish race.[2] He had assumed a Greek name. Many Semites adopted Greek and Roman names in the interest of business or to gain favor in the eyes of their conquerors. In the past century, many foreigners entering the United States did this same thing. Many Jewish people also changed their names when migrating to Europe, giving themselves German, Italian and other European names.

The writer of *The Gospel According to Luke*, whoever he may have been, was acquainted with the disciples of Jesus and their followers. He had heard the traditions about Jesus and had read manuscripts written by eyewitnesses who had seen and heard Jesus. This writer, with his unique opportunity and knowledge, examined the evidence and weighed the facts in composing his new and more convincing document. He omitted some material and changed other material that did not harmonize with certain narratives. For example,

---

[1] Lk. 1:1-4, Aramaic Peshitta text, Lamsa translation.

[2] Many modern scholars debate the notion that Luke was a Jew. Raymond Brown, NT scholar, claims that "the way that Col. 4:11 is phrased, i.e., all the men listed before that verse are of the circumcision, suggests that Luke who is listed after that verse is not a Jew." But as we also mentioned in the introduction, Luke, no doubt, was a Semite whether or not he was Jewish or Syrian.

like Matthew, he traced the genealogy of Jesus to David, but unlike Matthew, who traced through the kingly line, he traced through Nathan, another son of David. He also included in his gospel the events that brought about the birth of John the Baptist. We do not find these events described in any other earlier documents.

These changes were probably made to override certain prejudices that were prevalent. Galilean and Samaritan followers of Jesus would have had no interest in the royal Davidic descent of Jesus because the enmity between the house of David in Judah and the ten northern tribes, the house of Israel, still survived. The author attempted a compromise so that he could recommend Jesus' gospel of the kingdom to the Semitic peoples of both the north and the south.

Part 2—THEOPHILUS' FAITH AFFIRMED. Theophilus[3] had become a convert to the gospel of Jesus Christ. Evidently, he had embraced the gospel of the kingdom by hearing the stories of Jesus' life and teaching that were now widely circulated and popular among the people. However, at this time, there were many written scrolls and confusing stories that perplexed men like Theophilus. These stories varied widely. Some stated that Jesus was descended from David but no one had heard about a surviving descendant of David's royal family.

The high priests and scribes were totally ignorant of the existence of any heirs to the house of David. Jehoiachin, the last king of the Davidic dynasty, was carried captive by the Chaldeans about 500 years previously.[4] Even the Maccabees did not dare to connect themselves with the famous house of David. Nonetheless, the Jews literally expected the Messiah to come from the line or the house of David.

Although Luke's gospel traced Jesus to Nathan, a son of David, the writer was concerned about the teaching of Jesus and his mission.

---

[3]Theophilus is a proper name commonly used from the third century BCE on, found both in Greek papyri from Egypt and inscriptions. Jews and other Semitic races used the name "Theophilus." There is no reason to doubt that he was a historical person, most likely another Semite.

[4]2 Kings 25:27.

He tried to impress Theophilus with the truth of Jesus' words, whereby he had been converted. He also wanted to emphasize the works that the Galilean sage and prophet had done.

HEROD, ZECHARIAH AND ELISABETH

There was in the days of Herod, the king of Judaea, a certain priest named Zacharias, of the course of Abia: and his wife was of the daughters of Aaron, and her name was Elisabeth. And they were both righteous before God, walking in all the commandments and ordinances of the Lord blameless, And they had no child, because that Elisabeth was barren, and they both were now well stricken in years. Lk. 1:5-7.

Part 1—HEROD THE GREAT. Luke's dating of the births of John and Jesus, as far as Palestinian history is concerned, remains elusive at this point. "In the days of Herod, the King of Judea" at least informs us that Jesus and John were born before the death of Herod the Great.[5] Luke refers to Herod the Great, the son of Antipater, founder of the Herodian dynasty. He was an Idumean by race but a Jew by faith. His father served in the Roman army during the Roman conquest of Palestine and Egypt. He also won favors in the eyes of the Roman generals in Syria. When Herod was driven out of Palestine by the confederation of the Hasmoneans and the Parthians, Marc Antony gave him support and the Roman Senate accorded him the title "King of Judea" in 40 BCE.

After the capture of Jerusalem and the overthrow of the Hasmonean dynasty, Herod became sole ruler of Palestine. He married Mariamne, an Hasmonean princess, whom he killed later with her two sons, Aristobulus and Antigonus. This murderous and heinous act on his part put an end to the Hasmonean house; it established Herod and his sons as the sole heirs of this newly formed kingdom.

Herod, like his father, knew how to please Roman emperors and their high officials in Syria. He imposed high taxes so that he could

---

[5]Most scholars use 4 BCE for the birth of Jesus. Also see Mt. 2:1.

113

keep his post. He also built a magnificent temple to please his Jewish subjects. But the Jewish people despised and resented him because he was not a Jew by birth. Although Herod attempted to show that he was a benefactor of their religion, he really had no use for the Jews themselves. Jews and Idumeans had always hated each other.

Part 2—OF THE COURSE OF ABIA. The Aramaic word here is *tishmishta*—literally, "service, order"—and it refers to the daily service that the priests had to perform in the temple. The priesthood was divided into twenty-four orders called *mishmarot* in Hebrew, meaning "watches." Each watch or division was to serve in the temple twice each year for one week at a time, from Sabbath to Sabbath. Their times of service were appointed by lot. According to Scripture, King David had instituted this order of service and Abijah was of the eighth watch.[6] After the Chaldean captivity only four watches returned to Judea. Josephus, however, speaks of twenty-four divisions as well as four.

Part 3—ZECHARIAH AND ELISABETH. Zechariah literally means "God has remembered," implying that God has remembered him and Elisabeth by granting them a child in their old age. Elisabeth—*Eleeshwa* in Aramaic, *Elisheva* in Hebrew—was named after Aaron's wife. Aaron was appointed High Priest by his brother Moses while traveling in the wilderness. Both Elisabeth and Zechariah were pious people. Luke tells us that they were "righteous before God" so that it would be understood that their childlessness was not because of any evil or undeservedness in the sight of God. According to Jewish teaching a priest was not obligated to marry a woman of priestly descent, but commonly this was what happened. Elisabeth was "a daughter of Aaron." Since both Zechariah and Elisabeth were of priestly descent, their son John, who was yet to be born, was naturally expected to become a priest. But this was not to be the case. John became a prophet and forerunner of the Messiah.

Part 4—A BARREN WOMAN. "And they had no child." John's birth is patterned after biblical stories of barren women. (A few

---

[6] 1 Chron 24:10.

examples: Sarah, Genesis 16:1; Rebekah, Genesis 25:21; Rachael, Genesis 30:1; Samson's mother, Judges 13:2; Hannah, 1 Samuel 1:2.) The Aramaic text hints at something more. It reads: "They had no son because Elisabeth had become barren." Strange as it may seem, where ancient Semitic customs prevail, a Near Eastern woman, though she may have given birth to five or six girls, is often called "childless" if she has not given birth to a son. Girls do not inherit property from their parents, so a male heir is important.

In Elisabeth's situation, she probably had daughters but no son. At the time of the angel's visit to Zechariah, she was too old to bear any more children and therefore was barren. This was the reason it was difficult for Zechariah to believe the words that the angel spoke to him. (See Luke 1:11-20.)

THE ANGELIC APPEARANCE IN THE TEMPLE

According to the custom of the priest's office, his lot was to burn incense when he went into the temple of the Lord. And the whole multitude of the people were praying without at the time of incense. And there appeared unto him an angel of the Lord standing on the right side of the altar of incense. And when Zacharias saw him, he was troubled and fear fell upon him. But the angel said unto him, Fear not, Zacharias; for thy prayer is heard; and thy wife Elisabeth shall bear thee a son, and thou shalt call his name John. And thou shalt have joy and gladness; and many shall rejoice at his birth. For he shall be great in the sight of the Lord, and shall drink neither wine nor strong drink; and he shall be filled with the Holy Ghost, even from his mother's womb. Lk. 1:9-15.

Part 1—DUTY OF THE PRIEST. "His lot was to burn incense." The Jewish *Mishnah* describes in detail the system of choosing by lot: "He, the officer, said to them, 'You that are new to the incense preparation, come and cast lots,' and they cast lots and the lot fell upon whom it fell."[7] Zechariah was in the front part of the Temple

---

[7]M. Tamid 5:2 - 6:3.

115

where the altar of incense was present with the menorah and the bread of the presence. It was officially called "the holy place."[8] The hour of incense was offered morning and at twilight. Zechariah had to enter the holy place to clean the altar of incense and burn fresh incense. It was here that the messenger of the Lord came in a vision to Zechariah and announced the coming birth of his son. He was to call his name John. This kind of occurrence is common among devout Semites. To this very day, an earnest petitioner praying reverently and sincerely will wait until a revelation comes saying a child shall be born. Usually, a patron saint, a deceased relative, or a messenger from God will appear in a dream or a vision granting the petitioner's request and, at times, naming the child. To Zechariah, the whole affair was a total surprise.

Part 2 —STRONG DRINK. "And shall not drink neither wine nor strong drink." Nazarites were holy men, consecrated to God, and a type of prophet. The men abstained from strong drink because they could not receive God's messages if distracted or confused by alcohol.

Bishops and other high ecclesiastical authorities today are also selected from the ranks of the Nazarites. This ancient custom still prevails among the Assyrian clans, and these Nazarites are active among them. Assyrian Nazarites, known as *nater kurseh*, abstain from eating meat, shaving their heads or faces and from marriage. They are dedicated to God's work and are called *nazireh*—those who have taken vows.[9]

The ancient Hebrew people believed that after death life remained in the hair and that hair continued to grow. Hair was also the symbol of strength as in the case of Samson.[10] Samuel and Samson were both Nazarites and abstained from strong drink, cutting their hair and trimming their beards.

---

[8]1 Macc.1:21-22.

[9]See Errico & Lamsa *Aramaic Light on the Gospel of Matthew,* "Nazareth," pp. 29-30.

[10]Judges 16:19.

THE SPIRIT OF ELIJAH

And he shall go before him in the spirit and power of Elias, to turn the hearts of the fathers to the children, and the disobedient to the wisdom of the just; to make ready a people prepared for the Lord. Lk. 1:17.

The Aramaic text reads: "And many Israelites he will cause to turn to the Lord their God, and he will go before him with the spirit and the power of Elijah, to turn the hearts of parents to their children, and those who are disobedient to the wisdom of the righteous; and he will prepare a true people for the Lord."[11]

John's ministry is compared to the prophet Elijah. John is to be empowered with the prophetic spirit to help Israel turn to God in a more specific way. He will go before the God of Israel in the power and spirit of Elijah. According to the narrative in the Hebrew Bible, Elijah had promised his student Elisha a double portion of his "spirit" if Elisha saw him depart this world.[12] Elijah's great prophetic and miracle working power was well known. He was a reformer and a rebel against King Ahab and Jezebel.

John would have the same boldness as Elijah and point his finger of accusation against Herod and Herodia. He was to help bring the people of Israel back to the ways of the Lord their God before the great and awesome day of Yahweh.[13]

THE ANGELIC VISITATION TO MARY

And in the sixth month the angel Gabriel was sent from God unto a city of Galilee named Nazareth, To a virgin espoused to a man whose name was Joseph, of the house of David; and the virgin's name was Mary. And the angel came in unto her and said , Hail, thou that art highly favoured, the Lord is with thee; blessed art thou among women. Lk. 1:26-28.

---

[11]Lk. 1:16-17, Aramaic Peshitta text, Lamsa translation.
[12]2 Kings 2:9-10.
[13]Mal. 3:2 and Mal 4:5-6. See also *Aramaic Light on the Gospel of Matthew*, "Part B, The Sign of a Prophet," p. 32 and "A Messenger," p. 166.

Dr. Abraham Rihbany, who was born and raised in the Near East, makes the following remarks concerning the angelic visitations:

> In the gospel story of Jesus' life there is not a single incident that is not in perfect harmony with the prevailing modes of thought and the current speech of the land of its origin. I do not know how many times I heard it stated in my native land and at our own fireside that heavenly messengers in the forms of patron saints or angels came to pious, childless wives, in dreams and visions, and cheered them with the promise of maternity. It was nothing uncommon for such women to spend a whole night in a shrine "wrestling in prayer," either with the blessed Virgin or some other saint, for such a divine assurance; and I remember a few of my own kindred to have done so.
>
> Perhaps the most romantic religious practice in this connection is the *zeara* [Arabic]. Interpreted literally, the word *zeara* means simply "a visit." In its social use it is the equivalent of a call of long or short duration. But religiously the *zeara* means a pilgrimage to a shrine. . . . But much more often a *zeara* is undertaken by women for the purpose of securing the blessing of fecundity, or consecrating an approaching issue of wedlock.
>
> The *zuwar* (visitors) remain at the holy shrine for one or two nights, or until the "presence" is revealed; that is, until the saint manifests himself. The prayerfully longed-for manifestation comes almost invariably in a dream, either to the mother or some other worthy in the party.[14]

In the narrative, the angel Gabriel comes to Mary (*Mariam*) in a dream. He greets her in typical Aramaic style. *Shlam lekh* simply means "hello" but it literally translates as "Peace to you." *Malyath taybootha* means "full of grace," but among Semites, for a woman to be full of grace signifies that God has granted her divine favor because she is going to have a child. Naturally, this kind of greeting was strange and perplexing to Mary (see verse 29). For a Near

---

[14]Abraham M. Rihbany, *The Syrian Christ,* "Birth of a Man Child," pp. 12-13,15-16.

Eastern woman to bear a child is to be highly favored of the Lord God. "Children are a heritage from the Lord" (Psalms 127:3). It is God who turns barrenness into fruitfulness and works the miracle of birth. For Semites "every birth is miraculous, and childlessness an evidence of divine disfavor." (Rhibany, *The Syrian Christ*, pg. 20).This is the reason Gabriel tells Mary that she is "full of grace [divine favor]."

Gabriel is an Aramaic name and it means "man of God." Some also translate the name as "God has shown himself strong." It was also the angel Gabriel who had come to Daniel at the time of the evening sacrifice.[15] The only two names of angels that appear in the Hebrew Bible are Michael and Gabriel.[16]

SON OF THE HIGHEST

He shall be great, and shall be called the Son of the Highest; and the Lord God shall give unto him the throne of his father David. And he shall reign over the house of Jacob for ever; and of his kingdom there shall be no end. Lk.1:32-33.

Part 1—HE WILL BE CALLED. Many Bible students have often wondered why Gabriel did not say "he is the Son of the Highest" instead of "he shall be called the Son of the Highest." The verbal phrase is in the future tense because the gospel writer understood Near Eastern, Semitic, religious temperament, especially among the Jews. To say of a male child who is to be born "he is the son of the highest" would imply that Israel's God was married, just like other gods. Such a statement would be taken as a blasphemy and as a pagan teaching. But to say "he shall be called the Son of the Highest" would be well understood without any problem among all

---

[15]See also Gen. 18:11, 24:1;

[16]According to Jewish history Angelology came about after the exile from Chaldea. Resh Laqish, a Jewish scholar, said, ". . . Also the names of angels came with us from Babylonia."

Semitic people. For example, God had called Solomon "my son." (See 1 Chronicles 28:6.) Jesus called God his Father, and he is known as God's son in a spiritual and not in a physical sense.

Matthew's gospel reads: ". . . he that is to be born of her is of the Holy Spirit."[17] In other words, Jesus was conceived by the power of the Holy Spirit. Such terms of speech are common in Semitic languages and are understood and accepted.[18]

Near Easterners believe that what is impossible to man is possible to the power of God's Spirit. Nevertheless, the Jews and Moslems resent any remark that implies that God could be married or possibly conceived and born. To them God is spirit, life, and truth; and these attributes are not subject to conception and birth. Jesus said to the Samaritan woman: "For God is Spirit and those who worship him must worship him in spirit and in truth."[19]

The phrase "son of God" has been a stumbling block to millions of Jews and Moslems as well as some Christians. The reason for this is that their concept of God is exactly the way Jesus had expressed it, that God is spirit. Since God is spirit, God never begets nor is begotten but is from everlasting to everlasting.[20]

In the Roman imperial system, the emperors were worshiped as gods of the realm. Their sons were known as sons of god. Tiberias, Nero, and other emperors were all looked upon as deities. One of the reasons the Romans persecuted the Christians is because these Christians claimed that Jesus of Nazareth was also the son of God, hence, a deity.

Persian, Greek, Egyptian, and other pagan emperors were also worshiped as gods. Therefore, it was easy for Western people to believe and say that "God has a son." On the other hand, this notion was extremely difficult for Semitic people, who were taught that God is the eternal Spirit.

---

[17]Mt. 1:20, Lamsa translation.
[18]See Isa. 9:6-7; Jer. 33:15.
[19]Jn. 4:24.
[20]One can now understand why Moslems call Christians blasphemers.

Part 2—THE KINGDOM WITHOUT LIMIT. ". . . and of his kingdom there shall be no end." The Aramaic text reads: "There will be no limit to his kingdom."[21] The Semitic word *sop* means "end, limit, border, edge, boundary, the uttermost part." In ancient times, the Euphrates River and the Mediterranean Sea were considered the ends of the world. Palestinian kingdoms were limited in territory, embracing less than a hundred square miles, and the people did not realize the magnitude of the great empires of the world. Near Eastern kings were known by the size of their kingdoms—the larger the kingdom, the more famous the king. Kings and rulers always aspired for more territory. They were never satisfied with the size of their kingdoms. Their great ambition was to extend their borders as far as possible.

Before Israel occupied Palestine, each city had its own king and laws. The limits or borders of a city were its own walls. The Davidic kingdom was really very small compared with the empires of Assyria, Chaldea, Persia and Greece. Their borders were beyond the geographical concepts of the Hebrew people. These domains extended from the Mediterranean Sea to the Indian Ocean. Their kingdoms embraced the then known world.

The angelic message here is that the messianic kingdom would be without limit. It would penetrate into areas and lands unknown at that time and include all races and all countries and cover a territory larger than any emperor had ever dreamed about ruling. The prince of peace was to rule forever and his message of the gospel of the kingdom was to endure throughout all the ages, regardless of racial or geographical barriers and boundaries.

BLESSEDNESS

For he hath regarded the low estate of his handmaiden; for, behold, from henceforth all generations shall call me blessed. Lk. 1:48.

---

[21]Lk.1:33b, Aramaic Peshitta text, Lamsa translation.

Until the middle of the 20th century, and with the exception of Turkey and Egypt, there was very little change in the position of women in Near Eastern countries since biblical days. Women were mostly thought of as inferior and unimportant except for mothers of heroes and heirs apparent to thrones. These women were highly respected and admired.

Many Near Easterners are polygamists. Kings marry many wives. When a prince ascended a throne, his mother's position was immediately elevated and her authority increased. There are times when mothers of great men are invited to sit in counsel with the leaders of the state, but this is exceptional and contrary to Near Eastern custom. For example, Bathsheba, the mother of Solomon, king of Israel, served her son in an advisory capacity. When Adonijah wanted to marry Abishag the Shunammite, he sought to have Bathsheba intercede for him.[22]

The highest ambition of a Near Eastern mother is to see her son occupying an exalted station in life. When a son's name is mentioned, it is usually coupled with his mother's name. In the books of Kings and Chronicles, the mothers of kings are always mentioned.

The Aramaic word *tuwa* has several definitions. It means "good, blessed, something choice as in a choice fruit." It also refers to "someone deserving of admiration, congratulations, felicitation and one who is enviable." "All generations shall call me blessed" shows that Mary realized she would be admired and envied because she was the mother of the Prince of Peace. He was to reign forever and ever, and she would share this everlasting honor with her son. This is typical of Near Eastern Semitic culture and customs. An exalted son means an exalted mother also.[23]

---

[22]1 Ki. 2:17.

[23]"For he hath regarded his handmaiden," 1 Sam 1:11; Gen. 16:11, 29:32.

THE BIRTH OF JOHN THE BAPTIST

Now Elisabeth's full time came that she should be delivered; and she brought forth a son. And her neighbours and her cousins heard how the Lord had shewed great mercy upon her; and they rejoiced with her. And it came to pass, that on the eighth day they came to circumcise the child; and they called him Zacharias, after the name of his father. And his mother answered and said, Not so; but he shall be called John. Lk. 1:57-60.

Part 1—THE MERCY OF GOD. The Aramaic text reads: "And when her neighbors and relatives heard that God had increased [literally: made many] his mercies to her. . ."[24] which means God had multiplied his favor. How did God multiply his mercies? God did so in two ways: (1) By promising Zacharias and Elisabeth a child. Once she gave birth to the child, it removed the reproach of being a barren wife. (2) The child was a male. Semites regard a male child as God's special blessing, for he was to perpetuate the family line.

Part 2—THE NAMING OF THE CHILD AT CIRCUMCISION. The eighth day is usually the day for circumcising a male child. This carried out the mark of the covenant that God had made with Abraham.[25] There is no recent evidence from the first century that unequivocally proves that a male child was named at the time of his circumcision. Nevertheless, Rabbi Samuel T. Lachs says:

This was, however, the practice a few centuries later, and more than likely reflects a continuum which may well include the first century. There is an old *baraita* which records the benediction of the father at the circumcision, "Blessed art Thou . . . who has sanctified us by Thy commandments, and has commanded us to make him enter into the covenant of Abraham our father." The congregation then responds, "As he has been made to enter the covenant so may he also be made to enter into the study of the Torah, the *huppah* [bridal canopy], and the performance of good deeds." The use of the pronoun "him" in the benediction of the

---

[24]Lk. 1:58, Aramaic Peshitta text, Errico.
[25]Gen. 21:4; Lev. 12:2-3.

father and the response of the congregation seems to indicate that originally the child was named immediately after the circumcision.[26]

Easterners naming the child after the father was common at this time in history, but even more common was the custom of naming the child after the grandfather. There is evidence for this custom. Elisabeth, however, interrupts the procedure and tells everyone that the child is to be named John. Yohanan is a priestly name and it means "Yahweh has granted favor."[27]

THE HORN OF SALVATION

And hath raised up an horn of salvation for us in the house of his servant David. Lk. 1:69.

Before silver and brass musical instruments were known, horns of rams and oxen were used for worship and the procession of armed forces. A small hole was made in the narrow end of the ram's horn into which the musician would blow. When the Israelites had encircled Jericho, the priests kept blowing into the horns of rams until the walls of Jericho collapsed.[28]

When conquering armies would enter a city, musicians would raise their horns toward the sky and blow lustily and triumphantly into their instruments. But, when an army was returning home defeated, musicians would point their instruments toward the ground. Their music would be sad and melancholy. They would play their mournful melody in a minor key and hang their heads to express the distress and sorrow of their brave soldiers. This practice was also common at funerals.

---

[26]Samuel Tobias Lachs, *A RABBINIC COMMENTARY ON THE NEW TESTAMENT*, "The Birth of John the Baptist," p. 26.
[27]Neh. 12:12-13, 42; 1 Macc. 2:1-2.
[28]Josh. 6:4.

The expression "And hath raised up an horn of salvation for us" means he has defeated our enemies and brought our forces back with horns raised and shouting songs of victory. The gospel of the Kingdom of God that Jesus preached and taught was a gospel of triumph. This powerful message was first declared and sounded throughout Israel. But it was also to be proclaimed in every land and tongue. It brings victory and release to anyone who accepts the joyful message of the kingdom.

A BOY'S OCCUPATION

And the child grew, and waxed strong in spirit, and was in the deserts till the day of his shewing unto Israel. Lk. 1:80.

In these biblical lands where public schools and factories were unknown, boys of six or seven years of age were assigned to take care of sheep and cattle. These occupations were important and most boys were taught these vocations early in life as a means of livelihood.

Usually sheep are pastured at a distance from the village and the shepherds remain with them all year round. In the spring and summer months, women and children live in tents in the desert where they pasture their sheep. The word "desert" does not always mean an arid place but an open area not inhabited. The Aramaic word *horba* means "a place without inhabitants." In many regions of the Arabian desert, in the area of the Euphrates river and on the borders of Palestine, thousands of sheep and camels are found. The natives live in tents and move from place to place seeking grass for their flocks.

When some boys grow to manhood they return to their homes to take up other tasks and vocations. John remained in the desert caring for sheep until he reached manhood. He then returned to his village, probably to carry on the work of his father, who was a priest, or perhaps to engage in some other occupation. But instead, God's spirit led him to become the herald of the Messiah.

CHAPTER 2

THE CENSUS

And it came to pass in those days, that there went out a decree from Caesar Augustus, that all the world should be taxed. (And this taxing was first made when Cyrenius was governor of Syria.) And all went to be taxed, everyone into his own city. Lk. 2:1-3.

"And it happened in those days that there went out a decree from Caesar Augustus to take a census of all the people in his empire. This first census took place during the governorship of Quirinius in Syria. And every man went to be registered in his own city."[1]

Caesar Augustus was born Gaius Octavius in 63 BCE. In 29 BCE his earlier title, Imperator, was ratified, and in 27 BCE the Senate gave him the title of Augustus. He died in 14 CE. There exists no record or proof that there was a universal census during this period. A census did take place in Judea in 6 CE but it wasn't during the days of Quirinius. Augustus had appointed him to be the counselor of Gaius Caesar, the adopted son of the emperor, who was given proconsular power and made vice-regent of the Eastern provinces, including Syria.

When Augustus annexed Judea, Samaria, and Idumea to the Roman province of Syria, Quirinius was sent as legatus by the emperor to take a census of property in Syria and to sell the estate of Archelaus in Palestine. Luke knew of the census that did take place in Rome and Judea and probably adjusted it for his purpose in the gospel story. There have been many explanations concerning this census and how Luke intended its usage. Some suggest that the Greek text implies that it was before the time of Quirinius in Syria.

---

[1]Lk. 2:1-3, Aramaic Peshitta text, Lamsa translation.

SWADDLING CLOTHES

And she brought forth her firstborn son, and wrapped him in swaddling clothes, and laid him in a manger; because there was no room for them in the inn. Lk. 2:7.

A very old and common practice among Semitic people was the swaddling of newborn babies. In many areas of the Near East this custom still prevails today. According to this ancient habit, mothers first bathe their newborn infants, then gently rub on the baby's skin a very small amount of salt that has been finely pulverized in a stone mortar for this great occasion. They also sprinkle their infants with a powder made of dried myrtle leaves. Eastern parents believe that putting salt on the baby's body will make his or her flesh firm. This little ceremony also represents a symbolic testimony that the parents will raise the child to be truthful and faithful.

The swaddle is a square yard of cloth to which the parent attaches a long narrow band at one corner. Usually the mother wraps the infant in the swaddle with its arms close to its body and its legs stretched out; then she winds the narrow band around the body from shoulders to ankles. The infant looks like a tiny Egyptian mummy. Semitic people swaddle their babies several times a day for six months to two years. They believe this will help the little bodies grow straight and firm. Again, this is another sign that the parents will teach the child to become honest, straightforward, and free from crookedness.

The Hebrew prophet Ezekiel refers to this custom in his prophecy. He speaks out against the citizens of Jerusalem who were unfaithful to the Lord their God and his commandments. Ezekiel rebukes in this manner:

> Thus says the Lord God to Jerusalem: Your root and your nativity is of the land of Canaan; your father was an Amorite and your mother a Hittite. And as for the one who bore you, in the day that you were born she did not *cut your navel, neither did she wash you with water nor did she salt your body nor wrap you in*

127

swaddling clothes at all.[2]

We can see that this custom is very important and symbolically significant. It would be only natural that Mary, the mother of Jesus, would salt and swaddle her newborn infant. Jesus was to be true to God and God's word. Thus, his swaddling represented loyalty and faithfulness to his heavenly Father as well as to his parents. This custom and its spiritual meaning applied to all children who were swaddled. In the case of Ezekiel's prophecy, not being swaddled represented unfaithfulness.

CHRIST OUR HOPE

Glory to God in the highest, and on earth peace, good will toward men. Lk. 2:14.

The Aramaic text reads: "Glory be to God in the highest, and on earth peace and good hope for humankind."[3] The term "will" in Aramaic is *seweeyana,* but the Aramaic word in this verse is *sawra.* It means "hope, expectation, joyful message, good news, gospel." (See also Luke 2:10.) The angels brought glad tidings and hope of a better future, a better expectation of things to come, a future wherein the messianic hope would be fulfilled. Israel would be freed from her oppressors and the kingdom of God would be established all over the earth.

For centuries Hebrew prophets had expected the coming of the Messiah, who would establish a new kingdom, a new way of life and a harmonious order so that people of all races would dwell in peace, and great and small nations would respect one another. This was the greatest Jewish expectation and hope of salvation. And because this prophecy of an everlasting peace and God's reign has not been fulfilled, the Jews believe that the Messiah has not yet come.

---

[2]Ezk. 16:3-4, Aramaic Peshitta text, Errico
[3]Lk. 2:14, Aramaic Peshitta text, Errico.

Today, the wolf and the lamb are far from dwelling together; the leopard and the kid are not lying down together. (These metaphorical terms of speech refer to powerful nations and smaller, less powerful nations.) Many centuries have elapsed since the angels sang this song of a good future for all humanity; and still today, after 2000 years, powerful nations and strong political regimes oppress weaker, defenseless races.

Where is the kingdom of God that Jesus demonstrated and taught? It is up to the followers of Jesus to put into action what he taught and revealed. Without implementation and action there can be no universal establishment and reign of justice and peace.

PURIFICATION

And when eight days were accomplished for the circumcising of the child, his name was called JESUS which was so named of the angel before he was conceived in the womb. And when the days of her purification according to the law of Moses were accomplished they brought him to Jerusalem, to present him to the Lord. Lk. 2:21-22.

As with the story of John's circumcision, the official naming of Joseph's and Mary's son took place, according to custom, during the rite of circumcision on the eighth day after the birth. Moslems circumcise their boys when they are thirteen years old. This is because Ishmael was thirteen years of age when Abraham circumcised him. But, Abraham's son by Sarah was only eight days old when his circumcision took place. God had appeared to Abraham, commanding him to circumcise every male born in his tribal community. This became a covenant ritual. The one who is circumcised becomes a true son of Abraham and his covenant with God.

This ritual is equivalent to Christian baptism. In the Near East, as soon as a child is baptized he becomes a full fledged member of the Church. Both baptism and confirmation take place the same day and at the same time. Assyrian priests are empowered to exercise the office of confirmation.

129

According to Near Eastern religious custom, a mother must follow the purification laws for forty days after the birth of a child. She cannot bake bread, cook or touch sacred things, nor can she pray or go to church. Both mother and child have to be sanctified on the fortieth day. Once the mother's purification days have ended, the boy must be brought to the temple to fulfill the laws of Moses. (Interestingly, Assyrian Christians and other Near Eastern Semitic races continue to practice this purification tradition.)

The laws of Moses dictate that a woman who gives birth to a male child is unclean for seven days.[4] Then on the eighth day the child is circumcised. The mother is confined for thirty-three days "until the days of her purification were completed" (Leviticus 12:4). Only then could she touch anything sacred or enter the Temple precincts. These time limits double if the woman gives birth to a female child—two weeks instead of one—and sixty-six days for the purification to end. After her confinement, she was to bring a sacrifice to the temple of a one-year-old lamb for a burnt offering and a young pigeon or turtle-dove for a sin offering. If she could not afford a lamb, she brought two turtle-doves or two young pigeons.

THE BOY JESUS IN THE TEMPLE

Now his parents went to Jerusalem every year at the feast of the Passover. And when he was twelve years old, they went up to Jerusalem after the custom of the feast. And when they had fulfilled the days, as they returned, the child Jesus tarried behind in Jerusalem; and Joseph and his mother knew not of it. Lk. 2:41-43.

Most of the ancient Assyrian Christian churches are built similar to the pattern of the Jewish temple. The church has many chapels, but the most sacred place is the holy of holies. It is in this sacred place that the sacrament is consecrated. During the services, only priests and deacons may enter the holy of holies. The priests use the various

---

[4]Lev. 12:2-8.

chapels for different purposes—for baptism, for evening and morning prayer, as a sacristy for vestments and other sacred articles. The main temple is for prayer on Sundays and feast days.

In this place men and women, boys and girls are separated during the services. The men stand at the front facing the holy of holies, and behind them are the young men and then the boys. Behind this group are the girls, while the women stand at the end of the temple.

Some boys are trained as singers for the religious services. They also assist the priests and elders who read Scripture standing close to the holy of holies. They encircle a holy book near the entrance to the most sacred place. Other boys often enter the circle although they were not invited. The special place offers a vantage point for one to see the holy of holies and to hear priests and deacons chanting from behind the walls of the most sacred area. At the end of the service, the deacons and choristers sit down to eat bread and other foods brought by the worshipers as an offering to God.

When Mary, Joseph and Jesus entered the temple in Jerusalem, Mary went to the women's court near the treasury, called in Aramaic *beth-gaza*. Women were not allowed to participate in the holy ceremonies nor to stand by the side of the men during this time. Joseph and Jesus then went directly to the front of the temple and took their respective places. Jesus was so impressed that after the service he remained and was invited to share in the sacrificial meal. This was followed by religious discussions and debates in which provincial teachers often clashed with the highly educated teachers and priests of Jerusalem. In the Near East, debates and quarrels in churches and holy places are not unusual. This is how Jesus was led to speak, and his stay was prolonged.

Joseph and Mary supposed that Jesus had gone with the other boys and girls, who usually formed their own party on such days. Feasts are the only occasions when boys and girls are permitted to mix and converse with each other. Customarily, children march ahead of the caravan and only go back to their parents when they feel hungry or are in some need. Probably, when Jesus left the learned

131

men in the temple, he began his search for his parents in the various courts of the temple. When he failed to find them, he returned to the place where the debates and religious discussions were still going on.

Meanwhile the caravan had started the journey home, and it was not long before Mary and Joseph made the discovery that Jesus was not with the other young people. Naturally, they hurried back to Jerusalem thinking that something must have happened to him. After inquiring at their lodging place and at the inns where their neighbors were staying, they went to the temple and found him sitting with the learned men of Jerusalem. They immediately told their son about the frantic search and how concerned they were about his safety. Jesus' reply to his parents is different in the Aramaic text.

The King James Version of scripture says: "And he said unto them, How is it that ye sought me? Wist ye not that I must be about my Father's business?"[5] The Aramaic text reads: "He said to them, Why were you looking for me? Did you not know that I would be in the house of my Father?"[6] That is to say, "I have no other place to go but to wait for you in the temple." Jesus felt that his parents would know that he would be with the learned men and teachers and that he would be late in leaving the temple, as he was probably accustomed to doing in his home town of Nazareth.

THE SILENT YEARS OF JESUS

And he went down with them, and came to Nazareth, and was subject unto them: but his mother kept all these sayings in her heart. And Jesus increased in wisdom and stature, and in favour with God and man. Lk. 2:51-52

According to ancient Semitic custom, an Eastern boy is subject to his parents until he reaches manhood. Even after a young man is married, his parents will often guide him with sound, good counsel.

---

[5]Lk. 2:49, K. J. V.
[6]Lk. 2:49, Aramaic Peshitta text, Lamsa translation.

There is a certain period in a Near Eastern boy's life where a full, social recognition does not appear for him. No matter how brilliant he may be, people will not consider his counsel. It is only after he is thirty years of age that he can sit in the counsel of the elders. They now will grant him great respect. In the Near East of old customs and habits, the age of a man is what gives him his importance among his people. What a young man says does not count.

This rule applied to Jesus also. Nothing is known about the early life of Jesus—that is, between the ages of twelve and thirty. Nevertheless, there were certain customs a young man was bound to follow. "Being subject to the parents" does not only show social grace and natural affection. It was also a religious duty of far-reaching significance. According to Scripture, it is God who commands faithfulness to parents. This sense of meaning is what permeates the Semitic social world from the highest to the lowest of its rank. The commandment says: "Honor your father and your mother that your days may be long." It is again the wisdom and counsel of the parents that guide their children and keep them from getting into trouble and endangering their lives.

Jesus, as a young man, was probably engaged in the work of a shepherd or a farmer—most likely the occupation of a farmer. Most of his teaching reflects first-hand knowledge of seeds and also of sheep. When not employed, he sat around and listened to the elders talk about religious and political problems. This was about the only kind of education most lads received in those days. But this also holds true today in certain areas of Arabia, Kurdistan and other counties where there are no schools.

Jesus was never a student in Egypt or India as some have suggested. All his teachings were illustrated by stories of the common, everyday life of the people in his region around the Lake of Galilee. There is nothing in his gospel message of the Kingdom of God that is alien to Semitic ideas and ideals. Furthermore, there is nothing in the four gospels to indicate Jesus had visited any lands outside of Palestine.

Where was Jesus during these eighteen years? We might as well ask where the other prophets and leaders were of whom we know nothing until they became prominent. Today, also, we know little of the lives of youth while they are obtaining their experience. It is not until they have accomplished something worthwhile that they obtain a reputation. So where was Jesus? The answer is very simple. He was in Galilee, in his own town of Nazareth, in his own house, working like hundreds of other boys and young men, feeding sheep, plowing, cutting grass, buying and selling in the marketplace.

Part 1—JESUS' BOYHOOD. Jesus, like any other child, grew in stature, wisdom and experience and was subject to his parents and teachers. He had to acquire knowledge, experience, and learning like other young men. Luke records Jesus' circumcision, his presentation to the Lord at the temple to offer a sacrifice when he was a baby and his attendance at the temple with his parents during Passover. The gospel writer recorded these instances because they are important events in a young Jewish boy's life.

When he was a little boy, he played with other boys in Galilee. At the age of five or six he rode on donkeys. He carried a sling and pebbles, a small bow and arrows, and joined with children playing at war just as children do today. Once in awhile he had a fight with other boys. On occasion he went to the well to bring a jar of water for his mother, as children often do, and at times he went into the fields barefoot to gather stubble, thorns, and dry grass so that his mother might use this for cooking and heating the house. During festivals he accompanied boys and girls of his age to the mountains, where the girls made bread and cooked for them in their tiny utensils. Then, they would dance, celebrate, and return home at evening time.

Nevertheless, most of his early childhood was spent studying at the synagogue school. In those countries, boys began their religious studies at the age of three or four and continued until they were acknowledged as teachers. Jesus would sit with other boys in a circle at the feet of a learned teacher at the synagogue in Nazareth. He was also taught to read, write, and recite passages of holy Scripture. He would attend synagogue meetings regularly and thereby acquire more knowledge of the holy Book. That Jesus was a keen and brilliant student and a spiritual genius is clearly evidenced by his profound teaching, his debates with the scribes and Pharisees, his free quotations from Scripture, his expositions of the Torah and the prophets and his concept of God's kingdom.

Part 2—JESUS' HIGHER EDUCATION. Jesus was born, reared and truly nurtured in the bosom of the Judaism of his day; no doubt he and his family belonged to the prominent sect of the Pharisees. Jesus' sole interest in life was the fulfillment of the revelations of the Hebrew prophets and the creation of a universal state, a spiritual kingdom which the prophets had envisioned centuries before him. It would be a state wherein Jews and all other nations could live together in peace and war would cease.

For the most part, Jesus ignored the teachings of the Jewish authorities who emphasized traditional law and religious ordinances. He branded these teachings as "the doctrines of the elders." He saw that they had supplanted the word of God as revealed to the prophets. He minimized the importance of the sacrifices, rituals, temples, and man-made ordinances that had replaced the simple, pure Hebrew religion. For him, the temple religion in his day was a heavy burden for the people.

Jesus never contaminated God's truth, nor did he ever quote from the learned authorities of Jewish schools of thought. He went right to the source—the words of the prophets who acted as spokesmen for God and who had died for the sake of justice and the true meaning of religion. Jesus revived the school of the prophets with his emphasis on the spirit of the law and not on the letter of the law. He incurred the intense dislike of the priests, certain Pharisees and scribes, as well as other teachers whose main interest was the temple religion, and who had turned the temple worship into a den of thieves.

There were many diverse teachings in the days of Jesus. There were those who abstained from wine and strong drink, those who advocated asceticism and celibacy and made themselves eunuchs, and teachers who taught poverty as a means of salvation. Jesus had no ties with any of these teachings. He ate meat, drank wine, mixed freely with sinners, tax-gatherers and society's outcasts. His enemies called him "a glutton and winebibber."[7]

Jesus knew Scripture from memory and could quote freely from any book in the Torah and prophets. Those who were steeped in the tradition of the elders and well versed in Jewish commentaries scorned his provincial education. They said: "How is it that this man has learning when he has never studied?" The phrase "never studied" means Jesus never studied the doctrines of the elders or the hairsplitting commentaries such as the washing of cups and pots, walking on the Sabbath, times of the observance of the feasts and new moons, offering of sacrifices, and other obscure and controversial teachings of the Oral Law that for years had supplanted the simple and direct word of God.

Jesus' teaching is illustrated by things of nature that reveal the glory of God and capture one's imagination. He was intimately familiar with all aspects of his people's lives, their businesses, borrowing and lending, dishonesty in buying and selling, measuring with short or long measures and using diverse weights and crooked balances. At times, he saw partners in business, one with long arms who purchased goods and the other with short arms who then sold the goods to the people. (They used their arms to measure the goods.) He used this as an illustration when he said: "With the measure with which you measure, it will be measured to you."

Jesus also knew and understood the problems of householders and their servants, the employer and the laborer, the orchard owner and vineyard workers, the sheep and the shepherd (the good and bad shepherds), the bridegroom and the bride, rocky and fertile fields, and fields of briars. He had insight into the infinite power of the seed that multiplies itself; therefore, he likened his teaching and God's kingdom to the seed. Interestingly, nearly all Hebrew prophets had something to do with sheep, vineyards and orchards; almost all of them worked for their living tending sheep. This was Jesus' higher

---

[7]See Errico and Lamsa, *Aramaic Light on the Gospel of Matthew,* "A Madman, Glutton and Winebibber," pp.170-171.

education; he was not a graduate from any mystery schools of thought. He was simple and direct but a powerful spiritual genius. It is no small matter that he became known as "son of God, son of the Highest."

CHAPTER 3

TWO SHIRTS

And the people asked him, saying, What shall we do then? He answereth and saith unto them, He that hath two coats. Let him impart to him that hath none; and he that hath meat, let him do likewise. Lk 3:10-11.

The Aramaic text uses the word *koteenyan* and it usually refers to a linen garment, a tunic, sometimes reaching to or below the knees and with or without sleeves. We would call it a "shirt." *Saybartha* means "food, provisions or nourishment."

While some men and women have more than one robe and many shirts, there are others who walk about partially clad or wearing worn-out clothes. Frequently, beggars are barely covered not because they cannot obtain garments but because it is a custom. If any part of the body is uncovered it signifies poverty and distress.

Some Easterners give away their extra shirts or loan them to their neighbors and to those who are in need. Food is also shared during times of famine. Families who have stored abundant food distribute it among the poor of the town. John the Baptist calls upon the people to share their clothing and food to show that they have truly turned to God. (See Luke 3:8-11.)

WAGES AND GRAFT

And the soldiers likewise demanded of him, saying, And what shall we do? And he said unto them, Do violence to no man neither accuse any falsely; and be content with your wages. Lk. 3:14

Semites respected soldiers of the old Eastern autocratic governments as if they were sons of the kings. In many respects their authority was greater than their civil officials because they were the defenders of the crown and gave their lives for country and ruler.

Therefore, soldiers were the spoiled children of the king and, at times, were free to do whatever they pleased. Their wages, however, were meager. Generally, Near Eastern governments were bankrupt. Civil officials paid themselves first and then, if any money remained, a small portion of salaries due were paid to the soldiers. They were content with their pay when they received it; but often, they were left unpaid for years.

When money was appropriated from the treasuries of the central governments for soldiers' salaries, the red tape involved deprived them of their earnings. The reason for this was that as money was transferred from one department to another, each official took a share. Thus, the soldier's wages melted away like ice on a very hot, sunny day. The soldiers, caught in this predicament, relied heavily on authority and force to make a living. Although these men were also under authority, they did as they pleased because their superiors permitted them to rob and collect unjust taxes on a commission basis.

Travelers were robbed and towns looted by soldiers. When regiments were transferred from one place to another, small villages suffered heavy losses. These raiding soldiers took money, livestock, clothing and food.

Up until the 1930s the stipend remained very small for Near Eastern soldiers. Before World War I, Turkish soldiers were paid about one dollar a month and Persian (Iranian) soldiers were paid only about thirty cents a month.

The soldiers who came to hear and see John the Baptist may have been captains. Officers were often guilty of injustices and violent acts practiced on the public because they were not satisfied with their own stipends. They would send privates out to extract money or anything of value from citizens by unjust means. John was preaching the coming of a new age, a new kingdom, participation in which required the removal of sin—that is, unjust and violent acts—through repentance (turning to God) and doing good deeds. When one truly turns to God, violence and unjust practices would cease. John's cry to turn to God was not based on any proper belief system or ascetic behavior but on sharing food and clothing with the needy and not taking advantage in collecting taxes or abusing military authority by robbing the citizenry.[1]

ADAM—THE SON OF GOD

Which was the son of Enos, which was the son of Seth, which was the son of Adam, which was the son of God. Lk. 3:38.

When referring to Adam at the end of Luke's genealogical table, the Aramaic text reads *dmin-alaha*: "Who was the son of Anosh, who was the son of Sheth, who was the son of Adam, who was *of God*."[2] The Aramaic phrase "of God" means "created by God."

The Aramaic word for "son" is *bar*. Luke used this word throughout his lists of ancestors from Joseph back to Adam. But according to the Aramaic text, when Luke referred to Adam, he used the preposition *min*, meaning "from" or "of," instead of the noun *bar*, "son." Due to the mutilation of early manuscripts or to a misunderstanding, Greek translators probably misread the Aramaic word *min* for *bar*.

Luke traced Jesus' ancestry through King David's son Nathan and not through his son Solomon, who became king. Matthew's genealogy works through Solomon and only goes back to Abraham. Luke used the general lineage that we find in the book of Genesis. He traces the bloodline back to Adam, who was of God. By so doing, Luke presents a greater universal appeal of Jesus' ancestry, transcending ethnic limitations. It appears that there is no artificial pattern in this genealogy as there is in the book of Matthew.

Luke evidently did not agree with Matthew that Jesus was a descendant of David through the royal family. He knew the Pharisees and priests had rejected Jesus on the grounds that he was not of the kingly line. His writing was appealing to Jews, Galileans, Syrians and

---

[1]See Errico and Lamsa *Aramaic Light on the Gospel of Matthew,* "John the Baptist," pp. 31-33.

[2]Lk. 3:38, Aramaic Peshitta text, Errico.

Idumeans, who would not want to claim that Jesus was of regal blood. People of these regions detested David's lineage.

Seemingly, Luke tried to compromise so as not to offend the Jewish followers of Jesus in the south and yet satisfy the prejudices of those in the north. No objection would have been raised by the north to tracing the ancestry of Jesus back to Nathan, whose descendants never ascended the throne. Nearly a thousand years had elapsed since Nathan and his descendants could be called princely, but the lineage of Solomon had continued until after the Babylonian (Chaldean) captivity.

CHAPTER 4

STRIKING A STONE

For it is written, He shall give his angels charge over thee, to keep thee: And in their hands they shall bear thee up, lest at any time thou dash thy foot against a stone. Lk. 4:10-11.

Near Eastern courtyards are paved with large stones. Rocks and stones are also strewn about the streets and thoroughfares of towns and villages. People often stumble over them and hurt themselves. Children and older people sometimes fall from the housetops to the courtyards, injuring themselves on the stones.

The courtyard of the temple at Jerusalem was paved with large stones. When the thought occurred to Jesus to throw himself down from the pinnacle of the temple, he felt assured that not even his foot would touch a stone.[1] This would prove his claim that he was the Messiah. This thought was deceptive and satanic—that is, misleading.

In the Near East, people frequently say to each other: "The road is safe, even your foot will not strike a stone. Everything is all right." This means you will reach your destination safely without any trouble or misfortune.

JESUS READING SCRIPTURE

And he came to Nazareth, where he had been brought up: and, as his custom was, he went into the synagogue on the Sabbath day, and stood up for to read. Lk. 4:16.

Synagogue services were held on the Sabbath day. Attendance

---

[1]Mt. 4:9-11. For a complete commentary of Jesus' temptation in the Wilderness, see Errico and Lamsa *Aramaic Light on the Gospel of Matthew,* Chapter 4, "The Trial in the Desert," pp. 42-50.

was optional for the laity, and in case of any important business, people were justified in absenting themselves. It was not compulsory for Jesus to attend synagogue services regularly but, like most pious Jews, he did attend frequently. On this occasion one of the leaders of the synagogue had invited Jesus to read Scripture and to address the congregation.

It is still the custom for competent laymen to assist in religious services by reading certain parts of holy Scripture and commenting on them. Synagogues and churches are kept open all the time for any who desire to enter and pray.

A SCROLL

And there was delivered unto him the book of the prophet Esaias. And when he opened the book, he found the place where it was written . . . .And he closed the book, and he gave it again to the minister, and sat down. And the eyes of all them that were in the synagogue were fastened on him. Lk. 4:17, 20.

Jesus was most likely handed a scroll rather than a book for the reading. When he was finished reading, he handed the scroll back to the attendant. Both in Aramaic and Hebrew, though the words for scroll and book differed, they were used synonymously.

A scroll is a long piece of parchment about four and a half inches wide and five to twenty feet long, according to the content and length of the document. It is made of the skin of animals. The skin is first soaked in a solution made of ashes and the hair is removed; then the skin is washed, dried and smoothed.

Before paper was invented and manufactured in Baghdad about the ninth century CE, writing was done on scrolls made from the skin of young animals. Two small pieces of wood were fastened at each end of the scroll so that it might be rolled both ways. Paper scrolls containing sacred writings are still used in many areas of the Near East where the art of bookbinding is unknown. Binding was a later invention, probably begun in the early part of the second century CE.

143

Bookbinding was invented to preserve the holy writing and not because all the writings belonged to the same book. Scrolls were often loaned and the number given was forgotten; sometimes parts of the scroll were cut off. This could not be done with a book, where the pages are numbered. Loaning and stealing made it difficult for the scribes and copyists to obtain complete documents from which to copy. This is why some manuscripts of the same material differ as to length and content.

It is presumed that the president of the synagogue, who had the authority to choose those who would read from the Torah and recite the *haphtarah*, handed Jesus the Isaiah scroll. The Isaiah passage was probably the *haphtarah* recitation of the Sabbath. The *archisyagogos*, "president," also was responsible for maintaining order and removing disturbances from the synagogue.

JESUS ESCAPES PUNISHMENT

And all they in the synagogue, when they heard these things, were filled with wrath, And rose up and thrust him out of the city, and led him unto the brow of the hill whereon their city was built, that they might cast him down headlong. But he passing through the midst of them went his way, Lk. 4:28-30.

The crowd seized Jesus and took him to the edge of a hill to throw him down. They wanted to punish but not kill him. If they had desired to kill him, they would have stoned him in the town or slain him with a sword. They would not have bothered to take him to the edge of a hill.

In the Near East, when a man blasphemes or does something worthy of a minor punishment, he is humiliated and disgraced. His beard or mustache is shaved or he might be thrown into a body of water or openly punished in some other manner. The townspeople will quickly gather to see the dishonor inflicted on the offender.

Jesus' remarks in the synagogue about the widow of Zarephath and Naaman, the Syrian (see verse 26-27), aroused the anger of the men of Nazareth. They took him out to a hill behind the town. While some men were preparing to throw him down, others were pleading for mercy on his behalf and for the sake of Mary and Joseph. The rest of the group were debating and discussing what to do with him. While all the commotion and emotional outbursts were happening, Jesus slipped through the dense crowd and disappeared.

INSANE MEN CONFESS JESUS

And devils also came out of many, crying out, and saying, Thou art Christ the Son of God. And he rebuking them suffered them not to speak: for they knew that he was Christ. Lk. 4:41.

It was believed that demons came out of many men who were insane or mentally ill. According to the Aramaic version and Semitic manner of speech, when Jesus healed these men, they cried out and said: "You are the Messiah/Christ, the Son of God."

Devils would not have confessed or acknowledged Jesus' power and his messiahship nor could they have spoken to him. It was some of the men who acknowledged Jesus and his authority. They did this out of appreciation for his kindness in healing them. Jesus did not allow these men to say much because he did not want the populace to know that he was the Messiah/Christ.

His own disciples were not yet able to completely understand his divine mission. At times, Jesus warned them not to say that he was the Christ because such a confession would have been misunderstood and would cause confusion; it also would have created stronger opposition from the Pharisees and priests, many of whom were already antagonized by his teaching. Also, some men would not believe such healing had taken place. For instance, after Jesus had healed a man who had been born blind and his parents had testified to this fact, the Pharisees would not believe. They doubted Jesus and his power to heal.

CHAPTER 5

SCRIBES

And the scribes and the Pharisees began to reason saying, Who is this which speaketh blasphemies? Who can forgive sins but God alone?
Lk 5:21.

Sapreh is the Aramaic word for "scribes." It derives from *sipra*, meaning "reading" or "book." In Hebrew the word for "scribes" is *sopherim*. It comes from the same Semitic root and has the same meaning as the Aramaic.

They were called scribes because they were professional copyists. Their work was to copy holy Scripture and to read and write legal documents. Thus they had access to books and came to be known as authorities on the Torah. Their authority was difficult to dispute because books were rare and inaccessible to the public. People looked to the scribes for spiritual and moral interpretation of Scripture as well as for legal advice.

As this work was considered holy, no charge was made for their services. It was acquired freely and given freely. The scribes were not lawyers in the sense that we understand the term. They did not appear as barristers before ecclesiastical or civil courts. Their task was to read books and to explain their meaning. In those days, in some areas of the Near East, state and religious laws were one. (Moslems still carry on this practice. They accept the law of the Koran as the law of the land. They consider those who can read and copy sacred books as authorities on the law.) There are other less important scribes whose work is the writing and copying of commercial and legal documents. These men sit in the streets or in the tiny shops waiting for customers who cannot read or write. (See also Mark 1:22.)

EATING AND DRINKING

And they said unto him, Why do the disciples of John fast often, and make prayers, and likewise the disciples of the Pharisees; but thine eat and drink? Lk. 5:33.

Expressions of speech such as "eating and drinking" are very general in New Testament literature and still continue among Aramaic speaking people and other Semites. "He has eaten and drunk" means "he is fed and well taken care of." It is equivalent to the English expression: "He eats three square meals a day." The Aramaic phrase "The Son of man is come eating and drinking" means he is living a comfortable life. It does not mean he was drinking too much wine as the reading of the text might suggest.[1]

Water is scarce in Palestine. In some places there is abundant food but not much water. Therefore, a cup of cold water is precious. On the arrival of guests and strangers in a house, the first thing offered them is cold water, which is just as important as food. Aristocrats would not think of entertaining guests unless they had abundant water. Their wives, daughters and servants are sent out to the springs and wells to obtain water.

Wine is used at a marriage feast and on a few other occasions but is seldom used during a meal. An Eastern meal consists of food and water. Thus "eating and drinking" simply means a complete meal.

Some religious men deny themselves certain things that they consider luxuries. Others fast from food and water. John the Baptist followed this order. He fasted quite often. But Jesus accepted invitations and lived comfortably; that is, he ate what was put before him. He showed his religious character not through the denial of food and drink but through his gracious and cordial ways of living, supplying the spiritual needs of humanity. (See also Mark 2:16.)

---

[1] See Errico and Lamsa *Aramaic Light on the Gospel of Matthew*, "Part B—Jesus' Lifestyle," p.171.

OLD AND NEW WINE

No man also having drunk old wine straightway desireth new; for he saith, The old is better. Lk. 5:39.

Although wine and strong drinks were first used in the Near East, Semites drink little and know less about liquors. One hears of old wines in Europe and America as being the vintage of many years ago. This is not the case in the Near East, where any wine over six months is called old. Wine is made and drunk in the same year and one can seldom find wine over a year old. The majority of people drink new wine. The grapes are crushed in October and the wine is ready in two weeks. Rich families who have large vineyards produce more wine, which is kept for the spring and summer months until the new wine is ready. It could not be kept longer because glass bottles were unknown. Wine loses its flavor and turns into vinegar when kept in goatskins or earthenware.

The Jews were devoted to their theology and ancient customs and were reluctant to change for a new teaching. They preferred the old wine because it was better to them, and they had been drinking from their traditions and teachings for centuries. Jesus' teaching was new wine, and "no man drinks old wine and immediately wants new wine; for he says, The old is delicious."[2]

---

[2] Lk. 5:39, Aramaic Peshitta text, Lamsa translation.

CHAPTER 6

THE POOR

And he lifted up his eyes on his disciples, and said, Blessed be ye poor: for yours is the kingdom of God. Lk. 6:20.

Poverty is very common in all Near Eastern countries. People are divided into three classes—rich, poor and noblemen. The affluent are influential because of their wealth. A nobleman, whether he is rich or poor, is always highly respected, but the majority of the poor are despised. This is because of the belief that wealth is a blessing and poverty is a curse. Men who desire to rule must therefore amass considerable wealth.

Generally, a man who is poor remains poor and his descendants share the same fate. The poor are misruled and their property eaten by taxes and bribes. These people who barely subsist are the ones who support the central government, the needy nobleman and local officials. They carry the heavy burdens in life.

At the time of Jesus, most of the Jews were poor and in a helpless economic condition. They were unorganized and without leadership, so they could not protest or revolt against the unjust system of taxation. This world seemed a hopeless place for them, but they believed they were to find comfort in the world to come. This was the class of people who expected a sudden messianic appearance. They had turned their thoughts to Scripture for consolation and were patiently waiting for God's reign when justice would be executed. Once God's kingdom was established, the greedy rich would mourn while the poor would be joyful.

The term "poor," *miskeneh* in Aramaic, does not always refer entirely to the poverty stricken. It also means "the meek, the humble, the pious, the poor in pride." In Judaism of the last two centuries BCE, the term "poor" according to rabbinic sources had practically become a synonym for "pious" or "saintly." The poor were the ones who surrendered to God and let God guide them in everything. They relied completely on God and not on material possessions.[1]

REPROACH

Blessed are ye, when men shall hate you, and when they shall separate you from their company, and shall reproach you, and cast out your name as evil, for the Son of man's sake. Rejoice ye in that day, and leap for joy: for behold, your reward is great in heaven: for in the like manner did their fathers unto the prophets. Lk. 6:22-23.

Reproach and slander are common among the people of the Near East. In countries where newspapers, theaters and other amusements are not known, gossip is the general pastime. When there is nothing else to talk about, people begin to discuss the family affairs, reputation and religion of their neighbors.

Bishops, priests and missionaries are exposed more to public gossip because of their leadership in the community. Every unfamiliar act performed by them is quickly suspected. False and malicious remarks are spread from mouth to mouth and, in the process, are exaggerated. What appeared at first to be an innocent act may be construed as a religious or criminal offence.

Jesus' disciples would not escape such criticism. They would be regarded as lunatics and traitors. Many would think of their new teaching as subversive to the established religion; they would feel antagonistic toward these disciples. Officials would blame them for evils, despite the fact that their teaching had nothing to do with the misfortunes that befell the community. This would be unavoidable because the disciples would expose and correct false religious traditions and customs and therefore suffer the consequences. Jesus warned them not to be dismayed or discouraged because such reactions of reproach were bound to be their lot. (See also Matthew 5:11-12.)

---

[1] Mt. 5:5. See Errico and Lamsa, *Aramaic Light on the Gospel of Matthew,* "Poor in Pride," pp. 56-58.

WORLDLY SATISFACTION

Woe unto you that are full! For ye shall hunger. Woe unto you that laugh now! For ye shall mourn and weep. Lk. 6:25.

When Near Eastern men become wealthy, they believe they are blessed by God no matter how their fortunes may have been accrued. They rely on their earthly possessions for salvation although some may have confiscated the property of the poor and others may have acquired their wealth in other unjust ways.

This saying refers to men who have overlooked the spiritual side of life and have become totally satisfied with their worldly achievements. It tells them that they will soon discover the emptiness of only possessing materialistic things. They will regret their lack of spirituality, the possession of which is a treasure for this life and the life hereafter.

LENDING AND BORROWING

Give to every man that asketh of thee; and of him that taketh away thy goods ask them not again. Lk. 6:30.

The phrase "and of him that taketh away thy goods" implies that the goods have been taken by force. However, it is a common Near Eastern custom to lend garments, food and animals to those who would borrow them. But, that is not the meaning of this phrase.

Supplies are very scarce and neighbors depend on one another. Women go freely into each other's homes and even take articles without permission, returning them after they have used them. No one would refuse his neighbor because some day he might need his help. When neighborly relations are broken, borrowing becomes difficult. People become distrustful and request the return of borrowed articles although they may not be needed at that time. The borrower is embarrassed because he may not be able to return the wheat, oil or other articles right away.

151

Jesus wanted lending to include strangers, also, and even one's enemies. He knew such favors would be effective in creating and cultivating friendship and peace among all people. (See also Matthew 5:42.)

REWARDS FOR FAVORS

And as ye would that men should do to you, do ye also to them likewise. For if ye love them which love you, what thank have ye? For sinners also love those that love them. Lk. 6:31-32.

The Aramaic text reads: "Just as you want men to do to you, do to them likewise. For if you love those who love you, what is your blessing? For even sinners love those who love them."[2]

Easterners lend money and do favors to those from whom they expect to receive favors in return. People give precious gifts to government officials, politicians and those who are in power in exchange for favors. The poor find it very difficult to borrow money and wheat for seed because the lender does not trust them and knows they can do nothing for him. Therefore, he refuses to loan to the poor.

This discrimination also applies to guests. For example, a rich man is lavishly entertained. The host will slaughter a sheep or an ox for the guest because he knows that when he visits his guest's home the same will be done for him. A poor man usually only receives some bread and buttermilk because no return favors are expected from him.

Again, Jesus teaches his disciples and followers to do favors and to be generous to those who can not repay them. He also reminded them that their heavenly Father would reward them: "But love your enemies and do good to them, and lend and do not cut off any man's hope; so your reward will increase and you will become sons of the Highest; for he is gracious to the wicked and the cruel."[3]

---

[2] Lk. 6:31-32, Aramaic Peshitta text, Lamsa translation.
[3] Lk. 6:35, Aramaic Peshitta text, Lamsa translation.

THEY WILL POUR INTO YOUR ROBE

Give, and it shall be given unto you; good measure, pressed down, and shaken together, and running over, shall men give into your bosom, For with the same measure that ye mete withal it shall be measured to you again. Lk. 6:38.

Near Easterners often go from one house to another borrowing or buying a measure or a half measure of wheat. Most houses have their own measures and these vary in size. When the wheat is poured into the measure, if the good man of the house is doing the measuring for a neighbor or a friend from whom he expects favors, he shakes the measure several times. This process allows the wheat to settle and so he fills it to overflowing. He usually does not show this courtesy to strangers who come from distant places. The wheat salesman knows that he will probably not see the buyer again, so he does not give him or her a full measure.

As the distance between homes is short and bags are scarce, the borrower or buyer of the wheat holds the end of his robe with both hands, and the wheat is poured into it. Generally, Near Easterners wear long flowing robes that are often used for carrying food stuffs, such as fruit, vegetables and so forth. This was a general practice in most countries of the Near East and was followed by men and women. (See also Matthew 7:2; Mark 4:24.)[4]

---

[4]See Errico and Lamsa, *Aramaic Light on the Gospel of Matthew,* "Part C—The Bountiful Measure," pp 107-109.

CHAPTER 7

THE CENTURION

For he loveth our nation, and he hath built us a synagogue. Lk. 7:5.

This centurion may have been a Syrian or a Roman and not necessarily a member of the Jewish faith. Officers of ruling races, although adherents of other faiths, will sometimes help to build sanctuaries for their subjects. This does not mean that they contribute money but that they draft people to do the work.

Cyrus was a Persian King who levied heavy taxes and exacted gifts so that he could build a Jewish temple. This was also done by Herod the Idumean,[1] who built a most magnificent temple in Jerusalem. Some of the foreign officers, however, worshiped at the native sanctuaries because places of their faith were not available. This is true even today. Turkish officers will worship in Christian shrines when they have no mosques in the area to attend.

SEMITIC NEAR EASTERN FUNERALS

Now when he came nigh to the gate of the city, behold, there was a dead man carried out, the only son of his mother, and she was a widow: and much people of the city was with her. Lk. 7:12.

Cemeteries in the Near East were always outside cities and towns. Today cemeteries are often within the city limits, but they were originally outside when cities were smaller. As a city expanded these cemeteries were included within its boundaries as other locations were selected outside the city proper.

---

[1]Idumea—Edom, in Hebrew—a country conquered by John Hyrcanus around 128 BCE. It was incorporated into the Hasmonean kingdom and its inhabitants were forcibly converted.

154

The deceased are carried out of the city, but no dead person is allowed to be brought in. There are no exceptions. For instance, if a nobleman or a high official should die outside the city wall, his body cannot be carried into the city. Semites believe adversity would reign among the populace if a corpse were brought into the city. The dead individual is placed in a coffin or, in some cases, wrapped in bed clothes and laid on a stretcher and carried by friends.

The funeral is accompanied by priests, singers, men and women. These priests march at the head of the procession; then comes the coffin followed by family members and other mourners. At the beginning of the procession, the feet of the deceased are toward the city. This conveys the notion that the person who died was forcibly dragged out by the hair, as it were, and will soon surrender to the grave. When a certain point is reached outside the city, the pallbearers halt and the coffin is placed on the ground. Its position is then reversed and the head is towards the city. While this change of position is made, the women sit in a circle around the coffin weeping, singing, and saying their farewells. Women are not permitted to accompany the dead from this point on. Only men carry out the burial.

When Jesus was about to enter Nain, he was met by the funeral procession of the widow's son. It is very probable that he came upon the scene when they were reversing the position of the coffin. Immediately, he saw the grief-stricken widow wailing over her beloved son, who would no longer be the comfort and support of her old age. Jesus had compassion on her and raised her son from the dead.

AN ALABASTER OF OIL

And behold a woman in the city, which was a sinner, when she knew that Jesus sat at meat in the Pharisee's house, brought an alabaster box of ointment. And stood at his feet behind him weeping, and began to wash his feet with tears, and did wipe them with the hairs of her head, and kissed his feet, and anointed them with the ointment. Lk. 7:37-38.

Until modern machinery was introduced into the holy land and other areas of the Near East, oil was very scarce. Olive oil which is so plentiful in some regions of the country is scarce today in other districts. People keep small quantities of it in small containers for anointing and medicinal purposes. In some places where olive oil is scarce and expensive, sheep butter is used.[2]

Anointing with oil is a Near Eastern custom dating from ancient days. After bathing, women anoint their heads with oil to keep the scalp soft. Men rub olive oil or butter on their heads and other areas of the body. They often rub chapped hands and feet as well as wounds with olive oil. Travelers especially use oil in this way to refresh their bodies after weary journeys.

Those who are rich and extravagant use perfume and fragrant oils. In ancient days prophets and kings were probably anointed with butter carried in an ox horn. Perfume and liquid oils could not have been stored in such containers.

Mary had a small container of perfume for herself or her friends. As perfumes were rare, it was doubtless the most expensive thing she had in her possession and was the only appropriate gift she could bring to Jesus as an offering. Other people were entertaining him, but as Mary had a bad reputation, she could not invite him to her home. Poor people and men and women of questionable reputation hesitate to invite holy men into their homes. Instead they go to the homes of those who can entertain a holy man and there they offer their gifts.

JESUS UNDER SUSPICION

Now when the Pharisee which had bidden him saw it, he spake within himself, saying, This man, if he were a prophet, would have known who and what manner of woman this is that toucheth him: for she is a sinner. Lk. 7:39.

In the eyes of this Pharisee, Jesus' tolerance of the woman was

---

[2] See 2 Ki. 9:3.

inexcusable. Jesus was a prophet and need not have been warned of a sinner. (When Saul inquired of the woman of Endor who had a familiar spirit, he disguised himself, but she knew he was the king.)[3] The Pharisee was surprised to see Jesus allowing the woman, who was recognized as a sinner, to touch him. It was also a shock to many other guests who were present.

Generally, harlots are known in the Near East. They blacken their eyes and wear colorful dresses. Yet, there are women who are as pure as they can be but often others have misjudged and misunderstood them. As a result of this, a decent woman's reputation can be ruined. A casual remark to a stranger brands a Near Eastern woman as a harlot.

Jesus looked into the hearts of these women. He knew many of them were falsely accused, and some of them had fallen but wanted to be restored to the community again. He had come to help and save sinners and to heal those who were sick. It was difficult for him to shun the company of such people who recognized him as a prophet and sought his help. Jesus preferred to carry out his mission seeking lost sheep than to follow the formalities of tradition just to win the approval of religious leaders.

WATER FOR THE FEET

And he turned to the woman, and said unto Simon, Seest thou this woman? I entered into thine house, thou gavest me no water for my feet: but she hath washed my feet with tears, and wiped them with the hairs of her head. Lk. 7:44.

The offer of water to wash a guest's feet is a token of friendship and a hearty welcome. In some homes, the wives of the host or his servants wash the feet of honored guests. However, they will not perform this custom for ordinary guests or for teachers or prophets whose conduct or teachings are in doubt.

---

[3] 1 Sam. 28:12.

157

Simon, who was a Pharisee, knew Jesus was Galilean and not a strict practicing Jew. He had probably heard that Jesus did not follow certain protocol, such as washing his hands when he ate. Therefore, Simon did not receive Jesus with the special marks of honor and hospitality that a Semite bestows on an honored guest. Simon felt that Jesus did not deserve such recognition, so he received him as an ordinary guest and as a stranger who was not entitled to the exclusive treatment accorded to a Jewish prophet.

The woman was, no doubt, in the house when Jesus was received. She noticed Simon's attitude toward Jesus, who was a holy man. Perhaps, this is what prompted her to perform the immortal act. It was a rebuke to Simon but, at the same time, it won her fame in the gospel of her lord.

CHAPTER 8

SEVEN DEVILS

And certain women, which had been healed of evil spirits and infirmities, Mary called Magdalene, out of whom went seven devils, Lk. 8:2.

The Aramaic word for "demons" is *shedeh*. Aramaic speaking people used this term to explain the cause of insanity and incorrect thinking. *Shedana*, "demonic," refers to one whose mind has become deranged. However, this term does not always imply that the person suffers from severe mental illness or is violently insane. It can refer to sinners, those who behave strangely or make mistakes. It is also a general term commonly used in Semitic speech. For example, wise men may call each other *shedana* with reference to errors in judgment.

The number seven is symbolic of completeness. Luke tells us that Mary had seven devils which meant that she was completely under the power of evil thoughts or that her thinking was completely wrong. Jesus did not cast seven particular devils out of her. One devil would be sufficient to create misguided thinking and insanity if this statement is to be taken literally. This was not the case. Jesus restored Mary's genuine self by revealing the truth to her so that her former way of thinking had vanished forever. She was no longer subject to the earthly passions and desires that had weakened her faith in God.

When Mary saw Jesus and heard his sweet words, she felt there was something wrong within herself. She was ashamed of her behavior. Undoubtedly, she had always thought that she could never make good again. But now she heard a new prophet saying, "I came not to call the righteous, but sinners to repentance."[1] Jesus' powerful but simple truth is that God rejoices more over one repentant sinner than over ninety-nine pious persons. Mary was encouraged and

---

[1]Mk. 2:17.

strengthened. Jesus' assuring presence made her feel accepted and not rejected. His affirming and comforting teachings inspired her to turn to God and realize the new hope surging through her soul. Her attitude toward the world changed entirely. She began to lead a new life. Now she would seek after the things that concerned and nourished her soul; vanquished were her unhealthy desires. No longer was Mary dominated by wrong ideas and harmful practices.

CHAPTER 9

INSANE—LUNATICS

Then he called his twelve disciples together, and gave them power and authority over all devils, and to cure diseases. Lk. 9:1.

Again, Aramaic speaking people used the term *shadeh* to mean "the insane, lunatics or those who suffer from mental disorders." To this very day, this term is in common use in the Aramaic and Arabic languages. People refer to one who is mentally ill or possessed by a malevolent inclination as having an "evil spirit."

Since God is the only Spirit, how could there be an evil spirit? The Aramaic word *ruha*, "spirit," can also mean "a person, wind, rheumatism, pride, inclination." In Arabic, the insane are called *Magnooneen*. In Persian they are called *dewana*, meaning "those who live a wild, inordinate life" or "one suffering from mental disorders."

In the olden days, Near Easterners did not know any medical terms that describe mental disturbances. These conditions had no names so the people called them "devils and demons." Mark's gospel reads: "And unclean spirits, when they saw him, fell down before him, and cried, saying, Thou art the Son of God."[1] An evil spirit has no physical form with which to fall down and worship. The mentally ill men fell at Jesus' feet. As soon as Jesus healed them, they began confessing him as "the son of God."

IMMORTALITY

But I tell you of a truth, there be some standing here, which shall not taste of death, till they see the kingdom of God. Lk. 9:27.

One must not take such sayings literally. Statements such as the

---

[1]Mk. 3:11, K. J. V.

one in this verse are used as an expression of commendation concerning persons who have made some distinguished contribution to humanity. Semites often communicate with each other by saying: "If you do this thing you shall never die." This means that if the person does the particular thing, he will be remembered forever.

Hebrew Scripture tells us that Moses and Elijah had gone to heaven without tasting death. The Jews expected them to come back when the Messiah was to come. Jesus, on the mount, was talking about the coming of these two great prophets and the living work which they had done when they were on earth. These two prophets were the center of discussion among Jewish people. They were alive in the hearts of men and women who looked forward to their coming.

Jesus, in the above saying, was referring to his disciples. They were also to live forever until the coming of God's reign. They were soon to become the major topic of conversation among the various races of the world. These disciples died physically, but they have been living spiritually in the hearts of men and women who honor them.

Jesus spoke of the spiritual life and accomplishments that live forever. Corporeal life was not his major emphasis. Flesh and bones have no power—spirit is the source of all life and creates the growth of the bones and flesh The spirit lives forever because life is eternal.[2]

TRANSFIGURATION

And as he prayed, the fashion of his countenance was altered, and his raiment was white and glistening. And behold, there talked with him two men, which were Moses and Elias; Who appeared in glory and spake of his decease, which he should accomplish at Jerusalem. Lk. 9:29-31.

Just exactly what happened on the summit of Mt. Tabor on that historic day is very difficult to determine because the event was

---

[2] Mt. 16:28; Mk. 9:1; Jn. 8:52. See also Errico and Lamsa, *Aramaic Light on the Gospel of Matthew*, "Shall Not Taste Death," pp. 223-224.

probably not reported until many years after Jesus' death on the cross. Scripture informs us that the event was a vision. "And as they came down from the mountain, Jesus charged them, saying, Tell the vision to no man until the Son of man be risen again from the dead."[3]

Jesus and three of his disciples had climbed the mountain and were sitting at the top resting. The summit of the mountain was encircled by a luminous cloud. They could see all the surrounding areas. Some of the disciples were thinking of Israel's former glory and the messianic rule that was to restore the Davidic reign and establish God's kingdom on earth. Jesus had been talking about his journey to Jerusalem and his crucifixion. His disciples were interpreting events in their own way. They never imagined that the Messiah was to suffer before the kingdom was established. They expected immediate restoration of the kingdom of Israel and looked for Jesus' journey to Jerusalem to suddenly set up this long predicted messianic rule.

However, they were unable to explain the prophecies. The books of the prophets said that Moses and Elijah were to return before the fulfillment of the messianic rule. It was traditionally believed that these two great prophets had not died but had ascended to heaven—that they were awaiting the coming of the Messiah and would appear first to prepare the way before him. The idea of a suffering Messiah was strange to these simple disciples who had taken events literally. They thought the scriptures must first be fulfilled. Moses and Elijah must come back. Jesus, however, told them Elijah had already come but they did not know him. The disciples believed that no matter what happened, the kingdom would be established only through the fulfillment of Scripture. This necessitated the appearance of Moses and Elijah.

Wearied by the long, trying journey and discouraged with the sad news, they fell asleep although it was daytime. While their bodies were resting, their minds were awake and still pondering on the

---

[3]Mt. 17:9 K. J. V. See also Errico and Lamsa, *Aramaic Light on the Gospel of Matthew,* "The Vision of the Transfiguration," p. 225.

difficult question. Peter saw Moses and Elijah standing next to his master-teacher. Jesus' appearance began to glow. Then Peter spoke to Jesus, asking him to make three tabernacles—one for him and two more for Moses and Elijah. But when he opened his eyes, he discovered Jesus standing alone, encircled by a cloud. The two prophets who had appeared to him in the daytime vision seemed to have been enveloped by the cloud.

The transfiguration was a spiritual event. The law and the prophets were fulfilled through Jesus. Moses and Elijah had come. Their books had continually testified concerning the Messiah, and their words and commandments were committed to memory by the Jews. This transfiguration brought a sudden change in the lives of Jesus' disciples. They had the first glimpse of him in a spiritual way. Jesus' face shone like a white garment. His characteristics were no longer like those of an earthly ruler. His appearance resembled that of a suffering servant. Dreams of an earthly kingdom began to vanish from the minds of the disciples.

ENTERTAINING DIGNITARIES

And it came to pass, when the time was come that he should be received up, he steadfastly set his face to go to Jerusalem. And sent messengers before his face; and they went, and entered into a village of the Samaritans, to make ready for him. Lk. 9:51-52.

When a high government official or a religious dignitary contemplates a journey, one or two men are sent ahead to inform the people and make preparations. As hotels were unknown and it was difficult to procure food readily, it would have been embarrassing for anyone to invite such people to remain at a house on short notice.

Some townsfolk refuse to give lodging to a large group of traveling men, fearing that they might do damage. This is even more true of a religious man whose teachings are questioned by the ecclesiastical authorities. No one would be willing to risk his reputation by entertaining such a man and his followers. This would violate religious rules. Even casual conversations with such men would be regarded as a sin.

Many Jewish authorities considered Jesus a radical and a fanatic. Any welcome given to him would offend the religious conservative. His face set[4] towards Jerusalem meant that he was on his way to Jerusalem for the final conflict with authorities. An act of sympathy toward him might endanger the town, because he was also accused of political treason by trying to make himself a king.

JESUS REFUSES TO CALL DOWN FIRE

And they did not receive him, because his face was as though he would go to Jerusalem. And when his disciples James and John saw this, they said, Lord, wilt thou that we command fire to come down from heaven, and consume them, even as Elias did? Lk. 9:53-54.

While Jesus and his disciples were on their journey to Jerusalem, they had to pass through Samaritan territory. Galilee was close to Samaria and travelers journeying from Galilee to Jerusalem had to stop over in Samaritan towns. Although Easterners are hospitable and welcome strangers as guests, a little town may refuse to give shelter to a company of thirteen men because of fear or lack of accommodations. It would be difficult to provide food for such a large number.

The people of Samaria worshiped on Mt. Gerizim. They accepted the five books of Moses but followed the pattern of religion established by Jeroboam in the north. The people who dwelt north of Samaria on the borders of the Lake of Galilee accepted Jerusalem as the center of worship.

When the Samaritans refused to welcome Jesus and his disciples into their town, the sons of Zebedee asked their master to call fire from heaven on villagers but Jesus refused to do such a thing. He said

---

[4]In conversation among Semites, people often ask those who or about to travel or who are traveling: "Where are you facing?" meaning "Where are you going or heading?"

165

to them: "Ye know not what manner of spirit ye are of." This is a literal translation from Aramaic. It means "you do not know how bad tempered you are." The two brothers, Jacob (James) and John, were hasty and impulsive. People referred to them as "the sons of thunder" because of their hot tempers.

LOOKING BEHIND

And Jesus said unto him, No man, having put his hand to the plough, and looking back, is fit for the kingdom of God. Lk. 9:62.

Some men, while plowing, stop their oxen and turn to look backwards. They want to see how much of the ground is already plowed. This is done to determine how long it will take to complete the work. When they see the work is progressing slowly, they become discouraged. These men gain a reputation of being lazy workers. They are anxious to finish their job, regardless of how it is done, so they may leave the field and go home. They are not interested in their work but merely in the wages.

When a man hires servants, at times he secretly watches them plow to see if they will look back. If they do, he may discharge them immediately and hire others. Men who are known as good workers never look behind when plowing and harvesting. To them this would be a waste of time. They look forward and watch the uncultivated portion rapidly decreasing in size. They are interested in the field and its produce more than in leisure.

Jesus' disciples were not to look behind and count the few converts. This would discourage them. The work of the gospel of the kingdom might progress slowly, but it was to be done thoroughly so that the fields might produce rich crops. Besides, the field for the work of the kingdom was so large that the labor would continue forever.

CHAPTER 10

LABOR SHORTAGE

Therefore said he unto them, The harvest truly is great, but the labourers are few: pray ye therefore the Lord of the harvest, that he would send forth labourers into his harvest. Lk. 10:2.

Economic and social conditions are different in the Near East from those in the United States and Europe. Most people work for themselves. A few are employed as servants. Unemployment is almost unknown and the shortage of laborers has always been a problem because few Eastern people like to work for others. Employment, as understood in the Occident, was not understood in the Near East where a servant has practically the standing of a slave. Men of official position and nobility, when reduced to poverty, would rather see their children starve than work for others.

During the harvest season, labor becomes very scarce. Most people have their own crops and they take care of them first. Few people in town can be hired. Some men raise more wheat than they can consume. They use the surplus as a medium of exchange in bartering for other supplies, such as clothes, implements and household articles. Servants and laborers are also paid in wheat.

Initially, an owner of the field orders his servants to begin cutting the wheat. He prefers letting them do the work so he doesn't have to hire extra help. He makes excuses that it is difficult to hire laborers. The servants soon find the task too great, because they also have to perform their regular daily duties. Thus, the harvest becomes a problem. The servants fear that they may be caught in the rainy season. They beg their master to hire laborers. When the master sees that the servants cannot finish cutting the wheat in its due time, he rushes to hire men. He goes to other towns and marketplaces searching for workers who are idle.

Jesus had twelve specially selected men and seventy disciples to preach and teach the gospel of the kingdom. The field was too large

167

for them alone. Jesus' teachings were to reach throughout the world. His words were to be heard in every language. This was a tremendous task for only twelve men and seventy disciples. Jesus told them to pray that the lord of the harvest would send more workers into the field to spread the word of the kingdom. It is God who is the lord of the harvest. This need was met on the day of Pentecost. The Holy Spirit recruited more laborers and sent them into the field. Missionary work has continued for centuries. The harvest is still great although laborers are few. (See also Matthew 9:37.)

SALUTATIONS ON THE ROAD

Carry neither purse, nor scrip, nor shoes; and salute no man by the way. Lk. 10:4.

A salutation is an indication of friendship in the Near East. Semites are sociable and generally greet each other in the hometown and acquaintances on a journey. *Shalem* means "salute, greet." It comes from the Semitic root meaning "to surrender." To greet a stranger on the road exposes the solitary traveler to danger as some men take these greetings as a sign of fear and rob the unfortunate man.

Weapons are often concealed in the long robes; an unarmed man may be judged as armed if his speech does not give away the fact that he does not have a concealed weapon. Usually, people travel in a company or in caravans and will greet each other unless they are people of rival faiths and different nationalities, especially when hatred exists between them. They pass by silently, looking straight ahead.

When friends greet each other, they often engage in conversation that could result in a heated debate and injury could possibly ensue. (Recall the case of Abner and Joab, 2 Samuel 2:12.) Jesus did not mean that his disciples should be unfriendly and not greet acquaintances while traveling, but he did not want them exposed to the dangers that might present themselves on the road. In the Near East to this very day, when an Assyrian meets a Kurd, he is not supposed to greet him but should pass him by without fear. Parents and experienced friends always give this kind of counsel to young people and inexperienced travelers.

Then there is something more to consider. Besides the danger on the road, Jesus did not want to delay the work the disciples were sent to do. Dr. Abraham Rihbany details a typical conversation between two strangers meeting on the road:

> The Easterner's greeting is a copious flow of soul, whose intimacy and inquisitiveness are very strange to the mentality of the West. . . .
>
> May God [Allah] give you health and strength!
>
> O, may God [Allah] refresh and strengthen your life!
>
> Whence has your excellent presence come, and where are you facing?
>
> From Nazareth have I come, and I am facing Damascus.
>
> What is your precious name?
>
> Your humble servant Mas'ud, son of Yusuf of the clan of Job, and my years, friend, are four and thirty.
>
> All honor, all honor! May your life be long and happy!
>
> What children have you?
>
> Three sons in the keeping of God. . . .
>
> Thus the mutually complimentary conversation and the searching of hearts continue until each of the travelers is thoroughly informed concerning the personal, domestic and social affairs of the other. The trade, the income, the profession, the cares and anxieties, and even the likes and dislikes of each are

169

made known to the other before their ways part.[1]

Sometimes the traveler may also receive an oral invitation to the home of the person he has just met. And it might take three or more days before the traveler leaves.[2] When one does not greet on the road, Semites understand the wayfarer is on very urgent business. Jesus did not want his apostles detained as this would have delayed the spread of the message of the kingdom. Elisha, a prophet of God, gave a similar command to his servant Gehazi. His servant was sent on a mission of healing. Elisha did not want Gehazi delayed while traveling; thus, he forbade him to greet anyone on the road.[3]

EATING GENTILE FOOD

And into whatsoever city ye enter, and they receive you, eat such things as are set before you. Lk. 10:8

Antipathy to different religious practices has always been strong in biblical lands. Those of one faith never eat food prepared and served by members of a rival faith. Certain foods that are lawful to the adherents of one religion are an abomination to those of another.

Semites are usually hospitable to neighbors and strangers. In accepting hospitality, the person is expected to break bread with the family. To refuse to eat the host's bread is a breach of hospitality. There are some exceptions to this rule. Some hosts realize that certain foods are unlawful for guests who are of another faith. Thus, these guests, avoiding embarrassment, offer excuses such as "I am fasting" or " I am not feeling well."

At times, however, the refusal to eat bread at the home of a member of another religion can be regarded as an insult to that faith. The situation then becomes extremely complicated and embarrassing.

---

[1]Abraham M. Rihbany, *The Syrian Christ,* pp. 255-257.
[2]See Judges 19:4-9.
[3]2 Ki. 4:29.

This ultimately results in debates on theology and traditions that lead to bitterness, quarrels, hatred and sometimes physical injury and death.

Some hosts forget to ask the faith of the guest they have welcomed. They hasten to kill a sheep and prepare other foods, then are surprised and disappointed to learn the guest is a member of another religion which considers their bread and food as unclean. This, too, can make some hosts very angry and they put out their guest. Others reluctantly let him lodge for the night. While the family is eating, the guest sits in a corner by himself to eat the bread and cheese he has carried in his bag or hidden in his garments.

Today, some Near Eastern Christians will not eat bread baked by Jewish people. Likewise many Jews would be considered defiled and unclean if they ate cheese made by Christians or Moslems. The reason for this is that the rennet that makes cheese is taken from a cow killed by a non-Jew.

Jesus' disciples were of the Jewish faith. According to the traditions of the elders, they should not eat with Gentiles as we see in the case of Peter at Caesarea (Acts 10:14). Jesus knew these traditional customs created needless disturbances. He also knew that a continued observance of such traditions would hamper the work of his disciples and retard the growth of the gospel of the kingdom among the people. If the disciples refused to eat the bread of others, these people would consider the disciples as unclean. They would not be welcomed in Gentiles' homes and their glad tidings would mean nothing. This command was in line with Jesus' teaching: "What enters into a man from the outside cannot not defile him" (Mark 7:18).

HEAL THE SICK

And heal the sick that are therein, and say unto them, The kingdom of God is come nigh unto you. Lk. 10:9.

Where Western civilization has not yet penetrated the Near East, doctors, dentists, medicines and hospitals are unknown. Missionaries, consuls, travelers and strangers are often sought for healing. Foreigners are thought of as knowledgeable in ways of medicine and healing the sick. Native preachers and religious men also heal, but most people have more faith in strangers and out-of-town individuals. Easterners care little about preaching. They are more deeply impressed by what people do rather than by what they might say or preach. Religious men are expected to have extraordinary powers.

Jesus' disciples had to heal the bodies of men, women and children as well as healing their souls. If they cannot heal the sick who are brought to them, how can they preach to the people? They were to demonstrate the inner power of their religion by deeds as well as by words. An old Eastern proverb says: "Words without acts are like soft winds." His disciples had to show through their healing powers that God's reign had come.

I BEHELD SATAN FALLING

And he said unto them I beheld Satan as lightning fall from heaven. Lk. 10:18.

The word "Satan" derives from the Aramaic root *sata* meaning to "slide, go astray, turn aside or away, miss the mark." "I beheld Satan as lightning fall from heaven" means Jesus saw light driving out darkness, his truth triumphing over the power of evil.

Jesus' seventy disciples had just returned from their missionary endeavors. This was their first time to teach, heal and demonstrate the presence of God's kingdom among the people. They came back with good news that cheered their teacher and prophet. They had been eager to see if Jesus' teaching would be accepted and if they, personally, could heal the sick. They returned full of joy. Their mission was successful.

Jesus' disciples had shown their power not only by healing the sick but by curing mental and emotional illnesses, which were extremely difficult to treat. They told Jesus: "Even devils have been subject to us in your name" (see verse 17). This meant that people possessed with mental disorders had been healed and had embraced Jesus' teaching of the kingdom. "In your name" refers to Jesus' method of healing. The disciples restored the insane through the power of faith they had gained from being with their master-teacher.

TREADING ON SERPENTS AND SCORPIONS

Behold, I give unto you power to tread on serpents and scorpions, and over all the power of the enemy; and nothing shall by any means hurt you. Lk. 10:19.

Religious men must possess some sort of unusual miraculous power to have the confidence of Near Easterners. People think of them as being immune from the poison of snakes and scorpions. If religious healers do not evince such power, people would dispute their ability to heal, especially if affected by the bite of a snake or insect. On one of Paul's journeys, a viper had bitten him when he was seated by the fire warming himself. When the barbarians saw he was unharmed, they immediately thought of him as a god endowed with special powers.[4]

Semites also believe that fear can cure fevers. Moslem dervishes carry snakes with them on their preaching circuits. They tie them around their necks and carry them in their clothes. These dervishes claim they can perform cures. When those sick with fever are shown snakes by these so-called healers, they get up from the sick beds and run away in fear. In some cases they are immediately healed.

Jesus inspired his disciples and told them that they had power over anyone or anything that might harm them. His strong faith in them helped them overcome fear. He ignited their hearts with so much truth and love "they could tread on serpents and scorpions." This means they were not to fear anything. There would be nothing to retard or impede their progress in teaching God's kingdom, healing the sick and winning over some of the opposition.

---

[4]Acts 28:1-6.

WRITTEN IN HEAVEN

Notwithstanding in this rejoice not, that the spirits are subject unto you; but rather rejoice, because your names are written in heaven. Lk. 10:20.

The expression "your names are written in heaven" metaphorically has many meanings, such as "heaven acknowledges you, you are chosen ones, you will never be forgotten but remembered forever." In ancient times, the names of individuals who were to be honored and promoted were written in the Chronicles of the kings.

One must not take the expression "written in heaven" literally. Heaven has no bookkeepers and accountants. Nevertheless, every human act is evident and God sees and knows everything. These terms of speech were used because the names of valiant and faithful persons were written in the books of kings as a reward. (See the case of Mordecai, Esther 6:2-3.) Jesus tells his disciples not to rejoice because they had power to heal mental illnesses or that people who were deranged were subject to them, but to rejoice that they will never be forgotten. Their names would be remembered forever.

JESUS GIVES THANKS

In that hour Jesus rejoiced in spirit, and said, I thank thee, O Father, Lord of heaven and earth, that thou hast hid these things from the wise and prudent and hast revealed them unto babes: even so Father; for so it seemed good in thy sight. Lk. 10:21.

The Aramaic text reads: "At that very hour, Jesus rejoiced in the Holy Spirit and said, I thank thee, O, my Father, Lord of heaven and earth, because thou didst hide these things from the wise and men of understanding, and revealed them to children; yes, my Father, for so it was well-pleasing in thy presence."[5]

---

[5]Lk. 10:21, Aramaic Peshitta text, Lamsa translation.

Jesus felt the power of the Holy Spirit. He rejoiced and gave thanks to God for the anointing and power that his Father had given him. No other teacher of religion had been able to unlock the simple truths that he taught to his disciples. The Holy Spirit had revealed the teachings that were hidden from the eyes of men and made them manifest to even the simple and unlearned disciples.

All that Jesus taught was in accordance with the Word of God that had been revealed by the holy prophets. He did not supplant God's word as the Pharisees, scribes and elders had done with their own teachings.

Jesus was so humble as a teacher of religion that he refused to accept glory and honor. He told the people his teaching was not his own but was from the Father who had sent him. Therefore, he gave the glory to God. He rejoiced because God had fulfilled in his disciples the truth that Jesus had received from his Father. Now his disciples would be able to hand it down to their followers. Men of understanding did not grasp his teaching, but his simple followers did comprehend it and demonstrated its power.

THE UNEXPECTED HERO

And Jesus answering said, A certain man went down from Jerusalem to Jericho and fell among thieves, which stripped him of his raiment, and wounded him, and departed, leaving him half dead. . . . And went to him, and bound up his wounds, pouring in oil and wine, and set him on his own beast, and brought him to an inn and took care of him. And on the morrow when he departed, he took out two pence and gave them to the host, and said unto him, Take care of him; and whatsoever thou spendest more, when I come again, I will repay thee. Lk 10:30-35.

The Aramaic text reads: "A man was traveling from Jerusalem to Jericho. Suddenly robbers attacked him, stripped him, and left him half dead. Then they went away. And by chance, a priest was traveling down that road, saw him, and passed by. So then, a Levite also came and reached the same place, saw him and passed by.

"Now a man, a Samaritan, while he was traveling, came where he was, saw him, and had compassion on him. So he went to him, dressed his wounds, having poured wine and oil on them. Then he mounted him on his donkey, brought him to an inn, and attended to him. On the following day, early in the morning, he took out two denareen, and gave them to the innkeeper. He told him: Take good care of him. Whatever you may need in addition, when I come back, I will repay you."[6]

Part 1—THE PARABLE. All cultures, religious and racial orders, governments, and so forth, have always maintained a certain hierarchic system with invisible social and mental boundaries. In the ancient world, for example, there were Greeks and Barbarians, Jews and Gentiles. Biblical Israel also maintained a hierarchy among its own people. The order was priest, Levite, Israelite, proselyte, freed slave and so on.

When Jesus related this parable, he jolted his listeners by not following the usual hierarchic social system. He begins his story with an Israelite becoming robbed, beaten, stripped and left half dead. Then he brings in the appearance of a priest, followed by a Levite; but he surprises his audience with a non-Israelite hero. This was a shocker! Almost immediately Jesus begins breaking down social strata that religious notions and traditions had built. This simple but explosive story challenged his hearers and gave them a new look on the outworking of God's kingdom.

The road from the holy city to Jericho is about 17 miles and is extremely dangerous. It passes through mostly desert and rocky hills. This road was notorious for mugging and highway robbery. When the thieves took the poor man's clothes, they left the unfortunate fellow without any identification. In the Near East, clothes help identify an individual by telling about a person's class, religion, and village or clan of origin. These robbers had so badly beaten the victim, he appeared as dead. (We assume the victim is an Israelite because Jesus was most likely addressing a largely Jewish audience.)

---

[6]Lk. 10:30-35, Aramaic Peshitta text, Errico.

Interestingly, Jericho was the hometown for priests and Levites. Thus, it was no accident that Jesus had a priest and Levite traveling down that same road. According to Levitic law, a priest or a Levite must not touch a bloody or dead body. "The Lord said to Moses: Speak to the priests, the sons of Aaron, and say to them: None shall defile himself for a [dead] person among his kin, except for the relatives who are closest to him: his mother, father, son, daughter, and brother."[7] In Israel, the dead were considered unclean and therefore untouchable. Numbers 19:11 informs Israel that anyone touching a corpse will be unclean for seven days. So the priest and Levite were religiously correct to pass by the victim.

The story needs a hero, a rescuer for the poor, beaten man on the side of the road. Someone has to help the pathetic victim who fell prey to the highway criminals. The surprise element in the parable comes when Jesus says: "Now a man. . . .*a Samaritan*, while he was traveling came where he was. . . saw him. . . and had compassion on him." Undoubtedly, this part of the story agitated nearly everyone's racial and religious sensibilities. The hero was a non-Israelite. This Samaritan took care of the victim, dressed his wounds and brought him to an inn and took care of all his needs. Jesus had made his point.

The gospel of the kingdom—God's presence—subverts all hierarchic order of any present or future religious and political systems. In this kingdom there are no lines of demarcation—no boundaries—nor is there any social status. No one is greater than or above anyone else. According to Jesus' parable, an enemy who was considered culturally and religiously unclean by the people has compassion, heals, and cares for an Israelite. The Samaritan was not afraid to aid this needy human being on the roadside. The despised Samaritan transcended his racial and religious beliefs and helped the brutalized victim regardless of that man's faith.

Part 2—THE SAMARITANS. The Samaritans and Jews had long been enemies. This history goes back to the time of the rebuilding of Solomon's temple and the return of the Jewish exiles

---

[7]Lev. 21:1-2, Aramaic Peshitta text, Errico.

from Chaldea (Babylonia). We need to begin with Samaria, the capital of the kingdom of Israel. (The kingdom of Israel was comprised of the ten northern tribes. The capital of the southern kingdom of Judah was Jerusalem.) King Omri founded Samaria about 880 BCE. In 721 BCE, the Assyrians captured the entire northern kingdom of Israel, deported its people and resettled the territory with pagans from other parts of the empire.[8]

According to Jewish tradition, the Samaritans were the descendants of these settlers. We do not know the exact date when the Samaritans became a separate religious sect with a temple of their own on Mt. Gerizim. However, most scholars favor the fourth century BCE. Evidently, Jesus had sympathy for this group of people. This is shown through his parable of the "Samaritan" and the story of the "Ten Lepers" (Luke 17:11-19). Nevertheless, Jesus himself instructed the twelve apostles not to enter any town of the Samaritans, but rather to go to the lost sheep of the house of Israel.[9]

The Samaritans do not derive their name from any geographical designation but rather from the term *samerim*, "keeper [of the law]." John 4:9 tells us that the Jews had no dealing with the Samaritans. These Samaritans felt they were a special chosen group and called themselves the "sons of light." They criticized the Jerusalem temple, and they did not celebrate Purim or Hanukkah.

Samaritans also adopted their own specially edited Torah but did not accept the books of the prophets. They were a religious community that developed independently of the spiritual leadership of Jerusalem among a people who were, for cultural and historical reason, alienated from the Jews and could not maintain friendly relations. There is a proverbial saying about this hostility between Jews and Samaritans: "He that eats the bread of the Samaritans is like to one who eats the flesh of swine."[10]

---

[8]2 Ki. 17:1-41, 18:9-12,

[9]Mt. 10:5-6.

[10]Bernard Brandon Scott, *Hear Then the Parable: A Commentary on the Parables of Jesus*, "Who's that Masked man?" p. 197.

Part 3—NEAR EASTERN MEDICINE. Where drugs, medicines and doctors are unknown, Semites use oil, wine and honey as medicines. Other scarce articles are also sought as a remedy for the sick. Olive oil and butter cure chapped hands and feet and other areas of the body. When a sore develops, it is rubbed with oil. Dirt and carelessness create skin disorders. Water is scarce and bathing was rare and in some countries, hardly known. One often sees men or women with chapped hands and feet with a layer of hard dirt on them Sometimes, during the cold and hot seasons, the dirt breaks off leaving a deep hole in the skin. Oil softens the dirt and causes it to fall off and heals the skin underneath.

Some healers prescribe medicinal remedies that cannot be procured so that if the patient is not healed they cannot be blamed. For example, water from seven springs from which no one has drunk but virgin girls, soil from seven roads that do not cross each other and on which no one has traveled except virgin girls are recommended as the best medicines. Thus a patient who is not healed feels that the soil and water are not what the healer prescribed.

On one occasion, Jesus placed clay made with saliva on the eyes of a blind man. He did this because the man expected some sort of medicinal remedy. But Jesus simply told the man to "Go, wash and you shall be healed" (see John 9:607). Many ill people had seen other healers using herbs, sacred soil and prescribing complicated formulas. Jesus spat on the soil as a sign that he repudiated the blindness and not because clay would heal the man's eyes. This act proved to the blind man that matter could be changed and was not permanent. The act would make the supplicant wash his face and eyes.

MARTHA AND MARY

But Martha was cumbered about much serving, and came to him, and said, Lord, dost thou not care that my sister hath left me to serve alone? Bid her therefore that she help me. Lk. 10:40-41.

When an honorable guest is entertained, all women and servants in the house drop their other work to serve. In biblical lands, there is nothing more important than entertaining a holy man of great reputation. Women would neglect their babies, their bread in the oven and food on the fire to serve the revered guest first. No woman of the household is exempt from this duty. Some sweep, others rush to borrow bread, plates and other necessities, and still others are occupied with cooking and other preparation.

When the father and mother are deceased or not present, the eldest sister acts as hostess when an eminent person is received in the house. The guest, on his arrival, is immediately encircled by the people who had accompanied him and by those who come to greet him. Family members, although occupied with household duties and preparations, listen earnestly to conversations. Women who are acquaintances or relatives of the acclaimed guest would not hesitate to join the group to listen and to ask questions. Nevertheless, such a familiarity is often criticized by the older and more conservative women who adhere to strict Eastern etiquette.

Jesus was a friend of Lazarus and his sisters, Martha and Mary. He had known them for a long time and had been in their home on previous occasions. This is why Mary considered Jesus a close friend and sat talking to him freely. Although Jesus was a distinguished prophet, Mary treated him as a member of the family.

Martha was overly concerned about her sister. She was worried because she felt there was not enough homage paid to Jesus and she was not willing to see her sister sit idle in his presence. There was much work to be done as there were many guests to be cared for. There were also many curiosity seekers and beggars in addition to the honorable guest and his followers. In the Near East, on such occasions, women must not sit idle in the presence of a notable guest, even if there is nothing to do. In the eyes of strangers, such departures from social etiquette are frowned upon and considered as a lack of hospitality and interest.

Jesus told Martha that she was too careful about social graces and troubled herself over little things. He told her that it was all right for Mary to sit down and talk with him instead of rushing around busying herself with household duties. He needed no further attention. Mary was greatly interested in listening to his words and that was much more important than mere Eastern formalities. This is the reason Jesus said: "But one thing is needful; and Mary hath chosen that good part, which shall not be taken away from her." Mary entertained him with conversation, asked questions and poured her affection on him. She very carefully hung on every word that fell from his lips. For Jesus this was more vital than paying attention to household etiquette. Martha and Mary loved each other. Martha's rebuke to her sister was not due to jealousy but was like that of a mother to a daughter, which a younger sister in the Near East gladly accepts.

CHAPTER 11

NEAR EASTERN HOSPITALITY

And he said unto them, Which of you shall have a friend, and shall go unto him at midnight, and say unto him, Friend, lend me three loaves; Lk. 11:5.

In the Near East no house has a blessing if it does not entertain guests. The common proverb is: "Today he is my guest, tomorrow I will be his." Several extra loaves of bread are always baked for strangers. It often happens that travelers enter a house unexpectedly and bread has to be set before them. The owner of the house asks if they have eaten bread and they usually reply: "Yes, we are not hungry." It is customary for an Eastern guest to decline, at least seven times, when asked if he has eaten. But when the host keeps insisting that the travelers must eat, then they will gladly sit down to the meal.

Bread is baked from day to day and frequently the family supply is exhausted before night time. In the case of an unexpected visitor arriving at night, bread is then borrowed from neighbors. It would be embarrassing for the family to allow guests to depart without setting bread before them. Easterners practice this style of borrowing regardless of the hour of the night. Necessity forces the host to awaken his neighbor and ask him for a loan of three loaves of bread.

A NIGHT VISITOR

And he from within shall answer and say, Trouble me not: the door is now shut, and my children are with me in bed; I cannot rise and give thee. Lk. 11:7.

In the homes of the peasantry, and even in the homes of the fairly wealthy, one often finds two beds spread beside each other. One is used by the father and his sons, the other for the mother and daughters and little children. These two beds are surrounded by other beds on the same floor, occupied by the married sons or by other families sharing the home.

When a stranger knocks at the door at night, the head of the family answers the call because the identity of the stranger is unknown. On such occasions, the children may awaken, and it would be difficult to put them to sleep again. Some men, therefore, excuse themselves by saying, "My children are with me in bed. And if I wake them they will cry." But most men would rise at such times because of the emergency.

The Aramaic text reads somewhat differently: "Would his friend from inside answer, saying to him, Do not trouble me; the door is already locked and my children are with me in bed; I cannot get up and give you bread? I say to you that if because of friendship he will not give him, yet because of his persistence, he will rise and give him as much as he wants. I say to you also, Ask, and it shall be given to you; seek, and you shall find; knock, and it shall be opened to you."[1] So it is with our heavenly Father who will not refuse us when we call to him for our needs.

KNOCKING AND OPENING

And I say unto you, Ask, and it shall be given you; seek, and ye shall find; knock, and it shall be opened unto you. Lk. 11:9.

Borrowing and lending, asking and giving are characteristic of Semites, who believe in doing favors for one another without expectation of return. "Cast your bread upon the water and you will find it again" is a saying in the Near East. It means we should be generous and merciful so that generosity and mercy will be extended to us. Bread and clothing are given to neighbors whether they are able to return them or not. Recall how the Egyptians loaned to the Israelites not only clothing, shoes and other articles but even their

---

[1]Lk. 11:7-9, Aramaic Peshitta text, Lamsa translation.

183

expensive jewelry; but these were not returned by the Hebrews.

Money is loaned without a receipt and is returned with thanks to its owner when convenient to the borrower. Friends and strangers do not hesitate to go to a neighbor's house, knock at the door and ask for favors. Generally, these requests are granted if the seeker is worthy and the borrowing is for a good purpose, such as to pay taxes, buy food supplies and other necessities. When a man's reputation is bad and he is known as extravagant, no one grants him a loan.

Not everyone who knocks receives. There are many ways of knocking and different kinds of people who knock. Women in the house usually can identify the various kinds of knocks. They can easily tell the difference between the knock of a traveler and a beggar. Travelers and guests knock with a stick or a stone at the door. Beggars tap on the ground near the door. The sound of knocking also indicates the urgency. In response to the tap of a beggar, the woman goes to the door with a piece of bread in her hand. Travelers, merchants and preachers are always welcome and their needs are met.

If selfish and deceptive neighbors do favors for each other, how much more will the heavenly Father grant the requests of those who earnestly knock at the door for their needs. [2]

EGG AND SCORPION

Or if he shall ask an egg, will he offer him a scorpion? Lk. 11:12.

In many areas of the Near East, people keep their chickens in the family house. The nests of hens are made of straw, and scorpions are often found in the straw. This is the reason for the reference to egg and scorpion in the above scripture. At night people are afraid to put their hands in the nests, lest scorpions sting them. During the summer months, while people are living in the mountains taking care of their sheep, scorpions crawl into the tents looking for food and are

---

[2]Mt. 7:7, See also Errico and Lamsa, *Aramaic Light on the Gospel of Matthew*, "Asking: Bread—Stone, Fish—Snake," pp. 111-112.

frequently found in the bread and eggs.

GOD GIVES GOOD GIFTS

If ye then being evil, know how to give good gifts unto your children: how much more shall your heavenly Father give the Holy Spirit to them that ask him? Lk. 11:13.

The Aramaic text reads: "So if you, who err, know how to give good gifts to your children, how much more will your Father give the Holy Spirit from heaven to those who ask him?"[3]

The term "evil" in the King James verse of scripture does not mean "an evil one" or "evil things." It means "error, immature, imperfection." Such phrases are very common in the Bible. For example, Jeremiah says: "And as for the evil figs which cannot be eaten, they are so evil. . . " (see Jeremiah 24:3). Again, the Bible refers to trees as being "good or evil." In the case of evil figs, it means "unripe," and in reference to the evil trees, it means trees that produce inedible fruit.

The translation of *beesha* as "error" is more in line with the meaning of the word. A father, being human, may err in giving a gift to a child. During the night a child may cry because he is hungry. The father, instead of giving him a fish, could mistakenly hand him a snake. Or instead of handing him an egg, he could accidently take hold of a scorpion. (See above comment: "Egg and Scorpion.") Parents are always careful not to make these mistakes. They would not want to give wrong things to their children. How much more careful, then, is our heavenly Father who is the source of all knowledge and goodness in giving good gifts to his children.

God gives good gifts through the Holy Spirit. In other words, through the Holy Spirit, God guides those who are seeking gifts. We may ask for things that could be harmful to us and our family. The Holy Spirit will guide and reveal to us whether that which we are

---

[3]Lk. 11:13, Aramaic Peshitta text, Lamsa translation.

seeking is beneficial or not. Only God can discern the difference. The human mind has always failed to see the line of demarcation between good and harmful things. Most of our troubles in this life come because we do not seek God's counsel in the things we undertake and in the gifts we seek. When people are guided by God, they are inspired to do that which is good and beneficial.

STRONG MAN ARMED

When a strong man armed keepeth his palace, his goods are in peace. Lk. 11:21.

Nearly all Near Eastern homes have courtyards where sheep, oxen and cows are kept. In some towns, when a house is large the animals are kept in the home in a room adjoining the family living room. When houses are small, not only animals but wheat and other valuable articles are kept outside in the courtyard. In this case, the owner of the house or a servant sleeps outside to watch the animals and goods.

Banks were unknown in the Near East. Thieves usually attempt to steal animals and goods even though they are guarded day and night. When robbers attack a house, they first disarm and bind the owner so that they can make a safe escape with the stolen sheep or other animals. It requires a great deal of time to take them to a hideaway far away from town.[4]

AN EVIL EYE

The light of the body is the eye: therefore, when thine eye is single, thy whole body also is full of light; but when thine eye is evil, thy body also is full of darkness. Take heed therefore that the light which is in thee be not darkness. Lk. 11:34-35.

---

[4]Mt. 12:29; Mk. 3:27.

Beesha is the Aramaic word for "evil." It has many meanings; therefore, context determines its interpretation. In this verse of scripture, it refers to a "diseased eye." "If your eye is diseased, your whole body will also be dark" is the intended meaning. Semites also use the word *beesha* to express envy and jealousy. They often say, "He is struck by an evil eye," meaning someone envies him. Often mothers will blacken the faces of their children to protect them from men and women who are believed to have an evil eye. A woman never tells another that her baby is very good looking or handsome. Such an utterance could be considered as an evil eye—that is, an envious remark.

A diseased eye also refers to one who is covetous and desires property that does not belong to him. In such a case, the term means all his actions are poisoned and the whole body is dark. A person without envy or covetousness is known as having a "good eye." This refers to a person of pure character whose words and actions bring blessings to others.

Beesha also carries the idea of "naughty." A mother calls a child who misbehaves *beesha*. Easterners further apply the term to things that are unnatural and deceptive. For instance, a walnut with an extremely hard shell to crack open is called *beesha,* "evil walnut."[5]

ALMS INSTEAD OF CEREMONY

But rather give alms of such things as ye have; and behold, all things are clean unto you. Lk. 11:41.

The Aramaic word *zedhqatha,* "alms," derives from the Semitic root *zadaq,* "to become righteous." An Easterner is judged not by what he says but by what he does—that is, by the practice of alms giving and the hospitality he extends to the poor and strangers. Many

---

[5]Mt. 6:22. See also Errico and Lamsa, *Aramaic Light on the Gospel of Matthew,* "Part A—The Eye," pp. 76-77, "A Pure Eye," pp. 102-103.

people give about ten percent of their income as tithes. In the Near East, even thieves and bandits set aside a large share of their ill-gotten goods as an offering to God so that they may be forgiven on the last day. Rich men who have acquired wealth unjustly give alms very generously while they are alive, and gifts are offered at shrines in their names after death.

This utterance was a rebuke against certain Pharisees (see Luke 11: 39-40) who washed their hands before they ate and who prayed in the streets so that they might appear righteous. But they were not interested in showing mercy and compassion to the poor. The high priests and other religious leaders followed the traditions and received gifts but did not practice giving so that they might truly be clean.

GRAVES

Woe unto you, scribes and Pharisees, hypocrites! For ye are as graves which appear not, and the men that walk over them are not aware of them. Lk. 11:44.

In most Near Eastern countries, cemeteries are not taken care of like those in America. Graves soon become covered with weeds and the identity of those who were buried there is lost. However, the graves of prominent and distinguished holy men are usually marked; a stone is placed over them and a smaller stone is placed at each end. It is a sin for Semites to walk over the grave of a holy man. When such graves become a center of worship, a small tomb is built over them; these are decorated with plaster to be distinguished from other graves that are sunken.

THE TOMBS OF THE DEPARTED

Woe unto you! For ye build the sepulchres of the prophets, and your fathers killed them. Truly ye bear witness that ye allow the deeds of your fathers: for they indeed killed them, and ye build their sepulchres. Lk. 11:47-48.

Easterners build tombs only over the graves of rich men and saints, thus creating a small shrine. Some of these tombs become places of prayer and worship. Admirers and followers of the deceased visit them from time to time with offerings that are afterwards given to the poor and wayfarers. These tombs are always decorated with white plaster and are symbolic of purity. Generally, Moslems place a jar of cold water in the tomb so that thirsty travelers may quench their thirst and offer a prayer for the departed saint. Near Eastern Christians, on the anniversary of the death of the saint, go to the grave site with a company of people, kill sheep and cook them; then with bread that they brought from home, they eat the cooked sheep with all who have come to the shrine. (See also Matthew 23:29.)[6]

KEY OF KNOWLEDGE

Woe unto you, lawyers! For ye have taken away the key of knowledge; ye entered not in yourselves, and them that were entering in ye hindered. Lk. 11:52.

The scribes, who were also known as lawyers, had sole authority over the interpretation of Scripture. "The key of knowledge" refers to the authority of these scribes to dispense knowledge. "Key" means "right, authority, power, to open or lock." But they did not go deeply enough into scriptures so that they could understand their spiritual meanings, nor did they allow others to interpret Scripture. The scribes were opposed to all those who differed from them. (See Matthew. 23:13.)

---

[6]See Errico and Lamsa, *Aramaic Light on the Gospel of Matthew,* "Decorating Tombs," pp. 287-288.

The Pharisees and scribes relied on the doctrine of the elders (Oral Law), traditions and teachings of other Jewish teachers of the past. To this day, millions of Christians are supposedly guided by the theology of men who differ in interpretation from one another and are contradictory to the teachings of Scripture.

CHAPTER 12

SECRET COUNCILS

Therefore whatsoever ye have spoken in darkness shall be heard in the light; and that which ye have spoken in the ear in closets shall be proclaimed upon the housetops. Lk. 12:3.

The phrase "in darkness," in this instance, means "in secret." In the Near East, some important councils are held in partially dark places so that people will not know what is being said. A group of men can be seen assembled and seated in a corner of the house whispering to one another.

The inner chamber, or closet, is a small place (room) in the house wherein people find privacy. Some of the decisive secret councils are held in this inner chamber. In some homes these small, private rooms are used for sleeping and prayer, especially in the homes of the rich.[1]

When things are spoken secretly, they are generally made known, for people tell one another. Facial expressions and gestures of the hands give the secrets away. People will interpret what you say by these expressions and gestures. (See also Mark 4:22; Luke 8:17.)

ENEMIES OF THE SOUL

But I will forewarn you whom ye shall fear: Fear him, which after he hath killed hath power to cast into hell; yea, I say unto you, fear him. Lk. 12:5.

Jesus warns about the antagonists to truth—those who were opposed to the gospel of the kingdom. Many of Jesus' followers were sooner or later to die for the truth that they were representing and

---

[1]See 1 Ki. 22:25, 2 Ki. 9:2.

practicing. He admonished his followers not to fear those who kill the body because they cannot harm the soul. The physical form is but a garment in which the soul is clothed or manifested.

Jesus' disciples and followers were warned to be careful of false teachings, sin, and evil influences that can destroy not only the body but also the entire being. Some malevolent teachers caused the faithful to go astray from the way of God and worship pagan deities, thus succeeding in corrupting their souls.

The term "hell" means "mental suffering, continual regret." God, being a good and loving Father, is not the author of hell. Man creates his own difficulties and his own hell. The only way one can overcome these difficulties is with the help of God.

GOD'S DIVINE CARE

Are not five sparrows sold for two farthings, and not one of them is forgotten before God? But even the very hairs of your head are all numbered. Fear not therefore: ye are of more value than many sparrows. Lk. 12:6-7.

God's care is manifested throughout the universe. Jesus assures his disciples of God's guidance and continual protection against evil forces. God is constantly mindful of all creation and creatures; even the little sparrows that look so unimportant are clothed and protected through God's power and care. God is even aware when they are sold.

Humans are more important than sparrows and other creatures. Humans are created in the image and likeness of God, and therefore, when even a hair falls from a person's head, God feels it and knows it. God is the very essence of life and that life connects with all living creatures great and small.

JESUS REFUSED TO MEDDLE

And one of the company said unto him, Master, speak to my brother, that he divide the inheritance with me. And he said unto him, Man, who made me a judge or divider over you? And he said unto them, Take heed, and beware of covetousness: for a man's life consisteth not in the abundance of the things which he possesseth. Lk. 12:13-15.

Pious Eastern men and friends at the town gate or on housetops settle disagreements among the people. Most of the disputants avoid and shun government officials and regular judges. In regard to the case brought to Jesus, the man was probably testing him.

Jesus refused to become entangled in an inheritance argument between two brothers. It appears that the one who asked Jesus to speak to his brother about dividing the inheritance with him was greedy. He wanted him to induce his brother to give him a larger share, which he probably did not deserve; he may have been the younger son, who usually receives a smaller portion of an inheritance.

Jesus was not a judge or a divider of property. There were priests and scribes who took care of such matters. The lesson here is to not meddle with the affairs of others. However, one may provide assistance when people sincerely seek help and counsel.

BARNS

And he spake a parable unto them saying, the ground of a certain rich man brought forth plentifully: And he thought within himself, saying, What shall I do, because I have no room where to bestow my fruits? And he said This will I do: I will pull down my barns, and build greater; and there will I bestow all my fruits and my goods. Lk. 12:16-18.

Semites work for months plowing and harvesting and then rest the remainder of the year. They store family food and winter supplies, such as wheat, oil, olives and cereals in a barn. Owing to difficulties in transportation, every town depends on its own supplies for the winter and every family raises food for its own use. There is little buying or selling.

In good years, they store wheat and other supplies in barns against the bad years. At times, the crops continue to be abundant and fruitful for several years and the barns become filled with wheat. The owner of the barn then builds an extension or erects a new and larger barn where he stores the increased surplus. When abundant wealth is accumulated from the cornucopia of his rich crops, the owner ceases working and producing. He begins to live lavishly, eating, drinking and entertaining.

Money is scarce in the Near East and a man's wealth consists mainly of produce such as wheat, barley, beans and cereals. Easterners consider a man who has many barns as wealthy and they envy his position. Owing to luxurious living and the comforts of life, some of these men forget their God and their religious principles. They scorn others who have not succeeded in producing rich and abundant crops as they have done and are very happy when lean years happen. Their neighbors and friends are compelled to beg for supplies from these wealthy men.

They often think to themselves: "I don't care how long this condition continues in the country. I have everything stored for years. All I have to concern myself with is eating, drinking and having a good time." This happiness is not interrupted until a sudden illness or death takes place and the wealthy men are lowered into their graves. If they leave no sons, their food supplies are divided among the people of the town.

THE LITTLE FLOCK

Fear not, little flock; for it is your Father's good pleasure to give you the kingdom. Lk. 12:32.

Usually, a large flock is composed of several thousand sheep belonging to numerous Eastern families. Several shepherds take care of the large flock of sheep. Others are assigned to protect them from bandits. In this way the flock is very secure. Most people, therefore, prefer to have their sheep in a large flock rather than in a small one. Small flocks consist of the sheep of poor families. They have only one shepherd and are often victims of bandits. The owners are in constant fear of robbers.

Jesus' followers were a little flock in comparison to the organized religion of Palestine with its high priests and scribes. They were hated and persecuted but they trusted in their lord for protection against all enemies. Even after their lord's crucifixion, he promised to be with them as a guarantee of their security. He promised that the Holy Spirit would guide them in all their activities. The work of the kingdom would continue through them.

AWAITING THE MASTER'S RETURN

Let your loins be girded about, and your lights burning; And ye yourselves like unto men that wait for their lord, when he will return from the wedding; that when he cometh and knocketh, they may open unto him immediately. Lk. 12:35-36.

When a master of a house is visiting in the town or is on a journey, his servants have to wait for his return and keep watch. Eastern Semites do not follow any itinerary and they own no time pieces so punctuality does not mean anything to them. They have no formalities or certain protocol to meet. A man might be invited to dine around six in the evening at his neighbor's house, but the supper may not begin until eight or nine.

While the lord of the house is away, the women and children have their supper; after they have eaten, the servants are served. A portion of the food is kept for the master until he returns. While the women and children are asleep, the servants must keep awake and be ready to greet and serve their master upon his arrival home. Easterners have no regular hours for meals. They eat when hungry.

At times, a man may be invited to dine at a friend's home, but when he returns, he may be more hungry than when he left. Thus, if the master should find both the women and servants asleep with no one to set food before him, he becomes severely irritated. And in his anger, he may discharge his servants and punish the women. It is a terrible disgrace for the master to wait on himself or to be locked out.

Some servants are very shrewd. They study their master's movements and calculate when he might return. If they think he will be late, they go to sleep, expecting to awaken upon his arrival. Their calculations, at times, prove to be incorrect; they sleep so soundly that they do not hear when the master comes to the door. To their surprise, they are awakened with kicks. Faithful servants who love their master would never sleep. No matter at what hour their lord may return, they stay alert and watchful. At frequent intervals they go to the door and look outside to see if he is coming.

When he arrives, they immediately rush to take off his shoes, bring him water and set bread before him. Eastern masters are devoted to these kinds of servants. They tell them their secrets, their losses and gains, their happiness and sorrow. They share everything with them and when in difficulty, they seek their advice. Some masters would rather part with their sons than their faithful servants. There are also servants who would give their lives for their lord.

This parable refers to the sudden return of Jesus. Just as servants are unable to know when their lord will return, so his disciples cannot tell the time or the hour of their master's return. All the followers of Jesus' teachings must be alert and keep constant vigilance, like faithful servants who wait for their master. When Jesus comes, faithful followers will be ready to greet him with joy rather than be awakened from sleep with disappointment and regret.[2]

SETTING THE EARTH ON FIRE

I am come to send fire on the earth; and what will I, if it be already kindled? Lk. 12:49.

---

[2]Many modern NT scholars believe that early Christian scribes placed this parable on Jesus' lips. In other words, it did not originate with Jesus.

The Aramaic text reads: "I am come to set the earth on fire; and I wish to do it, if it has not already been kindled."[3] "To set the earth on fire" is a Semitic expression meaning "to upset, stir up trouble, to disturb its peace." When taxes are high, Easterners say, "The government is burning us."

Jesus' gospel of the kingdom of God was to upset the whole world, but he discovered that it was already upset and deeply troubled. The Jews were divided into sects, and bitter feelings of rivalry existed between them. There was much discontent among the people against the government and the ecclesiastic authorities who had betrayed them for the sake of retaining their social and religious positions.

There were rumors of wars, revolutions and uprisings. Jesus' teachings would add to the fire that was already kindled. His teachings also helped spread the flames abroad so as to upset the old order and bring in a better day for all humanity.

JESUS MINDFUL OF HIS DEATH

But I have a baptism to be baptized with; and how am I straitened till it be accomplished! Lk. 12:50.

The Aramaic text reads: " I have a baptism to be baptized with; and I am oppressed until it is fulfilled."[4] Jesus speaks of his death. He was to be sprinkled (baptized) with his own blood. The scene of his death on the cross was constantly and continually before his mind's eye and it oppressed him. (See Matthew 20:22.)

The Hebrew prophets had predicted the Messiah's rejection and death. They themselves had been put to death for the sake of the truth that they had preached. The political system of their times could not take the message of these men of God. They had to be killed. Thus, Jesus would not escape his destiny. His gospel of the kingdom was

---

[3]Lk. 12:49, Aramaic Peshitta text, Lamsa translation.
[4]Lk. 12:50, Aramaic Peshitta text, Lamsa translation.

dangerous to the existing order of things. Religious authorities and political powers had to silence the prophet from Galilee. Jesus knew that he faced the same fate as the Hebrew prophets.

WEATHER FORECASTS AND POLITICS

And he said also to the people, When ye see a cloud rise out of the west, straightway ye say, There cometh a shower; and so it is. And when ye see the south wind blow, ye say, There will be heat; and it cometh to pass. Ye hypocrites, ye can discern the face of the sky and of the earth; but how is it that ye do not discern this time? Lk. 12:54-56.

Meteorological instruments were not known in the Near East, but from ancient times the weather had always been forecast. The hot days in summer are predicted during the cold days in December and January. In the same manner, cold days of winter are predicted in the hot summer months.

The word for "predicting or prognosticating" is *bakhoreh*. Forecasters are generally illiterate men and women who have made a study of weather conditions. They are found only in certain places in the Near East. The method of calculating and forecasting is a secret that is handed down orally from one generation to another like the arts of healing and certain crafts.

Warnings about cold winters and hot summers are announced from month to month and precautions taken accordingly. Men and women who forecast weather conditions are called seers and fortune tellers. They also interpret dreams and predict periods of prosperity and peace, poverty and calamity. They are familiar with political situations and are consulted by the authorities. This was no doubt the power that Joseph possessed when he was in Egypt.

Jesus upbraided the people for not trying to discern and understand the situation of their day. He told them a change in their political, religious circumstances had to come if lasting peace was to be obtained. The poor and oppressed must be relieved.

To accomplish this, the Jews must be willing to share their

religion with the pagan world. God's truth that was revealed to Israel must be revealed to the Gentiles also. The people, at that time, failed to see the urgency of his message. They knew how to forecast the weather, but they did not know how to discern and interpret God's ways and the signs of the impending calamities so that they might escape.

CHAPTER 13

A FEAST, FEUD AND RAID

There were present at that season some that told him of the Galilaeans, whose blood Pilate had mingled with their sacrifices. Lk. 13:1

Sometime before Jesus began his ministry this bloody incident had taken place. It most likely happened in the early days of Pilate's administration. Dr. Lamsa suggests that this verse may refer to those Galileans who were the followers of Judas of Galilee. He was a radical dissident and leader (Acts 5:37) who attempted to free his country from Roman rule.

There exists, however, no other written historical record of this event. Nonetheless, it may have taken place in Jerusalem when some of these Galileans, after their leader's death, went to the temple to offer their sacrifices, and Pilate's troops caught and slaughtered them. Pilate seems to have been informed of their presence in the holy city and so had them executed.

In Near Eastern countries, a religious feast is the only occasion when government officials hope to capture bandits and insurgents. These officials know that dissidents will try to attend religious feasts; thus soldiers and secret service men are made alert and stationed at strategic places during the celebration. This special guard is also necessary to help keep the peace because many enemies attend these festivals, and old feuds are avenged with bloodshed during these times.[1]

"Whose blood Pilate had mingled with their sacrifices" means that they were slain on the same day as the animals that they brought for the temple sacrifices. Semites often say to each other, "I will mingle your goods with your blood," meaning "I will slay you for acquiring such goods unjustly."

---

[1] Acts 21:27.

SOME WILL NOT ENTER

When once the master of the house is risen up, and hath shut the door, and ye begin to stand without, and to knock at the door, saying, Lord, Lord, open unto us; and he shall answer and say unto you, I know you not whence ye are: Then shall ye begin to say, We have eaten and drunk in thy presence and thou hast taught in our streets. Lk. 13:25-26.

Jesus speaks of participation in God's kingdom. One must strive to enter (participate in) this kingdom. The gospel of God's kingdom is to be declared in all nations and among all peoples. Many will embrace Jesus' message and enter into his kingdom, but the day comes when the opportunity to participate in the kingdom will cease. In other words, the door remains open as long as people are alive. God's kingdom is for living here on earth. Only those who have accepted and practiced the principles of the kingdom enjoy its full fruits. Others who failed to practice what Jesus taught put themselves outside with the door shut.

Neither Jesus nor God shuts the door on anyone. People cut themselves off from the joys of the kingdom through their own willfulness and continuance in practicing evil. This saying is meant to encourage people to make great efforts to participate in the kingdom now so they won't find themselves left out.[2]

FIRST WILL BE LAST

And, behold, there are last which shall be first, and there are first which shall be last. Lk. 13:30.

Verses 29 and 30 in the Aramaic text read: "And they will come from the east and from the west and from the south and from the

---

[2]"The closed door" idea in this verse most likely is not Jesus' teaching. It follows the final judgment theme. This is not in keeping with Jesus' style of preaching. He admonished and encouraged his listeners to turn to God and warned of the consequences of practicing evils. However, he never threatened.

north, and sit down in the kingdom of God. And behold there are some who are last who will be first, and there are some who are first who will be last."[3] In the days to come many races from all over the world will embrace Jesus' teaching of the kingdom—nations that during the time of Jesus had not even been heard of; nations and peoples not yet born would enter into the kingdom.

Many in Israel, who had been called first, would be the last to realize Jesus' message of the kingdom. They were the first people in the world to whom God had sent prophets and had given his laws and commandments. The Jews were given the first opportunity to come to the great banquet and to enter the messianic kingdom. Many of them were among the first to accept Jesus' gospel of the kingdom, but there were others who had rejected him and his message. Those who rejected him would become last. When they refused to come, others such as the Galileans, Arameans and Syrians were called and therefore became the first

Jesus came first to the Jews because they had been called by God, and their prophets had shepherded them throughout the centuries. The Galilean prophet had also admonished his disciples to preach first to the Jews and the lost sheep of the house of Israel and then to the Gentiles. Israel was to be first and the Gentiles last, but it reversed.[4]

JESUS ANSWERS WARNING

And he said unto them, Go ye, and tell that fox, Behold, I cast out devils, and I do cures to day and to morrow, and the third day I shall be perfected. Nevertheless I must walk to day, and to morrow and the day following: for it cannot be that a prophet perish out of Jerusalem. Lk. 13:32-33.

---

[3]Lk. 13:29-30, Aramaic Peshitta text, Lamsa translation.
[4]See Mt. 19:30; 20:16; Mk. 10:31. See also Errico and Lamsa, *Aramaic Light on the Gospel of Matthew*, "The First Shall Be Last," p. 248.

The Aramaic text reads: "Jesus said to them, Go and tell that fox, Behold, I cast out demons and I heal today and tomorrow, and on the third day, I will be finished. But I must do my work today and tomorrow, and I will leave the next day, because it is impossible that a prophet should perish outside of Jerusalem."[5] (The word "fox" in Aramaic, just as it does in English, refers to someone who is shrewd or deceptive.)

The Aramaic word *mishtamleh* means "to be through, finished and complete." Jesus was asked to leave the town by those who knew Herod was planning to kill him. His reply to Herod was that he would remain until his work was done; that is, he would leave on the third day when he had completed what he came to do.

Herod was under the impression that John the Baptist had risen from the dead and was performing miracles. Besides, many people considered Jesus as a disciple of John the Baptist. Jesus was baptized by John and in his early ministry he followed in the footsteps of his predecessor. John was now deceased and the Herodians considered Jesus his successor. They were afraid Jesus might instigate a rebellion to avenge the blood of the beloved Baptist.

Jesus had important work to do before he could leave. There were many who needed their diseases healed. It was most probable that Jesus had promised to visit these sick people who desired his healing power. Jesus was not willing to depart before completing his mission.

---

[5]Lk. 13:32-33, Aramaic Peshitta text, Lamsa translation.

CHAPTER 14

THE SABBATH

And answered them, saying, Which of you shall have an ass or an ox fallen into a pit, and will not straightway pull him out on the sabbath day?.
Lk. 14:5

The Aramaic text reads: "And he said unto them, which one of you, if his son or his ox should fall into a pit on the Sabbath day, would not immediately pull and bring him out?" The Aramaic word for "ass" is *hmara*. The possessive case is *hmareh*, meaning "his ass." In Aramaic, "his ox" is *toreh* and "his son" is *breh*. It seems very likely that the Greek translator mistook the word *breh*, "his son," for *hmareh*, "his ass." This could easily occur especially if the manuscript was mutilated. Translators are aware of this difficulty when a part of a word cannot be read properly.

Jesus used a "son" and an "ox" as examples, contrasting both a human being and an animal falling into distress on the Sabbath. There were, no doubt, some religious extremists who would not render a service for the sake of an animal on the Sabbath day. They would let it stay in the pit until the next day, and if the animal died, it would not make any difference. In the Near East, there are some Jewish adherents who will not extinguish a fire on the Sabbath even if it threatens to destroy their own home. But in regard to animals Rabbi Samuel Tobias Lachs tells us:

There is sufficient material indicating that one could and should save an animal on the Sabbath or on a Festival. On the point raised in this verse it is not possible to say with certainty what the scribes would have said in our Lord's day. Opinions were still divided in the Rabbinical schools at a much later time. Some said that if an animal fell into a pit on the Sabbath, it was lawful to bring food to it there. Others held that it was further permissible to place a mattress and cushions under it so that it might get out

204

by its own exertion. The opposite of this approach has come down to us: "And if it [an animal] falls into a pit or a ditch, he shall not raise it on the Sabbath." This regulation, however, does not represent the view of rabbinic Judaism.[1]

If a man would not pull his ox out of a ditch on the Sabbath, he would certainly rescue his own son if he had fallen into a pit. The Sabbath was one of the most sacred Jewish institutions and strictly observed by the Jews in Judea. The province of Judea was where the priesthood was established and was the center of worship. This was not the case in Galilee where the people were non-Jews by race but adherents to the Jewish faith. Here the Sabbath was not so strictly observed. Jesus was often criticized for healing and performing miracles on the Sabbath.

If a father would lift his son from a pit on the Sabbath, how much more important it is to heal a sick man who is suffering pain from dropsy. In this way Jesus explained the importance of healing the infirm and relieving suffering every day. Humans are more important than the Sabbath because they are children of God. The Sabbath was instituted to help humanity—to provide a day of rest—so that people would not have to work seven days a week.

SPIRITUAL FOOD

And when one of them that sat at meat with him heard these things, he said unto him, Blessed is he that shall eat bread in the kingdom of God.
Lk. 14:15

"Eat bread" is a Semitic idiom that means "to be well received," in this case, to be well received in God's kingdom. To eat bread with a king or a prince is a great honor. Kings and princes never eat with those who are unwelcome in the palace. One can hear people say, "I

---

[1]Samuel T. Lachs, *A Rabbinic Commentary on the New Testament.* "What Man of You," p. 200.

dined with the ruler," meaning "I was well received and favored." The reference here is to the eternal joy in being present in God's kingdom. "Bread" also means "truth," that is, "the bread of life." Jesus spoke, as well, of drinking wine in the kingdom of God. "Wine" can also refer to "joy, teaching and inspiration." Jesus used these words metaphorically and the people of his day understood their meaning.

God's kingdom represents peace, eternal joy, harmony and an inner understanding of spiritual life. Those who suffer for the sake of the truth rejoice now in the kingdom's present manifestation and in its final consummation.

PARABLE OF A GREAT SUPPER

And they all with one consent began to make excuse. The first said unto him, I have bought a piece of ground, and I must needs go and see it: I pray thee have me excused. . . . And the lord said unto the servant, Go out into the highways and hedges, and compel them to come in, that my house may be filled. Lk 14:18, 23.

Part 1—THE PARABLE. With this parable, Jesus changed another invalid traditional idea about God's kingdom. This parable appears only in the gospels of Matthew and Luke. Some New Testament scholars believe that the Matthew version of this parable (Matthew 22:2-14) underwent heavy editing, so much so that the original intent has completely disappeared. They claim that Matthew's version of the parable does not carry the authentic voice of Jesus.[2] Matthew interprets the parable for his own teaching purposes. (This was a common practice for all three gospel writers—Matthew, Mark and Luke.)

Contrastingly, these scholars claim that Luke's version retains Jesus' initial structure of the parable or at least something close to it.

---

[2]See Errico and Lamsa, *Aramaic Light on the Gospel of Matthew,* "Parable of the Wedding Feast" and "A Wedding Garment," pp. 268-271.

Luke, evidently, had other sources for this story and did not rely on Matthew. The following is a translation from the Aramaic text:

A man gave a banquet, and invited many. Now at the time of the banquet, he sent his servant to tell those who had been invited: Look! Everything is ready for you. Come!

Every single one of them began to make excuses. The first one said: I have just bought a field, and I have to go and check it out. I beg you to let me be excused.

Another said: I have just bought five yoke of oxen, and I have to go and inspect them. So, I beg you to allow me to be excused.

Yet another said: I have just taken a wife, and because of this, I cannot come. Now then, the servant returned and reported to his master these things.

Then the master of the house became furious. He said to his servant: Go out quickly into the streets and marketplaces of the city. Bring back the poor, the afflicted, the maimed, and the blind, so that my house may be filled.[3]

In the Near East, one must have an abundance of food not only to serve the guests but to show one's wealth as well. Evidently, this was a wealthy man because he had the means to put on a huge supper. All the invitations, by word of mouth through the servant, had been issued. Everything was set for the feasting, so the servant was sent out again, according to the custom, to inform the guests that all was ready.

Now the guests began to make excuses. The first one bought a field and he had to look it over. In the Near East when a man purchases a field, he usually places a deposit on the land. Then the seller and purchaser agree on a specific time to inspect the field. If the purchaser fails to check the land during the specified time, he either loses the deposit or he must pay the balance upon which they had agreed.

The second invited guest told the servant that he had bought five

---

[3]Lk. 14:16-24, Aramaic Peshitta text, Errico.

yoke of oxen. Oxen and horses are purchased on a trial basis. The buyer is free to return the animals if they are not suited for his purpose. Usually the seller and the buyer must both be present when the animals are inspected. Also, witnesses must be present during this tryout period.

The third man's excuse was that he had taken a wife. According to Jewish law, men are excused from going to war if they are about to marry (Deuteronomy 24:5). In Islamic countries when a man marries, he is exempt from the military for a year and from any other governmental obligations that would take him away from his new wife. This law will also excuse the man if he should take a second wife the following year.

But as far as the parable is concerned, all three excuses were a charade. Why? Because all of them had been invited before any purchase of property or animals or taking a wife. They all had received and accepted invitations when the servant had first announced the dinner party. They were snubbing the host who was giving the great supper.

The guests simply did not want to attend the special feast. Their feeble apologies were contrived and the servant and the host knew it. The second appearance of the servant at their homes served only as a call that all was ready for them to participate in the celebration. These guests had slighted and insulted the servant's master and gracious host. However, the master's response to this social outrage was even more surprising!

The master commanded his servant to go out into the streets and gather the lame, the blind, the maimed and street people. Immediately, the servant obeyed his master's orders and brought in the outcasts. Although the dining room was now teeming with the "poor and afflicted," the host wanted more guests. So he sent his servant out into the highways and byways looking for additional people to attend. He ordered his servant to "urge" the people to come. This insistence on attendance is typical Near Eastern etiquette. Usually one must "urge" an individual no less than seven times.

Part 2—NEAR EASTERN HOSPITALITY. The Aramaic word

Alesso means "to urge, insist." A host will almost beg his guests to attend with such sayings as: "You must come to my house. By the head of my son, I will not eat if you are not present. My house is your house, and I am your servant." They do this because no party is a success without crowds of people and a long waiting line of guests outside. With such impressive attendance, the popularity and reputation of the host spreads throughout the town. In certain areas of the Near East, the host will give presents to his guests after the feast is over. The host of this great supper wanted his house overflowing with guests.

There is some of Jesus' humor in this parable, although it is sad and pathetic for the host. Imagine a wealthy man's house filled with poverty-stricken street people, the lame, the afflicted, and the blind at his sumptuous table? These people would not have the refinement of those who were originally invited. What must have taken place when they were dinning? And, of course, the parable is greatly exaggerated.

When the master invited all these despised and unfortunate people into his home, he lost his honor. But, by the same token, when he opened the supper to society's outcasts, he was mocking the ones who were previously invited. The rich man identifies himself with social and economic rejects. He had a dinner party full of society's nobodies. What a supper!

Jesus' reveals God's kingdom in a new way. God's presence is with the lower class, the poor and the outcasts. Jesus had declared in his beatitude: "Delighted are the poor for God's kingdom belongs to you."[4] Society's religiously admissible and professionally acceptable declined the invitation to celebrate God's presence in their midst. Now we discover God's sovereign presence in the oddest places and with the most inconceivable people. Jesus mixed socially with sinners, harlots and tax collectors and celebrated God's presence with them.

---

[4]Lk. 6:20, Aramaic Peshitta text, Errico.

COUNTING THE COST OF DISCIPLESHIP

For which of you, intending to build a tower, sitteth not down first and counteth the cost, whether he have sufficient to finish it? Lest haply, after he hath laid the foundation, and is not able to finish it, all that behold it begin to mock him, Saying, This man began to build, and was not able to finish, Lk. 14:28-30.

Towers were built around a city wall as a kind of fortification. In peacetime, watchmen generally manned these towers. They kept watch day and night. All ancient cities had walls with towers for the watchmen and soldiers during times of danger.

Towers were built in villages and in vineyards as well. What Jesus means here is this: Before laying the foundation to build a tower in his town or vineyard, a person first sits down and estimates the cost. He must see whether he has sufficient money to complete his project, lest he find himself in an embarrassing situation.

In Luke 14:26, we read: "He who comes to me and does not put aside his father and his mother and his brothers and his sisters and his wife and his children and even his own life cannot be a disciple to me."[5] The King James Version of this verse incorrectly translates the term "put aside" as "hate."

Jesus admonished his disciples and followers to sit down and examine their strength and courage before they joined his ranks. He wanted them to become aware that in following him and the principles of the kingdom that he taught, they placed themselves in danger. They might be arrested, convicted and forced to carry their own crosses to the place where they would be crucified. This serves as a warning to anyone who might think that becoming an adherent to the gospel of the kingdom is easy.

---

[5]Aramaic Peshitta text, Lamsa translation.

CHAPTER 15

A HUNDRED SHEEP

What man of you, having an hundred sheep, if he lose one of them, doth not leave the ninety and nine in the wilderness, and go after that which is lost, until he find it? Lk. 15:4

Near Easterners used to consider one hundred as the highest and most prized number. It was the largest figure that most of them could count and understand. Generally, sheep raising people and clans were simple and illiterate; figures over one hundred could only be understood by a few.

Most Semites either have one hundred sheep or strive to obtain that special number. People consider a man who owns a hundred sheep as a man of substance and living comfortably. The wealthy are the exception because they usually own several thousand sheep and goats.

The desire to have a hundred sheep is so strong that no one would like to see the number of his sheep fall below the coveted figure. Therefore, when a man who has one hundred sheep loses one of them, he feels totally devastated over the lost sheep more than a man who has only seventy-five and perhaps may have lost two or three. They are both concerned, but the one who had one hundred feels worse.

Jesus used this number because it was well known among the people. God does not reject anyone but ceaselessly searches for those who have lost their way and rejoices when they are found. So it is that God, like a good shepherd or as a man who owns a hundred sheep, always cares for his children—the human family. A parent's heart and mind will also be with the child who has gone astray and is more than happy when the erring child returns to God's kingdom.

At that time, many Pharisees and scribes doubted the wisdom and correctness of such close friendship with tax collectors and sinners. There is an old rabbinic rule from Mekhita that reads: "Let not a man associate with the wicked, not even to bring him nigh to the Law." This, of course, was a very pointed criticism against what Jesus practiced and taught. He opened the door of the kingdom to everyone. This parable reveals Jesus' attitude and concern for all people.[1]

THE LOST COIN

Either what woman having ten pieces of silver, if she lose one piece, doth not light a candle, and sweep the house, and seek diligently till she find it? And when she hath found it, she calleth her friends and her neighbours together, saying, Rejoice with me; for I have found the piece which I had lost. Lk. 15:8-9.

In a Near Eastern home, it is not unusual for five or six families to live under the same roof. Each family occupies a part of the square shaped house. Family ties are very sacred and Semites are extremely clanish. One often sees a father, his married sons and their uncles with their families living together. It is also common for families not related by blood to live together. The women of these families and their neighbors visit each other with utter freedom. They come and go, share food, work and gossip together.

Commonly, women admire one another's garments and ornaments. One of the first things to attract their attention is the necklace that is often made up of coins that a woman has earned. Or, the necklace may be a family heirloom which is a sacred treasure and very valuable. In the Near East, toys as we know them were unknown, so children often played with the necklaces of their mothers, at times inadvertently breaking them. The coins scatter everywhere and some become lost.

If a woman loses any of her coins, all the women in the house are alerted and become embarrassed. They are apt to be suspected of

---

[1]See Mt. 18:12-14 and Errico and Lamsa, *Aramaic Light on the Gospel of Matthew,* "Lost Sheep" p.233.

taking the coins. This makes all the women in the household and their neighbors diligently look for the coin or coins. The house is carefully swept, a candle is lighted and a close search is made around all the corners and in the dark places. If the coin is not found, women visitors leave with great regrets.

Then, within a few hours, the news spreads throughout the village that a coin is lost and may have been stolen. The entire atmosphere of the town changes. Some of the visitors will wish that they had never gone to the house on that day. But if the coin is found, its owner goes from house to house informing the neighbors of her joy. She will remove every thought of suspicion by saying with gratitude: "I have found my lost coin and I knew that no one had stolen it. It was in my house." All the women neighbors then rejoice with her and everyone breathes a sigh of relief.

The meaning is the same as in the parable of the hundred sheep. It is vitally important to reach everyone, including those who may have lost their way, and bring them into the kingdom. The strong desire to have one hundred sheep and the powerful emotional drive to find the lost coin is the attitude we are to maintain toward everyone. God's kingdom is all inclusive and excludes no one.

A FATHER HAD TWO SONS

And he said, A certain man had two sons: And the younger of them said to his father, Father, give me the portion of goods that falleth to me. And he divided unto them his living. And not many days after the younger son gathered all together, and took his journey into a far country, and there wasted his substance with riotous living. . . . And he said unto him, Son, thou art ever with me, and all that I have is thine. It was meet that we should make merry, and be glad: for this thy brother was dead, and is alive again; and was lost, and is found. Lk. 15:11-13, 31-32.

Part 1—THE BACKGROUND. Of all the stories that Jesus told, the most famous is the parable that Bible translators have named "The Prodigal Son." The truth is that Jesus never titled any of his parables. Many New Testament scholars believe that Jesus also never interpreted any of his narratives. Nevertheless, we find that the synoptic gospels—Matthew, Mark and Luke—record Jesus interpreting some of his own stories. Again, these scholars suggest that the gospel writers or scribes placed these interpretations on Jesus' lips. The gospel scribes were interpreting his parables to meet the growing needs of the new Christian communities. However, Jesus' purpose for telling these stories was to proclaim God's kingdom to everyone.

Jesus' parables are extremely important. They reveal his discernment of God's activity in a world that did not recognize how God's presence moves with, among and through humanity. It was Jesus' vision of God. He understood that God is always involved with humanity but not in the usual ways one often thinks. Jesus' narratives were meant to change people's thinking and perception concerning God's kingdom. Through these parables people learned about God's nature, ways and dealings with the human family.

The parable of the so-called "Prodigal Son" evolves around three main characters and not just the son who went astray. It tells us about the father's nature, and how this father responds to both his sons. This tale is about family relationships couched in an ancient, Semitic Near Eastern household. Jesus weaves his moving and dramatic story around a specific family idea, mainly parental guidance and love.

The psychology of a Semitic Near Eastern family is different from that of a Western family. The moment Jesus began his story with "A man had two sons," his listeners knew there was a problem. He introduces tension in his parable with his opening phrase. The Hebrew Bible contains many stories of friction between brothers—the narratives of Cain and Abel, Ishmael and Isaac, Jacob and Esau, Joseph and his brothers and many other family stories. The following is the entire parable of "a man had two sons" from the Aramaic Peshitta text.

Part 2—THE PARABLE: AN ARAMAIC TRANSLATION.

A man had two sons. Now his younger son said to him: My

father give me the portion that is coming to me from your house. So he divided his property between them.

And after some days, his younger son quickly collected everything that was his share and went into a far country, and there he squandered his substance living lavishly.

Now after he had spent everything, there happened a great famine in that country, and he began to lack. So he went and connected with one of the citizens of that country, and he sent him to his field to feed hogs. Now he was longing to feed his belly from the carob beans that the hogs were eating, but no one was giving to him.

And when he came to himself, he said: How many hired hands are now in my father's house abounding in bread and here I am perishing from the famine. I will get up and go to my father and tell him: My father, I sinned against heaven and before you. I no longer deserve to be called your son; make me as one of your hired hands. Then he got up and went to his father.

And while he still was at a distance, his father saw him and felt compassion for him. So he ran and fell upon his neck and kissed him. But his son said to him: My father, I sinned against heaven and before you; I do not deserve to be called your son.

But his father said to his servants: Bring out the best robe and clothe him, and put a ring on his finger, supply him with shoes. Bring out the fat ox, and let us eat and be festive. Because this my son was dead but is alive. He was lost but is found. So they began to be festive.

But there was his son, the elder one, who was out in the field. Now as he was coming, he came up close to the house, he heard the sound of many singing. He called to one of the boys and asked him: What is this? He said to him: Your brother has come, and your father has killed the fat ox because he got him back in good health.

Now he became furious so he was not wanting to go in. Then his father came out and pleaded with him. Now he said to his father: See, how many years I have slaved for you and never went against your orders. Yet you never gave me even a goat that I might throw a party with my friends. But this son of yours, after he had squandered your wealth with harlots, then came home, you killed the fat ox.

His father said to him: My son, you are always with me, and everything that is mine is yours. It was necessary for us to be festive and joyful because this brother of yours was dead but is alive and was lost but is found![2]

Usually a Near Eastern father centers his attention on the firstborn son. After all, he is the heir and successor. This special relationship between the father and the firstborn boy can and often does create problems with the younger son or siblings. Jealousy, disputes, and antagonism can arise between the oldest and the youngest. The older brother has complete authority over his mother, younger brothers and sisters, especially in the absence of his father. He can buy and sell, receive guests, hire and fire laborers and see after his father's servants. If it happens that the firstborn boy is young and lacks understanding, he often misuses his powers.

From early childhood, rivalry and competitiveness exist between the two brothers. The reason for this is that the younger brother does not receive the attention that the older brother receives. The best garments are made for the firstborn and a larger and more delicious portion of food is served to him. The younger brother is never consulted and even when he gives sound advice, his counsel is ignored.

While fathers invariably take sides with the elder son, the mother is more friendly toward the younger. But she has no say in household affairs, especially where money and property are concerned. Her task is solely one of reconciliation. She tries to make peace between her sons, but if she fails, the younger son secures his property and leaves home.

The younger boy either goes to the house of a friend or to another town where he would be away from the brother he dislikes. Rebecca advised Jacob to leave his father's house and go to Assyria, to the house of his uncle Laban, because his brother Esau hated him. Jacob despised Esau because he was the firstborn and his father's favorite son.

---

[2]Lk. 15:11-32, Aramaic Peshitta text, Errico.

According to Jesus' parable, the younger son asks for his inheritance right away. In the Near East, family property consists of sheep, food supplies, lands and a little cash. This property does not belong just to the father, as in America, but to all male members, who have an equal share in it. A son of twelve years of age is often married. Frequently, after the marriage, he lives with his father's family. Whether married or not, if the boy decides to leave his father's house, he takes with him his share of the entire property.

Leaving a father's house and going away is a common practice in the Near East. This is just about the only way a younger son can change his father's attitude toward him. Once the son leaves, the father's thoughts turn toward the younger son who is now absent. Worry begins to invade his mind. He will send servants out to search and inquire of travelers in the town whether they have heard of him. If the son returns, although he may have misused his fortune, his father receives him and celebrates with a feast of thanksgiving for his boy.

In this story, the father acquiesces to his son's wishes and divides the inheritance between his two boys. According to Jewish custom, this was a foolish act. The townsfolk would have considered the father as unwise and over indulgent. In small towns, news like this travels from home to home very quickly.

Jesus paints a vivid picture of how the boy wasted his inheritance and is caught in a famine. He is so destitute that he even has to feed hogs. This was unthinkable for an Israelite. The Talmud says: "Cursed be the man who would breed swine." The young Israelite was helping in their breeding. This part of the story is offensive and shameful!

"And he was longing to feed his belly from the carob beans that the hogs were eating." Jesus began to draw sympathy from his listeners. They felt sorry for the young man. He was starving, working for a Gentile, tending and feeding hogs, and he couldn't even take enough action to put a carob pod in his mouth. Jesus hints at how spoiled this rich young man was. He had been raised in a wealthy family and was used to being served.

Part 3—HUSKS OR PODS. The Aramaic word for husks is *haroobeh*, which derives from *horba*, "a lonely place." The *haroobeh* is an edible plant that grows wild in the open country of Syria. Its husks or pods are sweet and used for food by some people. Travelers and the poor eat many wild plants that animals eat also. During catastrophes, droughts and famines, when wheat is scarce, people subsist on wild fruits and plants.

Vegetables are seldom consumed. Bread, cheese, honey and curds are the principal foods. Occasionally, in the homes of the poor, a few wild vegetables are eaten raw or cooked. It would be a disgrace for the nobility and rich to eat vegetables since they consider them as a poor man's food. Ordinarily, the food of the wealthy consists of honey, raisins, molasses, some fruit and other sweet fare. A few years before World War 1, tomatoes and turnips were considered an abomination. Rich people would not touch them and looked down on those who did consume them. There isn't a more offensive remark than for one to say to his friend, "Eat turnips."

In this parable, Jesus compares the life of the younger son in his own home, where he lived in luxury, to the life he lived while feeding swine. Shepherds were eating husks or pods; this was normal to them. But to this son of a wealthy man, such food was repulsive. By eating carobs, he lowered himself to the state of poverty.

There is one thing more to consider. A rabbinic maxim says: "Israel needs carobs to be forced to *tishuva* (repentance)—that is, to turn to God." This means that any person who has to eat carob beans is in abject poverty. And usually when an individual hits rock bottom, that person will turn and find his or her way up and out of the predicament. According to rabbinic teaching, turning to God is the way out.

Upon returning home, the errant son meets his father and tells him that he has sinned against God and before his father. Interestingly, the father pays no attention to his repentance. He knows his son means what he says. The good father doesn't reprimand him and tell him "I hope you've learned your lesson" or any other kind of scolding. Instead the father commands the servants to bring out the best robe, a ring and shoes. He also has the fat ox slain so they can celebrate.

The boy's father knows the pain and sorrow that are in his son's heart. He calls for the family ring so his son may be fully reinstated. The son's adornment and the feasting lets the townsfolk know that the son has been well received and is in full restoration.

Part 4—THE MOTHER OF THE TWO SONS. In countries where old customs prevail, whatever the mother does for a family member is usually credited to the father. She works behind the scenes. In a Near Eastern family, the father looks after the sons and the mother looks after the daughters. A mother has more to say about her daughters but has no authority over her sons. Even during meals the father and his sons eat together and the female members eat afterwards.

Undoubtedly, the mother of the errant son rejoiced even more than his father. She was the one who had been inquiring of all wayfarers about him. She embraced him with abundant tears flowing down her cheeks when he returned home. As his mother, she prepared the calf and baked the bread for the banquet that his father was giving to welcome him home. She would hasten to make preparations for the reception. But it is the father who sits at the banquet, entertaining the guests and receiving praise and credit for his generosity. The mother is busy with the servants, but she is the main inspiration of the entire festival, although remaining in the background.

The story that Jesus told follows the old custom. The gospel writer makes no mention of the mother because whatever is done in a family must be said and done in the name of the father. If the father happens to be absent, the elder son takes his place.

Part 5—THE ELDER SON. The first part of the parable is about the younger son, who squandered his inheritance living a wild and degenerate lifestyle. In the second part, Jesus moves in the direction of the firstborn and centers around the father and both his sons—not just the prodigal.

The father had thrown a grand party for his youngest boy. He

219

killed the fat ox; musicians and entertainers were present; and the celebration was in full bloom. Jesus now introduces a new tension in the story with the coming of the older son. Once the older brother found out what was going on, he became furious. Why should he enter the house and join the festivity? So, he didn't. His refusal to participate in the celebration brought reproach on his parents. Not only was the older boy shaming the household with his behavior; he was also breaking the fourth commandment. He was not showing proper respect to his father and mother. By not participating in the celebration, he also shamed his brother.

The father went outside to plead with his firstborn son. The older son began to rant and rave. He complains about his dependency on his father and how he had worked as a slave for the household. In his mind, he was the abused one. He also reminds his father that the younger brother had violated the family bloodline by consorting with harlots. Family tension was at an all-time high. Jealousy, envy and resentment were predominant at this celebration. How would the father resolve the tension?

Part 6—THE STARTLING ENDING. The father of the two sons must answer the angry and resentful remarks of his older boy. In the closing lines of Jesus' story, the father responded to the indignation of his son by saying: "My son, you are always with me! Everything that is mine is yours! It was necessary for us to have these festivities and celebrate because your brother was dead and is alive. He was lost but is found!"

"My son you are always with me," means "you are my constant companion." "Everything that is mine is yours," means "you are co-owner of all I possess." What the older boy did not realize was that he had made himself a slave in his father's house; he was slaving for something that already belonged to him.

This Near Eastern father did not live up to being a stern, strict patriarch; he was a forgiving, all-inclusive father. He loved both his sons and desired family unity and solidarity. Yes, he did spoil his boys and brought some of the problems on the household. But in the end he was able to resolve it all.

God's kingdom doesn't divide the human family; it unifies it. God's presence is loving, harmonious and forgiving and works to bring harmony and peace among all nations. God is no respecter of persons. In this kingdom, love and forgiveness flow freely.

One race or nation may consider itself greater than another; one religious group may believe itself superior to other religious communities. Some groups may consider themselves holier and purer than others. But in God's kingdom, these imaginary lines of separation that human beings create between themselves do not really exist.

Religious notions draw lines of division between the older son and the prodigal, sinner and saint, good and bad. But Jesus made it very clear about the love of God through this parable. Such also is the joy of the heavenly Father and of the angels in heaven when an individual who has wasted his life returns from an erroneous path and begins a new life.

Jesus taught that God as a father lets his sun shine upon the good and the bad and lets his rain fall upon the just and the unjust. Jesus encouraged his disciples to be like their heavenly father—that is, all-inclusive.[3] This parable illustrates how the father refused to lose either son, the firstborn or the prodigal. And the older son learns from his father the true meaning of love and acceptance despite the erring ways of his brother. The father's loving kindness was sufficient for both sons, as God's grace is for all humanity. The kingdom is open for everyone.

---

[3]See Errico and Lamsa, *Aramaic Light on the Gospel of Matthew*, Mt. 5:48, "Perfection," pp. 89-90.

CHAPTER 16

THE PARABLE OF THE UNJUST STEWARD

And he said also unto his disciples, There was a certain rich man, which had a steward; and the same was accused unto him that he had wasted his goods. And he called him, and said unto him How is it that I hear this of thee? Give an account of thy stewardship; for thou mayest be no longer steward, Then the steward said within himself, What shall I do? For my lord taketh away from me the stewardship: I cannot dig; to beg I am ashamed. I am resolved what to do, that, when I am put out of the stewardship, they may receive me into their houses. . . . And the lord commended the unjust steward, because he had done wisely: for the children of the world are in their generation wiser than the children of light. Lk. 16:1-4, 8.

Part 1—THE PARABLE TRANSLATED FROM ARAMAIC.

A WEALTHY MAN HAD A STEWARD[1]

There was a wealthy man who had a steward. And they maliciously accused him of squandering his master's wealth. So his master summoned him and said to him: What is this that I am hearing about you? Give me an accounting of your stewardship because you can no longer be my steward.

The steward said to himself: What will I do because my master is terminating the stewardship from me? To dig, I am unable! To beg, I am ashamed!

I know what to do so that when I am removed from the stewardship they will receive me into their homes. So he called each one of his master's debtors, one by one, and he said to the first: How much do you owe my master? And he answered: a hundred measures of butter. Then he said to him: Take your bill, sit down quickly and write fifty measures.

And he said to another: Now how much do you owe my

---

[1] Lk. 16:1-8, Aramaic Peshitta text, Errico.

222

master? He said to him: One hundred bushels of wheat. Then he responded to him: Take your bill and sit down and write eighty bushels.

Now the master praised the unjust steward because he acted shrewdly.

Part 2— BUTTER, NOT OIL. The King James Version of verse six reads: "And he said, An hundred measures of oil. And he said unto him, Take thy bill, and sit down quickly, and write fifty." The Aramaic word for oil is *misha*, but it has many meanings, such as: "ointment, salve, unguent." And in this case, the word refers to "butter."

In many Near Eastern areas where money is scarce and ancient methods of trading continue, both the government and people use butter as one medium of exchange. People pay their taxes, tithe to the church and transact loans with butter. The price of animals, dry goods and food is often quoted in terms of butter. It is stored in sheep skins and carried by merchants from place to place for this purpose.

In this story the steward had loaned a hundred measures of butter to some borrowers who had probably used it to purchase articles or to pay taxes or debts. The business of making loans and collecting debts is left in the hands of the chief steward, who uses his discretion in making settlements. Most of these transactions are conducted orally; written agreements are seldom made. Even in the latter case, the name of the debtor is entered on the books merely as a matter of record; no signature is attached.

Aramaic numerals could easily be changed without arousing suspicion. This practice is still prevalent and causes no end of trickery and confusion. Many servants take undue advantage of their master's confidence in these business matters. They do this so that they may secure favors from debtors and exact more than is due. But this was not the case with the steward in Jesus' parable.

Part 3—THE UNJUST STEWARD. Stewards in biblical lands occupied a different position and sense of responsibility in the house of their lords than do the stewards and servants in Europe and America. They were the businessmen for their lords. Their task was

223

a rather peculiar one. A steward is neither a servant nor a partner, and yet he exercises great authority over the business affairs of the household. He is not only in charge of the servants and hired workers, but he must see after the women and children of his lord. He is empowered to transact business as he deems appropriate.

Generally, stewards are unmarried men or widowers who have an education and business skills seldom possessed by their wealthy masters. Some of them receive their position by pledging their services and loyalty to their master without pay. Thus, they become adopted members of the family. A Near Eastern steward may rebuke the master's wife and, if necessary, administer discipline to the children in the absence of his master.

Since these stewards receive no remuneration for their faithful services, they have great power and much to say about matters in the household. They act as if the house were their own. They will give their master's money to their own relatives and friends without the least thought of dishonesty. They also may cancel debts of those to whom they have loaned money and who were unable to repay.

The regular hired servants are invariably extremely jealous of a faithful steward and constantly conspire against him. They spy on him and protest to their master that his good steward is spending his wealth lavishly. They report that the steward is lending money to people whose reputations are bad and from whom debts cannot be collected. These hired men gossip about the steward and accuse him of being in love with certain women to whose relatives he has made loans.

At first the master of the house disregards all the gossip and complaints. He tries to make peace between the servants and steward, but when the malicious complaints and accusations continue coming, he is forced to take action and strengthen household affairs. He immediately begins an investigation by calling the servants to declare the charges and give the names of the people to whom the steward has loaned money and given butter and wheat. Next, he summons the steward and, after heated arguments, begins questioning his actions and generosity. The final outcome for the steward is usually a charge of embezzlement of his master's property. Of course, the steward will deny these outlandish charges and defend those to whom he had loaned money. He will tell his master that the loans were made to trustworthy people and that he had helped many poor families.

But as soon as the steward sees that his master's anger is not abated and that he is in danger of losing his position, he will call on the people to whom he made loans. He states his case to them and tells them that the servants have aroused his master's anger and made serious charges against him. He reminds them of these loans and favors in the hope that when he is put out of his master's house he may be welcome at their homes.

The steward secretly reduces the sums loaned, and where his master does not know the sum loaned, the entire amount is often canceled. The steward does these things with a certain sense of justification because he has spent years of faithful service without pay and has made money for his master. When he leaves he knows that his lord will not compensate him.

"Then the master praised the unjust steward because he acted shrewdly." Faced with a problem, the steward acted wisely. He was about to be put out in the streets so he knew how to use what was his to secure his future. There was no embezzlement and dishonesty in the work of his steward. He had given some money to his friends, reduced the loans of those who were unable to repay and done some charity with the wealth of his lord, but a part of this wealth belonged to the steward.

As a business manager, the steward was the one who made money and increased goods and property for his master; therefore, he was entitled to at least a share of it. So it was his share that the steward had reduced from the loans; by so doing, he was preparing a future position for himself in case his lord dismissed him from his post.

Jesus commends the steward because he handled his crisis with wisdom. "And I also say to you, Use this earthly wealth, however acquired, to make friends so that when it is gone, they will receive you and you will have everlasting habitations."[2]

The last part of verse 8, which we shall call 8b, "for the children of this world are in their generation wiser than the children of light," was most likely a comment, a marginal notation by a scribe, that became an integral part of the text.[3]

THE MAMMON OF THIS WORLD

And I say unto you, Make to yourselves friends of the mammon of unrighteousness; that, when ye fail, they may receive you into everlasting habitations. Lk. 16:9.

In the Western world, friendships usually result from mere acquaintances in churches, clubs, social and business relations. In Near Eastern lands, it is not an easy thing for one to make friends with influential people, as this kind of friendship comes about through money, favors and loans.

Peasants and common people are always eager to gain the friendship of the higher classes, publicans and government officials. The latter invariably expect to receive something for the favor of their friendship because in the Near East, men always need the protection of influential individuals.

Generally, one procures this kind of friendship through bribery, gifts or lavish banquets. When a person desires to become close to a certain official, he kills a sheep, buys wine and invites as many guests as possible in honor of the prospective friend. After the banquet, the honored guest is presented with a gift. It may be a sum of money, a horse, or a beautiful garment. It would be an insult to invite such men

---

[2]Lk. 16:9, Aramaic Peshitta text, Lamsa translation.

[3]Scholarly NT opinion has it that most of the verses from 8b through 12 was not said by Jesus. They believe these interpretations were added by a scribe or by Luke himself. We do not completely concur with this opinion for verses 9-12. Again, we must keep in mind that this commentary is not a critical, historical presentation of the gospel.

without being able to give them some appropriate gift. Government officials prefer cash.

(Dr. Lamsa's cousin, who was a mayor of a town, often invited government officials and influential men to their house. He and Dr. Lamsa slaughtered sheep, prepared a great feast and after the meal, his cousin gave his guests garments and sometimes money as presents. The recipient values these gifts and always remembers the act of generosity and hospitality extended to him. When his friend needs his influence, he does everything on his behalf. In countries where bribery and corruption predominate and where an unjust system of taxation prevails, friendship with men who are in power is essential.)

The so called unjust steward, who was called upon to account for his work, quickly went to his master's debtors and reduced their debts in order to gain their friendship. He did this so that they might return these favors in case he lost his position in his lord's household.

According to Luke, Jesus counsels his disciples to make friends with the wealthy of this world not by acts of bribery but by generosity, by reducing debts, extending credits, helping officials in their need. He would have us do for them what we would have them do for us in like situations.

THE OLD ORDER AND THE NEW

The law and the prophets were until John: since that time the kingdom of God is preached, and every man presseth into it. Lk. 16:16.

The law and the prophets spanned the period from Moses until John the Baptist. They were the heralds of the new law, the new covenant and the spiritual kingdom that was to come. John the Baptist was the last prophet of the old order and covenant. With Jesus a new order and covenant began.

Worldly men—kings, princes, and high priests—dominated the kingdom until the time of John the Baptist. Many of these men fought for power and oppressed the people of Israel. And from the time of

John's ministry until Jesus' ministry, God's spiritual kingdom suffered violence. It was dominated by force and only those who were powerful ruled over it.[4]

Jesus, through his teaching and his death on the cross, brought to the law and the prophets a new synthesis. He gave religion a new meaning. Jesus came not to weaken the Torah but to fulfill it—that is, to put it into practice. He came not to be ministered to but to minister. Now many men and women were pressing to enter into the kingdom of heaven.

THE PERMANENCY OF THE TORAH

And it is easier for heaven and earth to pass, than one tittle of the law to fail. Lk. 16:17.

The contrast is made in this verse between the probable end of heaven and earth as we know it and the positive permanency of the law. This style of comparison and contrast is very common in northern Aramaic speech. Semites often say: "I am so thirsty I could dry up the sea." They also express themselves by comparing the river with their tears: "The river may dry up but not the tears in my eyes." These sayings suggest the intensity of thirst and the depth of grief, but they are never taken literally. One may translate the Aramaic verb *nebran* as "will pass" or "may pass." The emphasis in this verse is on the eternal endurance of the Torah (law).

Jewish authorities suspected Jesus of weakening their religious laws. With this saying, Jesus answered those who falsely accused him. He declared that the law could neither be weakened nor abolished. The Torah is eternal and comes from God. What is of God is indestructible and everlasting.[5]

---

[4]Mt. 11:12-13. See also Errico and Lamsa, *Aramaic Light on the Gospel of Matthew,* "Corruption," pp 167-168.

[5]Mt. 5:17. See also Errico and Lamsa, *Aramaic Light on the Gospel of Matthew,* "Enacting the Torah,: pp 66-67.

THE RICH MAN AND LAZARUS

There was a certain rich man, which was clothed in purple and fine linen, and fared sumptuously every day: And there was a certain beggar named Lazarus, which was laid at his gate, full of sores. Lk. 16: 19-20.

Part 1—THE PARABLE TRANSLATED FROM ARAMAIC.

A WEALTHY MAN WORE PURPLE

Now there was a wealthy man and he wore purple and fine linen, and everyday he was having an extravagantly good time. Now there was a poor man by the name of Lazarus [Aramaic: Laazar], who was placed prostrate right at the gate of that wealthy one, afflicted with ulcers. For he was longing to fill his stomach with the crumbs that fell from that rich man's table. And even the dogs were coming and kept licking his sores.

Then it happened that the poor man died and the angels carried him away to the bosom of Abraham. Then that wealthy man also died and was buried.

And while he was tormented in *sheol*, he raised his eyes, and saw from a long distance Abraham and Lazarus in his bosom. So he cried out and said: My father, Abraham, have compassion on me, and send Lazarus that he may dip the tip of his finger in water to wet my tongue, because I am tormented in this blaze.

And Abraham said to him: My son, remember that you received your good things during your lifetime and Lazarus his hardships. So, look here! He is now at rest and you are in torment! And beside all these things, an immense chasm is fixed between us and you so that those who want to cross over from here to you [6] cannot; neither can they cross from there to us.[7]

Part 2—THE GATE AND THE CHASM. This is a parable, not a literal image of an afterlife. This narrative is filled with contrasts:

---

[6]The pronoun "you" is plural in Aramaic.
[7]Lk. 16:19-26, Aramaic Peshitta text, Errico. Many NT scholars believe that verses 27-31 were added and not a part of the original parable.

a rich man and a poor man; the rich man inside dressed in purple linen, the poor man outside afflicted with ulcers; the gate and the chasm; the poor man cannot pass through the gate to get inside and the rich man suffering in *sheol* cannot cross the chasm into the bosom of Abraham; in life the rich man had good times and the poor man, hardships; in the end, the poor man enjoys rest while the rich man endures torment.

The gates of rich men are always crowded with beggars, sick people and dogs—all of them expecting to receive food left over from the rich man's table. Some of the wealthy take care of these people and see to it that they are fed; others leave such matters to their servants. The lord of the house sees them but seldom talks to them.

Rich men are usually criticized and attacked by religious teachers who either have risen from poverty or whose followers are poor. No matter how a man acquires his wealth, he is suspected and exposed to verbal attacks.[8] This parable was either composed by Jesus or was a popular one in use at that time. Verbal illustrations are common in Semitic speech. Religious men, in order to pacify those in poverty and minimize their suffering, picture the poor in heaven with abundance and the rich in hell fire suffering for their greed and unjust ways of acquiring wealth.

When Jesus referred to wealth in his teaching, he admonished only those who relied on it for their sense of well-being and eternal salvation. He did not compel those who followed him to renounce all their wealth. For example, Zacchaeus gave away only half of his wealth and the other half he kept for himself and his family. Other disciples had nothing to leave. The old nets and boats that they left behind could not be sold. Perhaps they left them to some of their

---

[8]This parable might suggest that Jesus advocated communism and was opposed to capitalism. This would be a mistaken view. He was certainly opposed to those who acquire their wealth unjustly but he did not imply that any one should literally divest himself of his possessions and give everything to the poor and become destitute. Such a course of action would have created yet another evil. It would have simply made the poor rich and the rich poor. The problem of poverty and riches would not have been solved.

relatives.

The parable of the rich man who enlarged his barns and stored wheat and other food supplies clearly explains that Jesus depreciated only the hoarding and greedy rich. He spoke against those who were selfish and not against the godly rich who were entrusted with wealth and used it generously. (See Luke 12:16-24.)

In the Near East there was no recognized middle class. The people were either wealthy or extremely poor. This parable is intended to illustrate the gulf between the rich and the poor, whose property was confiscated by injustice and heavy taxation. It also shows the mental torment that the wicked rich will endure and the blessings of bliss that the pious poor will enjoy. A drop of water that the rich man desired is symbolic of his yearning for relief from suffering. This entire story is Near Eastern imagery, not reality. Jesus uses figures of speech and not literal terms. Once the greedy rich die they cannot come back to rectify their deeds. In other words, they suffer great regret and strong remorse. God does not do this to them. This is a result of their own acts. The symbol of the gate represents the opportunity to do good to those in need.

Part 3—THE GREAT GULF. "And beside all this, between us and you there is a great gulf fixed: so that they which would pass from hence to you cannot; neither can they pass to us, that would come from thence."[9] There is a measureless chasm between good and evil, like the distance between fire and water, truth and error.

In Jesus' time, just as today, many men and women were allured by false teachers of religion. They assured the people that after death, restitution could be made for the failures and evil deeds they had committed in this life.

This parable was to convince people that one cannot make amends after death. According to Jesus' teaching, the time is now. Amends must be made on earth so that the human community may live in peace and harmony. God's kingdom begins on earth and is available to all nations and races who wish to find the true way.

---

[9]Lk. 16:26, K. J. V.

Jesus cited another parable that touched on this same point—the parable of the shepherd separating the sheep from the goats. Jesus used this Near Eastern practice of separation to illustrate the final separation of the righteous from the wicked.[10] Again, we must understand that God does not discriminate between the righteous and the wicked. God is good to all and blesses everyone. (See Matthew 5: 43-47.) However, the evils and wrongs that people do to one another bring separation and division in the human community. God's presence and truth are to relieve human suffering, divisions and errors.

---

[10]Mt 25:31-46. See Errico and Lamsa, *Aramaic Light on the Gospel of Matthew,* "The Parable of the Sheep and the Goats," pp. 315-319, notes 11, 12.

CHAPTER 17

THE DONKEY'S MILL

It was better for him that a millstone were hanged about his neck, and he cast into the sea, than that he should offend one of these little ones. Lk. 17:2.

In Aramaic speech, Semites refer to a millstone as a donkey's mill. It is a large, round, smoothly hewn stone six feet in diameter and about a foot thick laid on the ground, on which another stone of the same size is placed. A hole is bored in the middle of each stone and an axle is fastened through them. The donkey is then harnessed at one end of the axle to turn the mill and grind the wheat and is driven by a man or boy. Some of these mills are also used as oil presses; in such cases, the upper stone is placed on its edge over the lower stone.

Such mills are still in use in many villages and in some cities. They are also found at the ruins of the ancient cities. These two pieces of stone are the largest to be seen in any town. Whenever people speak of a heavy object, they usually mention the donkey's mill. Everyone knows its size and weight. Jesus referred to the millstone because it was a stone familiar to all the people. The idea he wished to convey could readily be understood.[1]

INCREASING FAITH

And the apostles said unto the Lord, Increase our faith. And the Lord said, If ye have faith as a grain of mustard seed, ye might say unto this sycamine tree, Be thou plucked up by the root and be thou planted in the sea; and it should obey you. Lk. 17:5-6.

---

[1]Mt. 18:6. See Errico and Lamsa, *Aramaic Light on the Gospel of Matthew,* "Offences," p. 232.

The apostles, not being well trained in religion, thought that faith could be increased like material things—that is, by adding to it or acquiring it by means of knowledge. Jesus told his disciples that faith could not be increased by material means, nor can it be imparted from one person to another. For one to acquire faith one must become like a little child who has faith and trust in his parents and believes whatever they tell him. As Jesus puts it, faith is like a small mustard seed that can bore through rocks, absorb the sun and grow into a large, potent plant. All one needs is a spark of faith to ignite anything.

A single spark of fire can burn the world. When faith is put into action it increases. Through faith, we contact universal energies and forces that work with us. Faith ignites these powers that are latent within one's soul and gives that person the assurance of true success. It was Abraham's faith in God that enabled him to make his long and hazardous journey without harm. Abraham trusted in God and used that which he had at hand. It was the Lord God that did the rest. The disciples were to learn what it meant to work with God. A simple trust in God increases faith.

Jesus' disciples had been studying and traveling with him (like Elisha had traveled with Elijah, his master) and were afraid to practice healing on their own. They were like someone who is first learning to drive a car and is afraid to drive alone without the instructor. Also, in the Near East, students keep silent while their teacher is present. They refuse to try to do anything in the presence of their master, fearing that they will be unable to do well; generally, they expect their master to do it for them.

The disciples had always relied on Jesus; therefore, they were not taking any responsibility. This is the reason that the disciples did not have enough faith to heal the epileptic boy. After Jesus' ascension, they were forced to rely on themselves. Then they fully began healing people and preaching the gospel of the kingdom, demonstrating what Jesus had taught them.

IDLE SERVANTS

So, likewise ye, when ye shall have done all those things which are commanded you, say, We are unprofitable servants: we have done that which was our duty to do. Lk. 17:10.

The Aramaic text reads: "Even you also, when you have done all the things which are commanded you, say, We are idle servants; we have only done what was our duty to do."[2] *Bateeleh* in Aramaic means "idle" and not "unprofitable." This verse gives a clear and correct understanding of relations between master and servants in the Near East. In America and Europe laborers and servants work by the hour. Though they are required to be on duty, they do have intervals of rest. When their work is finished, they are free to return home.

This is not the way it works in the Near East where servants are hired to work throughout the year. They work constantly, ready whenever their lord may want them. They are assigned to perform various duties both in the household and in the fields. They must not remain idle. Even if there is nothing to do, they must make themselves busy and useful, especially when their masters are present.

Usually, Near Eastern servants do not complain of their continual labors and long hours. Instead, they always tell their lord that there isn't enough work to do and that they are idle. If they say otherwise, they are branded as lazy servants and no one would hire them. When a servant tells his master that he is idle because there isn't enough work, his lord trusts him more and gives him certain privileges. But to those servants who complain, their lord assigns more tasks or may lay them off.

EAGLES

And they answered and said unto him, Where, Lord? And he said unto

---

[2]Lk. 17:10, Aramaic Peshitta text, Lamsa translation.

them, Wheresoever the body is, thither will the eagles be gathered together.
Lk. 17:37.

The term "eagles" in this passage probably means "vultures." The latter are scavengers and devour dead bodies. The carcass in this instance represents the Jewish people of Palestine. The Jews had lost their political power and their prophets and seers. Now they were oppressed and harassed by the pagans and Gentiles who surrounded them. Thus the people of Israel and their leaders as a unit were like a corpse, ready for the vultures to pounce and devour them.

Israel had already been conquered—by Assyrians, Chaldeans, Greeks, Syrians—and soon the Romans were to trample on them. In the year 70 CE, Titus put an end to the Jewish state. He destroyed Jerusalem and its magnificent temple and dispersed the people.

CHAPTER 18

THE GODLESS JUDGE

. . . There was in a city a judge, which feared not God, and neither regarded man: And there was a widow in that city; and she came unto him saying, Avenge me of mine adversary. Lk. 18:2-3.

Part 1—THE PARABLE TRANSLATED FROM ARAMAIC.

A DISCREDITABLE JUDGE

There was a judge in a certain city, who neither had any fear of God nor had he any respect for human beings.

Now there was a widow in that city. She was constantly coming to him, saying: Vindicate me from my adversary! But he was not willing to do so for a long time.

But afterwards he said to himself: Though I do not revere God nor respect human beings, yet, because this widow causes me trouble, I will vindicate her—so that she may not be constantly coming and badgering me.[1]

Part 2—NEAR EASTERN JUDGES. In Israel, judges were to revere God; by so doing, they would comply with God's law (the Torah) and practice justice for all. "You will provide from among all the people, capable men who revere God, honest men who detest bribes and duplicity."[2]

Widows must be respected and cared for. Israel's laws protected widows, orphans and foreigners. "You will not abuse any foreigner nor oppress him. For you were strangers in the land of Egypt. You will not ill-treat any widow or orphan. If you abuse them, and they pray before me, I will surely hear their prayer; and my anger will burn, and I will slay you with the sword. Then your wives will

---

[1]Lk. 18: 2-5, Aramaic Peshitta text, Errico.
[2]Ex. 18:21, Aramaic Peshitta text, Errico.

become widows and your children fatherless."[3] Israel's prophets also cried out against injustices done to widows, orphans and foreigners.

Near Eastern Semites regard many of their judges as cruel and dishonest. They usually classify them with "tax collectors and sinners." No matter what kind of charitable donations a judge may make as a church member or how he may help the poor, people generally look upon him rather warily. They suspect him of practicing injustice.

Many Near Eastern judges are hesitant about taking cases for widows and poor people. They usually try to excuse themselves by saying that they are in poor health or that they are suffering from case overload. Others may promise aid but not follow through with their promises. Nevertheless, the poor and widows keep returning to the judge's home, begging and badgering him for a hearing.

In those ancient days, and even in some areas of the Near East at the turn of the century, judges did not receive any salary for their services. Thus, it was easy for them to accept bribes because of their need for money. Being aware of this situation, people sent their bribes a few days before they visited a particular judge. Many judges could tell when a poor person had come to their home because that individual had not sent any payment ahead of time. A servant would usually greet these petitioners with the depressing news that the judge was too busy and could not be bothered with them at that time. Many judges felt it would cost too much time to work with widows and the poor. On some occasions, however, judges were forced to help these needy petitioners.

The magistrate that Jesus describes is totally shameless and does not care about honor. But because the widow kept coming and pestering him for a very long time, he finally gave in and provided the justice she needed. Jesus' humor is in the irony of the story. This judge who was not afraid of God nor of any human being, finally comes to fear this poor widow. Imagine, a corrupt judge who was an outlaw magistrate, fearing no human being, having no respect for the

---

[3]Ex. 22:21-24, Aramaic Peshitta text, Errico.

law nor fear of God Almighty, becoming afraid of the weakest member of society. The woman was hassling him to death and he couldn't take it any longer!

Luke framed Jesus' parable around the notion that God will avenge those who seek justice from him. In other words, if a corrupt judge eventually responds and answers a destitute widow's plea, how much more will the gracious heavenly Father hear and avenge the prayers of his elect. "And the Lord said, Hear what the unjust judge saith. And shall not God avenge his own elect, which cry day and night unto him, though he bear long with them? I tell you that he will avenge them speedily . . . ."[4]

Aside from Luke's interpretation of this parable placed on Jesus' lips, another non-allegorical view is possible. Jesus surprises his listeners with a simple story that carries a profound message. God's kingdom is everywhere present, constantly coming and wearing down resistance. God's presence, through spirit and truth, doesn't come with a great display of awesome power; it comes like a nuisance that won't go away. This kingdom forever badgers human beings until they open to its power and grace. The ever-present and ever-working kingdom will keep manifesting itself until the nations of the world acknowledge its presence. God's ruling presence never gives up on anyone. Justice for all can only prevail through God.

FAITH MIGHT BE LOST

I tell you that he will avenge them speedily. Nevertheless when the Son of man cometh, shall he find faith on the earth? Lk. 18:8.

Jesus knew that a great many of his followers would recant and return to their former religions. He also knew that the material and physical world had many alluring rewards to offer. Some would regard living a temporal life more important than life eternal.

---

[4]Lk. 18:6-8, K. J. V. Many NT scholars believe that these words were added by Luke and were not the original words of Jesus.

By placing these words on Jesus' lips, Luke questions whether there will be faithful followers on the face of the earth when the full revelation of God's kingdom is realized. In a materialistic world, how many who claim to be Christians truly practice the teachings of Jesus and apply the principles of his all-inclusive gospel of the kingdom?

JESUS CRUCIFIED BY ROMANS

Then he took unto him the twelve, and said unto them, Behold, we go up to Jerusalem, and all things that are written by the prophets concerning the Son of man shall be accomplished. For he shall be delivered unto the Gentiles, and shall be mocked, and spitefully entreated, and spitted on: And they shall scourge him and put him to death: and the third day he shall rise again. Lk. 18:31-33.

Jesus was crucified not by the Jews but by the soldiers who were in the service of the Roman Army. The Jews had no authority to crucify or even to stone a man from Galilee. The Jewish high priest was an ethnarch—that is, the head of the nation, with spiritual authority but limited political power over his people.

Punishment for blasphemy was stoning. When Stephen was convicted of blasphemy, the religious authorities had him stoned to death. Stephen was a Jew from Judea and therefore was under the jurisdiction of the high priest.

However, Jesus' case was different. He was a Galilean and therefore under the jurisdiction of Herod Antipas. This is the reason Pilate, the Roman governor, sent him to Herod for his judgment. When the governor said to the high priest, "Take him and judge him according to your own law," the high priest answered, "We have no authority."

Jesus could not be convicted on religious grounds. Therefore, a political charge was made against him stating that he had told the people he was the king of the Jews. Thus, Pilate was the only one who could judge him and convict him under such a charge. So it was the Romans who had the final say in the execution of Jesus. They put him to death on the charge of making himself a king, and that was treason.

THE SON OF DAVID

And he cried, saying, Jesus, thou son of David, have mercy on me. Lk. 18:38.

Aramaic speaking people use the word *bar*, "son," not only to signify a blood son or relative but also to show likeness of character. *Bar David*, "son of David," means someone who is like David but not actually David's descendant. The blind man knew nothing of Jesus' ancestry.

Near Easterners customarily call their great men by the names of their distinguished heroes and beloved kings, with no thought of family ties. Some of these famous men may have lived a thousand years before, just as David was about a thousand years before Jesus.

David was the best loved king of Israel. He was not only the liberator of the Israelites from the Philistine yoke; he was also the founder of a kingdom that made Israel known among other nations. People expected the Messiah to be like King David. He was to free the Jews from the Roman yoke and reestablish the defunct throne of David.

Jesus never pretended that he had any connection with the royal family of David, but he accepted this title that the people bestowed upon him as a mark of distinction and honor. The Pharisees were annoyed when the people referred to Jesus as the "son of David." This honor or title was appropriate for the Messiah only. He was to be born in Judea and, of course, be a blood descendant of David. Religious authorities understood Scripture literally and could not associate the Galilean teacher with the house of David. But God's promises to David were spiritual. (See Matthew 20:30, Mark 10:47.)

CHAPTER 19

TO RECEIVE A KINGDOM

He said, therefore, A certain nobleman went into a far country to receive for himself a kingdom, and to return.. Lk. 19:12.

"To receive a kingdom" means "to be confirmed as a ruler." The Romans were the rulers of Palestine and Syria as well as all the countries around the Mediterranean basin. They appointed indigenous men to rule over small territories largely inhabited by tribal people. There were also Roman viceroys and governor-generals who acted as supervisors in various regions of the Eastern empire. The native rulers were not kings but tetrarchs who ruled in the name of Caesar. When their people were discontent, they were recalled by the governor-general or by Rome. Then, other men were appointed to take their places.

These positions were usually procured through bribery or political intrigue. When high officials were recalled or the emperor died, these positions become insecure and depended largely on favors received from the new ruler. They could be obtained only by a special trip to the capital city of Rome or to a seat of the provincial government. This is how Herod and his sons obtained their kingdoms. Jesus refers to this political practice in his parable.

Where ancient civilization still predominates, the ruler of a town of two hundred families is still called a *malka,* "king." Today, they call him a *melick.* The Aramaic word *malka* means a "ruler or counselor."[1] *Melick* is used for a chieftain of a small territory or a mayor of several districts.

---

[1] Isa. 9:6.

SERVANTS ENTRUSTED WITH MONEY

And he called his ten servants, and delivered them ten pounds, and said unto them, Occupy till I come. Lk. 19:13.

Usually, noblemen and rulers of small territories receive no salaries. Their people are poor and burdened with heavy taxes and tithes imposed by their own rulers and with tributes to the central government. Noblemen and rulers of cities prosper by trading. They entrust their servants with money so that they may use it for commercial purposes. It is loaned to merchants and traders with interest and used to buy and sell sheep and wheat.

Sheep are bought from small herdsmen in country places and sold in cities for food. Large profits come from these transactions. The business of buying and selling sheep continues during the summer months, so the money turns over many times and the original capital invested is multiplied. Then there is the money that is loaned to farmers to buy seed. During the harvest season farmers give one fifth of the total wheat raised to the money lenders.

Near Eastern rulers, noblemen and officials of high rank entrust their entire business to their servants. It would be a disgrace for these men to buy and sell and perform such tasks. These business obligations are for servants and stewards, who at a certain time during the year give account to their lord of all their transactions—profits and losses.

If the servants happen to lose the money entrusted to them through carelessness or otherwise, they are held responsible. The property of these servants who failed their lord is confiscated and they are dismissed. Some servants, out of fear, hesitate to use the money entrusted to them and hide it in their homes and return it at the end of the year.

According to the parable, this nobleman was a ruler of a city. He went on a journey to pay his respects to the king and to seek confirmation of his official position. He entrusted his servants with small coins called in Aramaic *menin*. On his return, he rewarded his servants who had traded and made large profits with *kakhreh,* the largest coins in those days. The *kakhrah,* "talent," was a large coin of silver or gold probably worth about 3000 shekels. A man could carry only one of them. The Greek translators made an error when translating this word *kakhrah* for *karkhah,* a province. The difference between these two words can only be distinguished with a single dot placed over one of the Aramaic consonants and can be easily confused.

This nobleman could not have given his servants ten and five cities as a reward for their faithfulness. For this nobleman had only one city over which he ruled. Furthermore, his servants were not qualified to be rulers. Because of their business acumen and fidelity, these servants were entrusted with larger sums with the prospects of greater profits for the future. This is characteristic of Near Eastern rulers or noblemen to first begin with small sums of money for their servants until honesty and ability are demonstrated.[2]

ONE SOWS, ANOTHER REAPS

For I feared thee; because thou art an austere man: thou takest up that thou layedst not down, and reapest that thou didst not sow. Lk. 19:21.

In the Near East, it often happened that one sowed but another reaped. One planted a vineyard, but another drank its wine. The reason for this was that during wars and persecutions, farmers and owners of vineyards were either slain or had fled to another country. The persecutors reaped their crops and picked their grapes.

Israel's prophets had planted the vineyard—that is, the kingdom of God. They had sown the seed of God's word and many of them had died for its sake. But now the apostles were reaping the fruits of the Hebrew prophets' labors.

To this day, it is true that some men work hard but never taste of

---

[2]Mt. 25:14-30; Lk. 19:16-19. See Errico and Lamsa, *Aramaic Light on the Gospel of Matthew,* "Servants Appointed Guardians," pp. 311-314.

the fruits of their labor, while others reap the reward. Nevertheless, all those who labor and suffer for the sake of their good work shall live forever. The generations that come after them will praise their names. For example, all the prophets who died for the sake of their teaching are now living through the holy literature that they left behind as a great heritage. Their names are remembered and handed down from one generation to another. Their lives are emulated and their words are published and read in hundreds of languages.

The fearful servant of the nobleman was accusing his lord of being a harsh and demanding man. His master should be satisfied that he hadn't lost the money. Fear kept him from investing for his lord. Fear paralyzes movement. The servant froze his future because he feared his master. One must be free of the worldly system of gains or losses. In God's kingdom no such worldly rules apply. There is no fear in God's kingdom; one is free to act.

TO HIM WHO HAS SHALL BE GIVEN

For I say unto you, That unto every one which hath shall be given; and from him that hath not, even that he hath shall be taken away from him. But those mine enemies, which would not that I should reign over them, bring hither, and slay them before me. Lk. 19:26-27.

Most of the land in the Near East is owned by princes and rich landlords who lease it to farmers. These farmers, in turn, raise the crops and divide them with the owner. In some cases, the peasants receive a small portion of the produce that is barely enough to supply them with food until the next harvest.

Those peasants who work diligently and raise good crops are granted more land, but those who fail have their land taken from them and given to those who were more productive. According to Luke, Jesus illustrated this point by the parable of the talents. Those who had made good were given more money. To the one who hid his money, what he had was taken from him and given to those who had done well. This is also true in business or trade. To those who succeed, more is given; to those who fail, even what they have is lost. In this instance, Jesus means that more power and knowledge will be given to those who do well preaching, teaching and demonstrating the gospel of the kingdom. But to those who are negligent, even what they have will be taken away.[3]

JESUS WAS REJECTED

And when he was come nigh, even now at the descent of the mount of Olives, the whole multitude of the disciples began to rejoice and praise God with a loud voice for all the mighty works that they had seen. Lk. 19:37.

According to Luke, Jesus had predicted his rejection by the temple authorities, his judgment before the Roman governor and his crucifixion. Many times he had warned his disciples of impending disaster. The prophecies had to be fulfilled. The great prophet Isaiah had predicted that the Messiah would be rejected and put to death.[4] Jesus expected no welcome from the authorities. This is the reason he rode on a donkey when entering Jerusalem during Passover week. The donkey was the most despised animal, but for Jesus it was a symbol of meekness.

As we see from the gospel of Luke, Jesus was greeted by a crowd of his own followers who had come to the feast ahead of him. It was these people who went out to greet him and hail him as the mighty conqueror of the Davidic kingdom. There is no mention in the gospel that Jesus and his disciples were greeted by the priests, Pharisees, Sadducees, scribes or Jewish dignitaries. The religious authorities had rejected Jesus and turned a deaf ear to him.

After his arrival in the historic city, no one took salt, water and bread to welcome him according to the custom. He was not invited to anyone's home. Jesus and his disciples spent most of that week in

---

[3]Mt. 13:12 and 25:29. See Errico and Lamsa, *Aramaic Light on the Gospel of Matthew,* "To Him Who Hath It Shall Be Given," pp. 314-315.
[4]Isa. 53:1-5.

the garden of Gethsemane—a public park—sleeping under the olive trees.

In John 12:12-13 we read: "On the next day, a large crowd which had come to the feast, when they heard that Jesus was coming to Jerusalem, took branches of palm trees, and went out to greet him, and they cried: Hosanna! Blessed is the King of Israel who comes in the name of the Lord."[5] But when the Pharisees heard the people singing, they rebuked them and asked Jesus to stop them. Jesus' entry into Jerusalem was a spiritual triumph and not a political one. It was a triumph of truth over error, meekness over force, and life over death and the grave.[6]

JEWISH PEOPLE BACK JESUS

And he taught daily in the temple. But the chief priests and the scribes and the chief of the people sought to destroy him, And could not find what they might do, for all the people were very attentive to hear him.
Lk. 19:47-48.

Jesus had a large following of people in Judea. Although the majority of his followers were Galileans, many Jews in the south who were tired of the priestly system and the corrupt Herodian dynasty looked to Jesus as their savior from these things. They were wearied of the imperial Roman government that constantly taxed them and added to their burdens. These Jewish people felt fresh hope for a new way of living by listening to the prophet from Galilee.

The religious authorities had to arrest Jesus at night and bring him to trial during the dark hours because they feared the masses of Jewish people who had sided with him and his message. Additionally, these authorities were afraid of the people who had been flocking to Jesus and declaring him a reformer. Some were proclaim-

---

[5]Aramaic Peshitta text, Lamsa translation.
[6]See Errico and Lamsa, *Aramaic Light on the Gospel of Matthew,* "Riding on an Ass," pp. 257-259.

247

ing him as a prophet and even as the great Messiah.

Every attempt to reform the corrupt government in Judea was crushed by Roman powers and the supporters of the Herodian dynasty. The religious authorities were afraid that resistance against the government might cause the Romans to deprive them of their religious freedom and power.

CHAPTER 20

HUSBANDMEN AND THE VINEYARD

Then began he to speak to the people this parable; A certain man planted a vineyard, and let it forth to husbandmen, and went into a far country for a long time. And at the season he sent a servant to the husbandmen, that they should give him of the fruit of the vineyard: but the husbandmen beat him and sent him away empty. Lk. 20:9-10.

Rich, Near Eastern landlords plant vineyards, build towers and erect wine presses, and then lease them to others. In some cases the lessee agrees to take care of the vineyard, prune and cultivate it and give one-third of the fruit to its owner. Other vineyard workers lease vineyards for a lump sum of money to be paid according to the terms of the contract. Generally, vineyards are leased for a number of years, and the workers pay during the season, either in cash or with produce.

The leasing of a vineyard is not always profitable. Droughts and unseasonable rains often create heavy losses, and the workers have to pay whether the vineyard produces or not. They must meet the terms of the agreement at any cost; otherwise they will lose their reputations. Then when their contract expires, no man would be willing to rent them another vineyard or trust them with anything.

Some owners, although they have leased their vineyards, expect produce from them free of charge. Workers who desire to retain the good will of the owners, during the season send baskets of grapes and other fruits to them. The landlords especially enjoy receiving fruits from the trees that they planted with their own hands. When the workers fail to do this, the owner does not hesitate to send his servants to the vineyard to pick as much fruit as they wish without the permission of the husbandmen. The owner feels that the vineyard belongs to him and he has a right to its produce. Some of the tenants who are humble and generous men raise no objection, but others resent such interference.

During bad years, vineyard workers are very careful and try to make as many sacrifices as possible so that they can meet their obligations. They will not even allow their own children to pick grapes. In such trying times, there is nothing that will arouse their hatred against the owner of the vineyard more than to see the owner's servants walking on the grounds, picking, eating and filling baskets with grapes to take away. The workers hate the owner who compels them to pay the last cent, although he knows the vineyard has not produced sufficient fruit that year and still wants the grapes without paying for them. Then there are soldiers and government officials who take whatever they please, adding to the anger and frustration of the husbandmen.

Some of them, because of worry, lose their tempers and beat the servants of the landlord. The workers would be glad to see the owner take the vineyard away from them, rather than pay the rent and give the fruits of their labors to the owner's servants, who didn't earn the right to partake of the vineyard. The servants, however, feel that the property belongs to them and that they have the right to pick the grapes, in spite of the fact that the grounds were leased. Some of the servants choose to fight rather than return in humiliation with empty baskets. During such quarrels, servants as well as workers are often wounded and killed.

Allegorically interpreted, the vineyard was the symbol of the Jewish faith and its people. It was entrusted by God to the priests and elders, but they had not been faithful workers. They had not taken good care of it and had not offered fruits in due season to its owner nor had they paid the rent. Their rule was one of injustice and extortion. They were greedy and corrupt workers who had completely forgotten the rights of the owner.

God sent his prophets to warn the priests and leaders of this sacred trust, but they stoned and killed them. In the parable, the owner thought that the workers would feel shame if he sent his son to collect the produce. But the workers took him outside the property and slew him so that they could take possession of the vineyard. Finally, the landlord demanded vengeance and sent a foreign army to invade and destroy these wicked workers. This, of course, was symbolic of the Roman army that destroyed the temple, its system of worship, the high priests, elders and other religious authorities. God transferred the trust of the vineyard—that is, the kingdom—from the religious authorities to Galileans, Syrians and other Gentiles.[1]

Most modern New Testament scholars debate whether this parable comes directly from Jesus. They suggest that originally, without the reworked elements of Christian overtones, it did derive from Jesus. Regardless of how one interprets the parable, destruction comes from people's own misconduct and behavior. God does not practice vengeance.

A reminder: This book is not a critical commentary. Therefore, we do not discuss the scholarly textual problems and the pros and cons concerning the parable. This commentary works with the Aramaic language, its word meanings and Near Eastern, Semitic culture. (Please see the bibliography for critical works on the New Testament.)

---

[1]Mt. 21:35; Mk. 12:1. See Errico and Lamsa, *Aramaic Light on the Gospel of Matthew,* "The Wicked Vineyard Workers," pp. 263-264.

CHAPTER 21

THE TIME OF THE GENTILES

And they shall fall by the edge of the sword, and shall be led away captive into all nations: and Jerusalem shall be trodden down of the Gentiles, until the times of the Gentiles be fulfilled. Lk. 21:24.

During the time of Jesus, the Jews were ruled by the iron rod of the Romans and oppressed by people of other races who acted as cohorts of the Romans. For example, King Herod the Great, an Idumean by race but a Jew by religion, was a vassal in the hands of the Romans. He collected heavy taxes and tribute which he shared with the Roman officials.

The Roman rule lasted until the early part of the seventh century CE, when it was superseded by the Arab conquest. Nevertheless, other stern Gentile rulers reigned over Palestine, oppressed the Jews, murdered them by the thousands, and carried many of them away captive.

When the kingdom of God is established on earth, people of all races and religions will live together peacefully and love one another. Then a lasting peace will reign and the predictions of the prophets will be realized. (See Micah 4:1-5.)

THE FULL REVELATION OF THE CHRIST REALIZED

And then shall they see the Son of man coming in a cloud with power and great glory. And when these things begin to come to pass, then look up, and lift up your heads; for your redemption draweth nigh. Lk. 21:27-28.

Part 1—COMING IN A CLOUD. Metaphorically, the term "cloud" means "glory, honor, and majesty." "To come in the clouds" also means "to succeed in a mission." Jesus used symbolic language so that he could explain his coming to simple people who did not

252

understand philosophical and metaphysical terms. Jesus is present with all humanity right now. He said, "Lo, I shall never leave you." He also assured his disciples and followers that whenever two or three of them are gathered together, he would be with them.

Whenever Near Easterners meet, following the greeting they ask one another: "What is your way?" This means, "What is your religion?" Then they begin to discuss religious matters. Therefore, whenever people are spiritually minded, thinking and talking about God's kingdom, the presence of the Christ is there among them.[1]

Jesus' coming will be a glorious victory; that is, good will triumph over evil. Hence, every eye will see him coming in glory and every heart will feel his presence. In other words, his spiritual kingdom, the reign of God, will be fully established on earth and all the nations of the earth will finally find peace. Jesus' mission then will have succeeded, his gospel fully realized and demonstrated throughout the world.

Part 2—SALVATION. In Aramaic, verse 28 reads: "But when these things begin to happen, have courage and lift up your heads, because your salvation is at hand."[2] *Porkana* in Aramaic means "salvation." The term "redemption" is not present in the Aramaic text.

There is a great deal of difference between these two terms. Salvation comes without paying a price or indemnity; it comes from God's love and grace. God saves his children just as a father would save his very own. But redemption means one has to pay a price to redeem. Slaves were redeemed by paying a price to their owner; prisoners of war were redeemed at prices according to their nobility and rank.

The mistranslation of the term *porkana* has led many Western scholars to use the word "redemption" erroneously. Some of them say that God, being just, had to pay a price to redeem the people of the world. Humanity is God's image and likeness. There was no one to

---

[1]Rev. 1:7.
[2]Lk. 21:28, Aramaic Peshitta text, Lamsa translation.

whom God owed a debt to redeem his children. God, being the only power in the universe, does not have to pay a price to anyone. To whom would God pay a ransom? Is anyone or anything greater than God?

Jesus told his disciples to have courage and lift up their heads when they saw the catastrophe taking place. They were to realize that their salvation was at hand, coming directly from God. Those who trusted in God and believed in the teaching of Jesus would escape the disaster. The disciples would be saved from the sudden destruction. God always spares a remnant. Even during the darkest days in the history of Israel, when people forsook the truth and gave themselves to the worship of Baal, God spared a remnant

"Lift up your heads" means "Don't be sad anymore." When people are sad, worried or uncertain, they hang their heads. When they hear good news, they lift up their heads and are happy. In the book of Second Kings, we are told that the King of Babylon lifted up the head of Jehoiachin—that is, honored the King of Judah. He had been in prison, but the Babylonian King raised him up and seated him among royalty.

CHAPTER 22

THE TRAITOR

But, behold, the hand of him that betrayeth me is with me on the table.
Lk. 22:21.

Among Semites of the Near East, the worst breach of friendship is for one to eat another's bread and secretly plot against him. To eat bread together is a token of loyalty, love and devotion. This sacred trust is seldom betrayed by a Semite. It is well illustrated in an eastern saying: "He is eating my bread and is disgracing my table." There is an Aramaic colloquialism that says: "His hand is on the table," meaning "he is eating my bread and yet he is plotting against me."

All the disciples were picking and eating food from the trays with their hands, as knives and forks were unknown. Jesus knew that Judas was plotting secretly against him. None of the disciples suspected Judas' treacherous act, nor did they understand about whom Jesus made the remark. They were all eating bread at the same time; thus, each one of them applied it to himself. Hence the question put by each one: "Is it I?"

DESTINED TO DIE

And truly the Son of man goeth, as it was determined: but woe unto that man by whom he is betrayed! Lk. 22:22.

The Son of man was destined to die. Scripture had predicted the manner of his death, and under no circumstances would Jesus reverse the course of prophecies about the suffering servant. Indeed there was no other way to ultimate victory except by the cross. Jesus did not want his disciples to be sorrowful on account of his departure or of the way he was to die by crucifixion. He impressed on their minds

255

that this was God's plan and that his death on the cross was his destiny. What was written must be fulfilled! This is typical Near Eastern thinking and feelings about life—nothing happens without God's will.

THE KINGS OF THE GENTILES

And he said unto them, The kings of the Gentiles exercise lordship over them; and they that exercise authority upon them are called benefactors. Lk. 22:25.

The Aramaic text reads: "There was also a dispute among them as to who was the greatest among them. Jesus said to them, The kings of the Gentiles are also their lords, and those who rule over them are called benefactors; But not so with you: let him who is great among you be the least, and he who is a leader be like one who serves."[1]

In countries where autocracy is the only form of government, kings and rulers exercise a tremendous power over their subjects. They regard their people merely as property, and their services can be exchanged or sold. Their possessions can be confiscated at any time if the ruler so desires or can even be killed at the behest of their leader. This was the case with Naboth. (See 1 Kings 21:13.)

The officials of these rulers and kings are empowered to levy taxes and collect revenues from their subjects. During difficult times, however, these monarchs or lords act as benefactors by distributing wheat and other supplies to their needy people. It is a characteristic of Near Eastern rulers and of the rich to acquire wealth unjustly so that they may distribute it generously in the times of depression. Some of these men would even share their supplies of bread with their famine-stricken people.

Jesus clearly censured this type of false generosity because these rulers were distributing in charity what they had confiscated from these same people by force and violence. They were benefactors only

---

[1]Lk. 22:24-26, Aramaic Peshitta text, Lamsa translation.

256

in name. And yet, the unfortunate subjects called their leaders benefactors because it made it easier to receive back what was unjustly taken from them.

Jesus' disciples were to avoid all forms of injustice and were to act as brothers toward each other. The chief among them was to be their servant. They were to teach meekness, love, and kindness and were to manifest these attributes themselves. They were not to be lords to each other but rather expressions of true friendship and care for one another.

JESUS APPOINTS A KINGDOM

And I appoint unto you a kingdom, as my Father hath appointed unto me; That ye may eat and drink at my table in my kingdom, and sit on thrones judging the twelve tribes of Israel. And the Lord said, Simon, Simon, behold Satan hath desired to have you, that he may sift you as wheat. Lk. 22:29-31

Part 1—AN ARAMAIC SAYING: "I appoint unto you a kingdom" is an Aramaic colloquialism. People often say to each other, "God gives you the kingdom of heaven," meaning "God gives you peace and tranquility." It does not mean that God will make you a king or ruler of a kingdom. One must not take this literally.

The disciples were expecting to be rulers of a kingdom on earth. According to the Jews, the Messiah was to be a king among kings, but Jesus' predictions about his death shattered all the disciples' dreams of earthly peace and prosperity. Disappointment took possession of their hearts. Jesus was attempting to cheer them by promising them everlasting peace and happiness in the kingdom of God. They did not realize yet what kind of vision and kingdom Jesus was teaching. The reign of God requires no thrones, princely rulers or hierarchy.

Part 2—SIGN OF THE KINGDOM. God, through the prophets, promised a universal kingdom based on justice and righteousness. A Messiah, the prince of peace, was to be the ruler over this spiritual domain. In due time, this kingdom was to embrace the whole world and bring all nations to the way of God.

The Aramaic word *malkutha,* "kingdom," also means "counsel."Hence, the kingdom of God refers to God's counsel, God's way of ruling the world—God's way of life.

Eating, drinking and sitting at the table in the kingdom are figures of speech and are not to be understood literally. These terms are symbolic of a righteous reign of joy, truth, harmony and prosperity. These things are the eternal bread of life that makes life worth living. The truths that Jesus taught his disciples not only judge Israel but all nations and peoples. When ones does not live in joy, peace and harmony, then misery and suffering become the end result of living— hence, judgment.

Part 3—THE DISCIPLES TESTED. The Aramaic text reads: "sift all of you," not just Simon. In Aramaic, the pronoun "you" is plural. The reference here is that all the disciples of Jesus were to be sifted like wheat. "Sift all of you as wheat" means "to test all of you." Wheat is sifted to separate it from the tares and soil. In this process of purification, it is constantly shaken in the sifter until the tares appear on top, the soil falls below and the wheat is at the bottom.

The ranks of Jesus' disciples had already been weakened and those who remained would be tested further. Their faith would be shaken; Judas would be separated from them; Peter would deny his lord; and the rest of them would flee. They would be shaken just like wheat; temptation to break rank and forsake everything would be strong. These trials would overtake them unexpectedly in the dark hours of the night.

SWORDS

Then said he unto them, But now, he that hath a purse, let him take it, and likewise his scrip: and he that hath no sword, let him sell his garment, and buy one. Lk. 22:36.

In biblical lands, during revolutions and wars, people sell their valuables and buy weapons. At such times, when wealth is endangered, swords and other arms are in demand and valuable. It would not be embarrassing for a man to exchange his coat or even his trousers for a dagger or sword and return home clad only in his long undershirt. Such forms of bargaining are very common in market places and streets even to this day.

This saying of Jesus is proverbial concerning an alarming situation. He did not literally mean that his disciples were to sell their cloaks and buy swords. This would have been a departure from his messianic understanding and interpretation. It would have been accepted as a signal for a revolution to establish the kingdom of Israel by force.

What Jesus meant was that danger was approaching and he would soon be betrayed into the hands of sinful men and be crucified. The disciples were never armed and had nothing to sell to buy arms. However, they took this saying literally and replied, "We have two swords." Jesus said, "This is enough." He dismissed the entire matter because he knew they were taking what he said literally. Had he wanted them to be armed and fight for him, more than two swords would certainly have been necessary.

ENTER NOT INTO TEMPTATION

And when he was at the place, he said unto them Pray that ye enter not into temptation. Lk. 22:40.

"Enter not into temptation" means do not be carried away by material things that weaken the forces of the spirit. Aramaic speaking people often say: "Do not let us be in need." When a husband goes on a journey, his wife's last farewell remark to him is, "Do not leave us in want." The Aramaic word for "temptation" also means "trial and difficulty." In the Lord's prayer, "do not let us enter into temptation" is the proper rendering of the verse. "Lead us not into temptation" implies that God might tempt us or try us out. God never leads anyone into temptation; but God will prevent us from going astray, consciously or otherwise, when we seek divine help.

Judas, when he betrayed his master, was tempted by the love of money and not by God. James in his epistle says: "Let no man say when he is tempted, I am tempted of God: For God cannot be tempted with evil, neither tempteth he any man."[2] God guides those who pray and look to him for help to overcome the temptations of life.

Jesus knew his disciples and followers would meet worldly temptations just as Judas did. He saw from the very beginning that his teaching would have a universal appeal and would overthrow the existing religious systems of his day. His followers would receive honor and fame, but pride and greed would entice them and weaken their unity.

Jesus even anticipated the strife and divisions that took place after his death. These divisions would be the results of ambitious men who, during their temptations, did not seek God's help. They placed more value on honors and material things than on the things of spirit.[3]

PRAYING ALONE

And he was withdrawn from them about a stone's cast, and kneeled down, and prayed, Lk. 22:41.

How the disciples recorded these sad moments has been a puzzle to a great many Bible students. When Jesus arrived at Gethsemane, the disciples sat down and he separated from them just a short distance. He did this, probably, because he did not wish to alarm them by what he might say in his prayer. Jesus knew Judas was already in league with the religious authorities and that he might come at any time with the soldiers. His disciples were not aware of the seriousness of the situation. They were tired, sleepy and fearful, but they were not asleep. The Aramaic verb *damkeen*, "sleeping," also means "dozing" and "reclining."

---

[2]James 1:13, K. J. V.

[3]Mt. 6:13. See Errico and Lamsa, *Aramaic Light on the Gospel of Matthew,* "Lead us not into Temptation," pp. 99-100.

260

Jesus was praying aloud, for he had reached a crisis within his soul. During such times of stress, Near Easterners usually raise their voices and pray to God as though conversing with him. Undoubtedly, the disciples heard some of their master's utterances. If they had been nearer to him, they might have reported all that he said. In these last moments, Jesus was entrusting himself to the will of his Father. He was talking to God as a son would talk to his father or one friend to another. But there were times when he was deeply moved and yielded to tears and his words were not distinct. (Matthew 26:39.)

SWEAT TURNED INTO BLOOD

And being in an agony he prayed more earnestly: and his sweat was as it were great drops of blood falling down to the ground. Lk. 22:44.

"And his sweat was as it were great drops of blood falling down to the ground" is a Near Eastern saying for overwhelming distress and suffering. It does not mean that his sweat literally turned into blood. The Semitic writer describes in figurative speech the agony through which Jesus was passing during his time of prayer in Gethsemane. He was emphasizing the temptation, suffering and fear that befell Jesus.

Perspiration turning into blood means that the agony and torment in Jesus' soul were excruciating The mental and emotional anguish was unbearable. When a man is very fearful, people say "he has turned white" or "his sweat has turned into blood." Semites also speak of a murderer's leaven turning into blood. These descriptive expressions are symbolic of Eastern thought concerning some of life's intense experiences and are never taken at face value.

THE KISS OF JUDAS

And while he yet spake, behold a multitude, and he that was called Judas, one of the twelve, went before them, and drew near unto Jesus to kiss

261

him. But Jesus said unto him, Judas, betrayest thou the Son of man with a kiss? Lk. 22:47-48.

Some Near Eastern men very seldom kiss their wives and children, but they kiss their friends on the cheek when greeting them. A host kisses his guests on their arrival at his house. Friends who have not seen each other for a long time show their affection for each other in this way. When enemies reconcile, they kiss each other as a sign of friendship.

In the Near East, kissing is an indication of sacred friendship; but occasionally, it can be deceptive and misleading. For example, while Joab was kissing Amasa, he plunged his sword into Amasa's body.[4] When a man desires to destroy his enemies, he invites them to his home and greets them with a kiss; then, after entertaining them lavishly, he orders his servants to kill them.

Although a kiss is a sacred bond between two men, it is shameful to kiss a woman, even one's own wife, in public. If a single girl happens to be kissed, she is immediately humbled, humiliated and disgraced—so much so that she may not easily be married. Her reputation has been tarnished. If her parents happen to be influential, they will attempt to avenge her, even to the extent of murdering the man who kissed her.

Judas kissed Jesus not only to point him out to the soldiers and the servants of the high priests but also as a mark of his discipleship. He did not want Jesus to know he was implicated in the scheme. He pretended he was innocent and that he was not responsible for the soldiers who followed him.

By kissing Jesus, Judas implied that he himself was in danger as were the rest of the disciples. This is evident because Judas did not appear at Jesus' trial. He could have been used as a witness against Jesus and perhaps his words might have carried more weight in convicting his master. But Judas fled and secretly kept in touch with the high priests to see what was going to happen to Jesus. When he

---

[4]2 Sam. 20:9-10.

discovered that his lord was condemned to die, he regretted what he had done. He did not expect such a result. He had been disappointed in his lord and felt that he had wasted his time with him. But he thought that the authorities would only chastise and threaten him and then set him free. When things turned out differently, Judas came back to the high priests and returned their money. He told them that it was blood money and that he was deceived by them. They replied to him that it was his own affair.[5]

YOUR TURN

When I was daily with you in the temple, ye stretched forth no hands against me: but this is your hour, and the power of darkness. Lk. 22:53.

The Aramaic word *shaa*, "hour," also means "turn" or "time." In the present instance the reference is to "turn" and not "hour." When Semites are persecuted, they say: "It is your time [or turn], do what you please."

Some Pharisees and priests had sought to seize Jesus, but they were afraid of the people. On certain occasions, he had escaped out of their hands. Now it was their turn. Now their time had come. Jesus had accomplished his mission and was ready to go with them.

Jesus had preached for three years and laid the foundation of a new order. He was now ready to die. He need no longer flee from his accusers. He was in their hands and they could have their own way. They could put him to death in any manner they wished and he would make no protest or defense.

---

[5]Mt. 26:48; Mk. 14:44. See Errico and Lamsa, *Aramaic Light on the Gospel of Matthew*, "The Traitorous Kiss," pp. 336-337.

THE RIGHT HAND OF GOD

Hereafter shall the Son of man sit on the right hand of the power of God. Lk. 22:69.

Semites think of God in a spiritual way and not in physical terms. But when they refer to God's qualities, they speak in human terms. They describe God as having hands and feet, but this is figurative and not literal. The right hand symbolizes power and authority. Semitic kings place their loyal subjects on the right at official banquets as a sign of honor and appreciation. Queens also sit at the right of their kings.

Near Easterners suspect anything that is done with the left hand. It is a bad omen. A present is always offered with the right hand. Saluting, likewise, is always done by the right hand. A Semitic bishop blesses the people with his uplifted right hand and people kiss his hand of blessing.

Jesus was God's beloved son. His triumphant victory on earth would accord him all honor and glory. He was to sit on the right hand of God; that is, all power and authority would be entrusted to him. From now on, Jesus' power and authority would increase and he would be recognized and acclaimed all over the world.[6]

---

[6]Mk. 14:62.

CHAPTER 23

BEARING THE CROSS WITH JESUS

And as they led him away, they laid hold upon one Simon, A Cyrenian, coming out of the country, and on him they laid the cross, that he might bear it after Jesus. Lk. 23:26.

Simon was probably from the city of Cyrene in Africa. Either his family or he had migrated to Palestine. In the Near East, strangers and immigrants are always called by the name of the city or country from which they or their ancestors originated. Simon was compelled to help Jesus carry his cross but not to relieve the teacher from Galilee of his heavy burden as most suppose.

The Aramaic text reads: "And while they took him away, they laid hold of Simon, a Cyrenian, who was coming from a village, and they placed the end of the cross on him, to carry it with Jesus."[1] The King James Version says: "And on him they laid the cross, that he might bear it after Jesus." This means that Jesus was bearing the front part and walking ahead while Simon carried the lower end. The heaviest part of the cross rested on Jesus' shoulders because it had the cross bar. His position was more trying and exhausting as he climbed the steep hill with this burden. It was difficult for him to hold on to the cross and ascend, especially as the arm of the cross grazed the ground.

GREEN AND DRY TREES

For if they do these things in a green tree, what shall be done in the dry? Lk. 23:31.

The Aramaic text reads: "For if they do these things with the

---

[1] Lk. 23:26, Aramaic Peshitta text, Lamsa translation.

green wood, what will be done with dry wood?"[2] This is an Aramaic figurative saying referring to fire and wood. Fire consumes green wood slowly but dry wood burns quickly.

Jesus used this metaphor to refer to himself and the people who were weeping over him as he was carrying his cross, climbing the steep hill of Golgotha. He told the daughters of Jerusalem: ". . . Do not weep over me; but weep over yourselves and over your own children. For behold, the days are coming in which they will say, Blessed are the barren and the wombs that never gave birth and the breasts that never gave suck. Then they will begin to say to the mountains, Fall on us; and to the hills, Cover us."[3]

Green wood is symbolic of innocence and dry wood of guilt. If suffering was inflicted on an innocent man, how much more would be done to the guilty? Jesus was the green wood that the religious authorities were kindling, but the days were to come when the Romans would inflict great suffering on the religious authorities and the people.

The Jewish nation was like dry wood ready to be consumed when Jerusalem was conquered. Their suffering and destruction would be greater for they would be killed along the roadside, women would leave their children and flee for their lives, husbands and wives would be separated and carried captive, the dead would be left unburied with no one to weep over them.

Jesus had many mourners who after his death would anoint his body and bury him. But, he knew what would befall the people of Palestine. This was what made him so apprehensive even at the hour of his own approaching death. He wanted to warn the women who had come from Galilee with him and the daughters of Jerusalem who had come to see him die. Jesus did not want them weeping over him but to weep for themselves because they would have no mourners in the day of their desolation.

An unjust person need not lament over the death of a righteous

---

[2]Lk. 23:31, Aramaic Peshitta text, Lamsa translation.
[3]Lk. 23:28-30, Aramaic Peshitta text, Lamsa translation.

individual but should rather mourn over his own grievous errors. The world need not mourn over the death of Jesus for he did not regard his own death as a loss. He knew that the nails and spear would not prevent him from giving new life to the human family.

CRUCIFIED

And when they were come to the place, which is called Calvary, there they crucified him, and the malefactors, one on the right hand, and the other on the left. Lk. 23:33.

The Aramaic word *zakpo* means "to stretch out the arms and nail the hands to the cross." Criminals were nailed and not tied on a cross, as some commentators and pictures suggest. The latter method would have prolonged death and the pain would have been less. The victim would be exposed to thirst, cold and heat, and finally die of starvation. On the other hand, the nails would cause severe suffering and quick death. The loss of blood would make thirst more intense

The public demanded crucifixion so that they could be sure that the criminal was dead. No spectator would be willing to remain more than three or four hours on the scene, nor would the soldiers keep guard for several days. In the case of Jesus, the high priests wanted execution to take place promptly so that it would be possible to lower the bodies from the crosses before the Sabbath began. The whole drama took four or five hours. If the victims had not been nailed, they would not have died during this period of time.

Even today in Eastern countries, criminals are put to death very quickly because of the spectacular appeal. In Persia, they are placed in front of a cannon; the entire procedure lasts only a few minutes.[4]

---

[4]Mt. 27:33; Mk. 15:22; Jn. 19:17.

PARADISE

And Jesus said unto him, Verily I say unto thee, Today shalt thou be with me in paradise. Lk. 23:43.

The term *pardesa* is a Persian word meaning "garden." This word is also used in Semitic languages to mean a beautiful garden full of trees, abundant flowers and fresh cool springs. Persia is famous for its roses and stunning gardens. Most regions of the country, especially those bordering Mesopotamia, are very fertile and well watered by rivers and brooks. Flowers grow wild and nature has endowed the land with all that makes for beauty and loveliness.

On the Western border of Mesopotamia are Arabia, Syria and Palestine, where trees are few and water scarce. Persia looks like paradise to the eye of a traveler who enters it by way of these countries and the Arabian desert. The contrast is so strong that to the people of these other lands, Persian gardens are symbolic of the gardens of heaven.

When nomadic Moslem forces conquered Persia, they were amazed with the splendor and attractiveness that surpassed anything they had seen in their own desert countries. Moslem theologians pictured heaven as a Persian garden full of trees bearing fruit, their branches hanging down to the ground so that people could easily pick the fruit while they reclined under the shade of these trees. Abundant water streamed from cold springs and ran through the garden. Green gardens, trees and cold water were alluring to people born in an arid land where such luxuries existed only in dreams and folk tales. Among these desert people, who were raised with hardships, nothing could satisfy their desire of fulfillment more than Persia, a place of comfort and luxury.

The thirst and suffering of the penitent thief on the cross were to cease and his dreams of comfort and bliss would soon be realized when he entered heaven's paradise. This was the assurance that Jesus promised the dying criminal.

According to Aramaic manner of speech, the emphasis in the

text is on the word "today." It should read: "Truly I say to you today, you will be with me in paradise." The promise was made on that day and it was to be fulfilled later. This is characteristic of Semitic speech, implying that the promise was made on a certain day and it would surely be kept.

BURYING A STRANGER

This man went unto Pilate, and begged the body of Jesus. And he took it down, and wrapped it in linen, and laid it in a sepulchre that was hewn in stone, wherein never man before was laid. Lk. 23:52-53.

Births and deaths carry no expense for Near Eastern families. They are regarded as natural events. Infants are born in homes without the aid of doctors or nurses. The burial of the dead is a responsibility of the town. Among Semites the birth of children brings joy to the entire town, while a person's death creates great sorrow for everyone.

Near Eastern generosity is never so lavishly shown as at the funeral of a neighbor. The immediate relatives of the deceased are completely relieved of all duties and expenses. Men and women volunteer their services in taking charge of the house. Food for the professional mourners and the out-of-town guests is furnished by the townspeople. All the articles for the burial are usually given by friends and nearest relatives. The townsmen open the grave site.

In the case of strangers who die or are killed, burial articles are contributed by rich and religious men. It is sacrilegious to leave the dead unburied. Joseph of Arimathea (Aramaic—*Ramtha*) was a rich and religious Jew who used his influence with Pilate. He was of Judea but he did not wish to see even a Galilean religious leader, though he had been condemned as a criminal, left unburied. People considered such occasions to bury the dead as opportunities to do good.

CHAPTER 24

GOLGOTHA—A CEMETERY

And as they were afraid, and bowed down their faces to the earth, they said unto them, Why seek ye the living among the dead? Lk. 24:5.

"Why seek ye the living among the dead?" means "Why do you search in a cemetery for someone who is alive?" Golgotha, "the skull," was a cemetery.

Some of the women followers of Jesus who had come with him from Galilee had watched the men put his body temporarily in an empty tomb. And now, very early on Sunday morning, they had returned to the sepulcher and brought spices with them to give Jesus' body a proper and final burial. His body had been hastily placed in the tomb on Friday evening because the Sabbath was drawing near.

Evidently the sepulcher was close to the place where Jesus and the two criminals were crucified. At that time, the top of this hill was a cemetery for foreigners who had died in Jerusalem. The Jewish cemetery is on the other side of the brook of Kedron, across from the holy city.

(Dr. Lamsa suggests that the reference to the temporary sepulcher was one of the caves across from the Damascus Gate. These three caves look like the face of a man—two eyes and a mouth—and the top of the hill resembles a human skull, hence, the name Golgotha, "the skull.")

The two men were surprised that the women were looking for Jesus in a cemetery. Their master had told them that he would be arrested, condemned, crucified and buried, but that he would rise again. Nevertheless, as one can see from reading the gospels, neither the women nor the disciples had taken his words seriously. They could not understand how anyone could triumph over death and rise from the grave.

270

CHRIST'S SUFFERING FORETOLD

Ought not Christ to have suffered these things, and to enter into his glory? And beginning at Moses and all the prophets, he expounded unto them in all the scriptures the things concerning himself. Lk. 24:26-27.

Jesus, prior to his crucifixion, had told his disciples and followers that he would be rejected, condemned and crucified. He had wanted to prepare them for what they thought was a tragic end. Nevertheless, his followers could not understand how such a great and holy man, who had worked miracles and wonders, could meet with death on the cross. Nor did they expect him to rise from among the dead.

Jesus' disciples reasoned that the holy prophets were still in their graves so how could their master escape the grave? To the minds of the unsophisticated disciples, death was an end to all things—a total finality. But to Jesus, death was not the end. His death was nothing but a triumph over fear and evil and the beginning of a new life.

FLESH AND BONES

Behold my hands and my feet, that it is I myself: handle me, and see; for a spirit hath not flesh and bones, as ye see me have. Lk. 24:39.

Spirit has neither flesh nor bones; it is invisible and the finest essence in the universe. Spirit is everywhere and all-encompassing. Human beings can sense spirit because it is life and truth; but it is formless and intangible.

Jesus rose from the dead in a new body, a spiritual body, free from all physical elements, limitations and hindrancess. Paul says in his first letter to the Corinthians 15:42-44, Aramaic text: "So also is the resurrection of the dead. It is sown in corruption; it is raised in incorruption: It is sown in dishonor; it is raised in glory: it is sown in weakness; it is raised in power: It is sown a natural body; it is raised a spiritual body. There is a natural body and there is a spiritual body."

Jesus, having a spiritual body, was able to enter a room when the doors were closed. He could appear and disappear among his disciples. Prior to his death and crucifixion, he had never done this.

Christ in Jesus had the power to materialize and dematerialize his form. On some occasions, such phenomena took place when the disciples were in a deep, ecstatic state—that is, when they were in the spiritual realm of divine mind.

Apparently, some of his disciples were not completely convinced that their master had broken the bars of *sheol* and had risen from the dead. When Jesus suddenly appeared in their midst, they thought he might be a ghost in human form. In the Near East today, many people claim they have seen ghosts appearing to them in human bodies.

Jesus admonished his disciples for their lack of faith. He told them that he was the risen Christ and that they could touch him. Jesus assured them he was not a ghost but the triumphant Messiah who had conquered the grave and won a victory over death and *sheol*. He had opened the doors of the everlasting spiritual kingdom.

THE ASCENSION

And it came to pass, while he blessed them, he was parted from them, and carried up into heaven. Lk. 24:51.

Over the Arabian desert where the stars near the horizon look as though they touch the ground, heaven does not seem so far away. The Assyrians and Chaldeans, although they were advanced in astronomy, had but a vague idea of the distance between the stars. They knew about the stars, their position and their movements. They invented the calendar and measured time, but they knew very little of the tremendous distance between heaven and earth.

Ancient people thought it would be no problem to enter the heavens. This notion is illustrated by their attempt to ascend into heaven by building the tower of Babel. They thought heaven was not more than a mile or two above the earth, just a little distance above the clouds. Their concept of the earth was totally different from ours.

They believed heaven was above the earth and there was also an unknown place under the earth. People either ascended or descended. This theory still exists among many tribal Semitic people in the Near East who believe the stars and the moon are little lamps hung in heaven for the benefit of the earth.

Jesus, after conversing with his disciples and followers at this last appearance, disappeared. They saw him go up into the heavens. At that time, Jewish people believed that certain prophets could ascend to heaven. Moses and Elijah had already demonstrated this power. It was not difficult for the early followers of Jesus to believe their lord also had ascended.

The ascension was a spiritual event. Jesus ascended with a spiritual body with which he arose from the grave. In Aramaic and Hebrew the word "universe" also means "heaven." Heaven is a later term that was used when the question of the resurrection developed. In reality and in the realms of heaven there is no distance, no north, south, east or west. These are relative, conventional terms invented by the human mind for the sake of convenience. They do not exist in spirit.

Jesus has always been present with his disciples and followers. He said: "For wherever two or three are gathered in my name, I am there among them."[1] ". . . and, lo, I am with you always, to the end of the world."[2] The universal presence of Jesus is continually working to achieve the aim of his mission—to bring the everlasting kingdom into full realization and manifestation.

---

[1]Mt. 18:20, Aramaic Peshitta text, Lamsa translation.
[2]Mt. 28:20, Aramaic Peshitta text, Lamsa translation.

BIBLIOGRAPHY

ARAMAIC AND SEMITIC STUDIES

Black, Matthew, *An Aramaic Approach to the Gospels and Acts*, Peabody, Mass., Hendrickson, Third edition, 1967&1998.

Burkert, Walter, *The Orientalizing Revolution*: *Near Eastern Influence on Greek Culture in the Early Archaic Age*, Harvard University Press, 1992.

Charlesworth, James H., *Jesus Within Judaism*: *New Light from Exciting Archaeological Discoveries*, New York, Doubleday, 1988.
_____, *Jesus' Jewishness*: *Exploring the Place of Jesus in Early Judaism, New York*, Crossroad Herder, 1996.

Chilton, Bruce, *Pure Kingdom: Jesus' Vision of God*. Grand Rapids, Michigan, Eerdmans, 1996.

Chilton, Bruce & Neusner, Jacob, *Judaism in the New Testament*, London, Routledge, 1995.

Eisenberg, Azriel, *The Synagogue through the Ages*, New York, Block Publishing Company, 1974.

Errico, Rocco A., *Setting A Trap For God*: *The Aramaic Prayer of Jesus*, Unity Village, Unity Books, 1997.
_____, *Let There Be Light*: *The Seven Keys*, Smyrna, GA, Noohra Foundation, 1994.
_____, *And There Was Light*, Smyrna, GA, Noohra Foundation, 1998.
_____, *The Mysteries of Creation*: *The Genesis Story*, Smyrna, GA, Noohra Foundation, 1993.
_____, *The Message of Matthew*: *An Annotated Parallel Aramaic-English Gospel of Matthew*, Smyrna, GA, Noohra Foundation, 1991.
_____, *Aramaic Light on the Gospel of Matthew*: A Commentary on the teachings of Jesus from the Aramaic and unchanged Near Eastern Customs, Smyrna, GA, Noohra Foundation, 2000.

Falla, Terry C., *A Key to the Peshitta Gospels*, New York, Brill, 1991

Fitzmyer, Joseph, *A Wandering Aramean: A Collection of Aramaic Essays*, Chico, CA, Scholar Press, 1979.
_____, *Essays on the Semitic Background of the New Testament*, Chico, CA, Scholar Press, 1974.

Gibson, Margaret D., *The Commentaries of Ishodad of Merv: The Gospel of Matthew and Mark* (Aramaic) Cambridge, University Press, 1911.

Hitti, Philip K., *The Near East in History*, Princeton: D. Van Nostrand Co., 1960.

Lach, Samuel Tobias, *A Rabbinic Commentary on the New Testament*, Hoboken, NJ, KTAV, 1987.

Lamsa, George M., *The Oldest Christian People*, New York, Macmillan, 1926.
_____, *My Neighbor Jesus: In the Light of His Own Language, People, and Time*, Philadelphia, A. J. Holman, 1932.
_____, *New Testament Origin*, New York, Ziff Davis, 1947.
_____, *The Kingdom on Earth*, Unity Village, Unity Books, 1966.
_____, *The Holy Bible: From the Ancient Eastern Texts*, San Francisco, Harper Collins, (originally A. J. Holman) 1957.
Lawrence, T. E., *Seven Pillars of Wisdom*, Garden City, New York, Doubleday, 1926.

McCullogh, W. Stewart, *A Short History of Syriac Christianity to the Rise of Islam*, Chico, CA, Scholars Press, 1982.

Moffett, Samuel H., *A History of Christianity in Asia*, Vol. 1, Harper, San Francisco, 1992.

Overman, J. Andrew, *Matthew's Gospel and Formative Judaism: The Social World of the Matthean Community*, Minn., Fortress Press, 1990.

Rihbany, Abraham M., *The Syrian Christ*, Boston, Houghton Mifflin, 1916.

Stewart, John, *Nestorian Missionary Enterprise*: *The Story of a Church on Fire*, Kerala, India, Mar Narsai Press, 1961.

Torrey, Charles Butler, *The Four Gospels*: *A New Translation*, New York, Harper and Publisher, 1947.

Vermes, Geza, *Jesus the Jew*, Philadelphia, Fortress Press, 1981.
_____, *Jesus and the World of Judaism*, Philadelphia, Fortress Press, 1983.
_____, *The Religion of Jesus the Jew*, Philadelphia, Fortress Press, 1993.

Wigram, W. A., *The Assyrians and Their Neighbors*, London, G. Bell and Sons, 1929.

Zeitlin, Irving M. *Jesus and the Judaism of His Time*, London, Polity Press/Basil Blackwell, 1988.

STUDIES ON THE HISTORICAL JESUS

Chilton, Bruce & Evans, Craig A., *Studying the Historical Jesus*: *Evaluations of the State of Current Research*, New York, Brill, 1998.
_____, *Authenticating the Words of Jesus*, New York, Brill, 1999.
_____, *Authenticating the Activities of Jesus*, New York, Brill, 1999.
_____, *Jesus in Context*, New York, Brill, 1997.

Evans, Craig A., *Jesus & His Contemporaries*, New York, Brill, 1995.

Meier, John P., *A Marginal Jew*, *Rethinking the Historical Jesus*, New York, Doubleday, Vol 1—1991, Vol. 2—1994.

GENERAL

Brown, Raymond E., *The Death of the Messiah*, Volumes 1 & 2, New York, Doubleday, 1994.
_____, *The Birth of the Messiah*, New Updated Edition, New York, Doubleday, 1993.

Burkitt, F. Crawford, *The Earliest Sources for the Life of Jesus*, New York, E. P. Dutton, 1922.

Charlesworth, James H., *Jesus and the Dead Sea Scrolls*. New York, Doubleday, 1992.

Dalman, Gustaf, *Jesus—Jeshua*, New York, Macmillan Co., 1929.

Dungan, David Laird, *A History of the Synoptic Problem*: The Canon, the Text, the Composition, and the Interpretation of the Gospels, New York, Doubleday, 1999.

Farmer, William R., *The Synoptic Problem: A Critical Analysis*, North Carolina, Western North Carolina Press 1976.

McNicol, Allan J., *Luke's Use of Matthew*: Beyond the Q Impasse, Valley Forge, PA, Trinity Press International, 1996.

Stanton, Graham, *Gospel Truth?* New Light on Jesus & the Gospels, PA, Trinity Press International, 1995.

Renan, Ernest, *The Life of Jesus*, New York, World Publishing, 1941.

ABOUT THE AUTHOR
George M. Lamsa

George M. Lamsa, Th.D., a renowned native Assyrian scholar of the Holy Bible, translator, lecturer, ethnologist and author, was born August 5, 1892 in a civilization with customs, manners and language almost identical to those in the time of Jesus. His native tongue was full of similar idioms and parables, untouched by the outside world in 1900 years.

Until World War 1, his people living in that part of the ancient biblical lands that today is known as Kurdistan, in the basin of the rivers Tigris and Euphrates, retained the simple nomadic life as in the days of the Hebrew patriarchs. Only at the beginning of the 20th century did the isolated segment of the once great Assyrian Empire learn of the discovery of America and the Reformation in Germany.

Likewise, until that same time, this ancient culture of early Christians was unknown to the Western world, and the Aramaic language was thought to be dead. But in this so-called "Cradle of Civilization," primitive biblical customs and Semitic culture, cut off from the world, were preserved.

Lamsa's primary upbringing as a boy was to tend the lambs. But, as the first-born in his family, while yet an infant he was dedicated to God by his devout mother. Years after her death, when Lamsa was 12 years of age, her vow was renewed by native tribesmen, an ox killed and its blood rubbed on his forehead. This vow to God, Lamsa claimed, had always been part of him. "God's hand" he affirmed, "has been steadfastly on my shoulder, guiding me in the divine work."

Lamsa's formal education and studies began under the priests and deacons of the ancient Church of the East. Later he graduated with the highest honors ever bestowed from the Archbishop of Canterbury's Colleges in Iran and in Turkey, with the degree of Bachelor of Arts. Lamsa never married, but dedicated his life to "God's calling." He spoke eight languages and his lowest grade in any subject was 99.

At the beginning of World War 1, when Turkey began its invasions, Lamsa was forced to flee the Imperial University at

Constantinople where he was studying. He went to South America where he endured great hardships during those years. He knew but three words in Spanish at that time—water, work and bread. As best as he could he existed—in the British Merchant Marine for a time, then working on railroads, in mines and later in printing shops, a trade he had learned while attending college in Iran.

After arriving in the United States in his early 20s, Lamsa worked by day as a printer, and by night he went to school. He later studied at the Episcopal Theological Seminary in Alexandria, Virginia, and at Dropsie College in Philadelphia.

It was through his struggles, during these years, with the English idioms that Lamsa gradually launched into his "life's work" of translating the Holy Bible from Aramaic into English. Yet many years were to pass before the world received his translations.

First as a lecturer in churches and seminaries, in halls and auditoriums, before statesmen, theologians, groups of artists, actors and others, Lamsa received recognition as a poet-philosopher and as an authority on all phases of Near Eastern civilization.

It was his own inner compulsion, and the urging of hundreds who heard him, that drove him forward and brought about—after 30 years of labor, research and study—his translation of the Holy Bible from a branch of the ancient Aramaic language that the earliest Christians used. (It is a know fact that Jesus and his followers spoke Aramaic.)

There were times that he was temporarily stopped in his translations when the idioms in the manuscripts could not be given correct English equivalents. It was Lamsa's firm belief that his translation from Aramaic would bring people closer to the Word of God and would facilitate understanding between the East and the West. For forty years, he produced commentaries and many other works based on the Aramaic language. The last ten years of his life, Dr. Lamsa tutored and prepared Dr. Rocco A. Errico to continue with the Aramaic approach to Scripture. He left this earthly life on September 22, 1975, in Turlock, California.

ABOUT THE AUTHOR
Rocco A. Errico

Rocco A. Errico, Th.D., D.D., is the founder and president of the Noohra Foundation of Smyrna, Georgia. The Noohra Foundation is a nonprofit, nonsectarian, spiritual educational organization of Aramaic biblical studies, research and publications. Dr. Errico is an ordained minister, lecturer, author, Bible authority, translator, Aramaic instructor, educator and spiritual counselor.

For ten years he studied intensively with George M. Lamsa, Th.D, world-renowned Assyrian biblical scholar and translator of the *Holy Bible from the Ancient Eastern Text*. Dr. Errico is proficient in Aramaic and Hebrew exegesis—Old and New Testaments—and in the customs, idioms, psychology, symbolism and philosophy of Semitic peoples. Errico has translated the Gospel of Matthew from Aramaic into English. He is also fluent in the Spanish language and has translated his book *The Ancient Aramaic Prayer of Jesus* into Spanish.

Dr. Errico holds a doctorate in Letters from the College of Seminarians, The Apostolic Succession of Antioch and the Church of the East—American See, a doctorate in Philosophy from the School of Christianity, Los Angeles, a doctorate in Divinity from St. Ephrem's Institute, Sweden, and a doctorate in Sacred Theology from the School of Christianity, Los Angeles. He also hold a special title of Teacher, Prime Exegete, *Malpana d'miltha dalaha*, among the Federation of St. Thomas Christians of the order of Antioch.

Dr. Errico serves as a professor and dean of Biblical Studies in schools of ministry for many denominations and is a regular feature writer for Science of Mind magazine, Los Angeles. He formerly served as an editor and writer for *Light for All*, a religious magazine. He has held advisory positions with many boards of ecumenical religious organizations. Dr. Errico lectures extensively throughout the country and is widely known for his numerous radio and television appearances.

Under the auspices of the Noohra Foundation, Dr. Errico continues to lecture for colleges, civic groups and churches of various denominations in the United States, Canada, Mexico and Europe.

For a complimentary catalog of Aramaic Bible translations, books, audio and video cassettes, and a brochure of classes, retreats and seminars, or for any other inquiries, write or call the Noohra Foundation. Those interested in scheduling Dr. Errico for a personal appearance may also contact:

Noohra Foundation
4480H S. Cobb Drive #343
Smyrna, GA 30080

E-mail: noohrafnd@aol.com

Phone: 770-319-9376
Fax: 770-319-9793

Noohra Foundation web-site: www.noohra.com

In addition to *Aramaic Light on the Gospels of Mark and Luke* and its predecessor (*Aramaic Light on the Gospel of Matthew*—$29.95), the Noohra Foundation is pleased to offer the following books by Dr. Rocco A. Errico and Dr. George M. Lamsa.

Books by Dr. Errico:

LET THERE BE LIGHT: THE SEVEN KEYS

The Bible is more than anything else a Near Eastern account of spiritual events and teachings. In this illuminating work, Dr. Errico builds a bridge between Western ways of understanding and the Near Eastern social realities that are embedded in the Bible. He helps us to see the Bible through Semitic, Aramaic eyes. Bypassing doctrinal creeds and rigid interpretations, he corrects numerous errors and misleading literal translations that have caused confusion for centuries. This book equips the reader with seven key insights to understand the allusions, parables, and teachings of the Bible, opening the door to the ancient Aramaic world from which the Bible emerged. $17.95

AND THERE WAS LIGHT

Like its predecessor *Let There Be Light*, this books takes us through the heart of the Hebrew Bible and New Testament by working with Aramaic—the language spoken by the Patriarchs, Jesus, his apostles and their contemporaries. Once more, Dr. Errico unlocks puzzling passages with the Seven Keys. Suddenly the Bible, from Genesis to Revelation, becomes clearer and more relevant for Western readers. The teaching ministry and parables of Jesus come alive as you've never read before. $19.95

SETTING A TRAP FOR GOD: The Aramaic Prayer of Jesus

What exactly does the word "prayer" mean? What does it accomplish? Dr. Errico focuses on original Aramaic manuscripts and the ancient culture of the Near East as he answers these questions in his revised and expanded edition of the Lord's Prayer. Discover the way of peace, health, and prosperity as you learn to "set a trap" for the inexhaustible power of God. $10.95

THE MYSTERIES OF CREATION: The Genesis Story

A challenging new look at the processes and mysteries of the primal creation account. Dr. Errico uses his own direct translation from the Aramaic-Peshitta text of Genesis 1:1-31 and 2:103. He discusse the Semitic meaning, names and theories of the origin of God. Where appropriate, he borrows insights from the world of both quantum physics and biblical scholarship. *The Genesis Story* introduces to humankind its responsibility to the earth and its environment. $16.95

THE MESSAGE OF MATTHEW: An Annotated Parallel Aramaic-English Gospel of Matthew

Dr. Errico's stirring translation of the ancient Aramaic Peshitta text of Matthew is further enriched with his stimulating and illuminating annotations. The style of writing in *The Message of Matthew* is simple and direct. The English translation is printed on the left side of the page with footnotes. The Aramaic text is printed on the right with additional footnotes in English. These valuable footnotes explain the meanings of Aramaic words and customs with supplementary historical information. $24.95

CLASSICAL ARAMAIC: Book I

Learn to read and write the language of Jesus in a self-teachable format. Classical Aramaic is a practical grammar that prepares you to read the New Testament in Jesus' own native tongue. $24.95

LA ANTIGUA ORACIÓN ARAMEA DE JESÚS: El Padrenuestro

Dr. Errico's own translation into Spanish of his book *The Ancient Aramaic Prayer of Jesus*. $8.95

ACHT EINSTIMMUNGEN AUF GOTT: VATERUNSER

German translation and publication of Dr. Errico's book *Setting a Trap for God.*

Books by Dr. Lamsa

THE HOLY BIBLE FROM THE ANCIENT EASTERN TEXT

The entire Bible translated directly into English from Aramaic, the language of Jesus. There are approximately 12,000 major differences between this English translation and the many traditional versions of the Bible. One example: "For I the Lord thy God am a *jealous* God." (Exodus 20:5 King James Version) "For I the Lord your God am a *zealous* God." (Lamsa translation) Another example: "And *lead us* not into temptation . . ." (Matthew 6:13 KJV) "And *do not let us* enter into temptation . . . (Lamsa translation). $35.00

IDIOMS IN THE BIBLE EXPLAINED and A KEY TO THE ORIGINAL GOSPELS

Two books in one. In Book 1 (*Idioms in the Bible Explained*) Dr. Lamsa explains nearly 1000 crucial idioms and colloquialisms of Eastern speech that will enrich reading of the Old and New Testaments for student and general reader alike. Obscure and difficult biblical passages are listed and compared with the King James Version. These make clear the original meaning of such ancient idioms and assure that our grasp of the biblical message is more sound and rewarding. Example: "Lot's wife became a pillar of salt" means she suffered a stroke, became paralyzed and died.

Book 2 (*A Key to the Original Gospels*) explains how the gospels were written, the reason for two different genealogies, the conflicting stories of the birth of Jesus, and more.

$14.00

THE KINGDOM ON EARTH

Part One—The Beatitudes, Part Two—The Lord's Prayer. Many scholars and teachers have dealt with the Sermon on the Mount, which has been called the "constitution of the Kingdom of heaven." None is more eminently qualified than Dr. Lamsa because no one else with his background has a similar knowledge of the Bible and of biblical times. With a warmth and understanding seldom equaled among contemporary scholars, Dr. Lamsa teaches the Beatitudes and the Lord's prayer in the light of Jesus' own language, people and times. $9.95

THE SHEPHERD OF ALL: The Twenty-Third Psalm

The Twenty-third Psalm, considered by many to be the most meaningful psalm in the Bible, is brought to life in a most vivid manner. Dr. Lamsa's ancestors for untold generations were sheep raising people and he was raised in a sheep camp. Based on his own personal experience as a shepherd, Dr. Lamsa interprets this beautiful and moving psalm in the light of Eastern biblical customs. $5.95

NEW TESTAMENT ORIGIN

Dr. Lamsa presents his theory for Aramaic as the original written language of the New Testament. To quote Dr. Lamsa in the forward of *New Testament Origin:* "The Aramaic text speaks for itself; it needs no defense. It is strongly supported by internal evidence, by the Aramaic style of writing, idioms, metaphors, and Oriental [Semitic] mannerisms of speech. Since Christianity is an Eastern religion, the Scriptures must have been written in an Eastern tongue. This fact will be recognized easily by any philologist familiar with Semitic languages. I am one of the millions in biblical lands—both Christians and Mohammedans—who believe that the New Testament was first written in Aramaic, and that our texts were carefully handed down from apostolic times." $5.95